We Escaped

We Escaped
©2015 Alexander H. ter Weele

ISBN: 978-1-939739-80-3

Published by
Piscataqua Press
142 Fleet St.
Portsmouth, NH 03801

Printed in the United
States of America

We Escaped

A Family's Flight from Holland
during World War II
(with the Gestapo in hot pursuit)

The song and dance of *The Sound of Music* ...
seasoned with the terror of war

Alexander H. ter Weele

For
Francine

And

Kerst, Cathy, Alex, Simonne, Maria, Jan; France, Daniela, Jakob, Joshua, Kiki; Eric, Amie, Stafford, Everest; André, Katy, Nicolas, Lauren, Margot.

In memory of my parents, Carl Frits ter Weele and Margery Ethel ter Weele-Crane, whose bravery in the face of Nazi persecution saved my life; and to Jan, Margery, and Fenneke, who shared in the danger and joy of our saga.

Prologue

18 februari 1938: Schuschnig cedes to Hitler's Berchtesgaden threat of 12 February to invade Austria, invites Nazis into government.

11 maart 1938: Seyss-Inquart seizes chancellorship, requests German invasion of Austria to guarantee smooth transition to Nazi rule.

30 september 1938: After flight to Berchtesgaden, Chamberlain hails breakthrough in negotiations, lauds Hitler's largesse to limit German annexation in Czechoslovakia to Sudeten areas, announces "peace in our time."

15 februari 1939: Franco declares victory in civil war as Nationalist forces secure Catalonia with Axis support.

16 maart 1939: With German troops in full control after marching into Czechoslovakia yesterday, Hitler declares Bohemia-Moravia a German protectorate.

7 april 1939: One hundred thousand Italian troops accompanied by 400 aircraft swarm into Albania on Good Friday. Mussolini declares invasion a total victory for the Italian people.

22 mei 1939: Germany and Italy sign Pact of Steel military alliance.

2 september 1939: Forty Nazi infantry divisions supported by fourteen mechanized divisions invaded Poland yesterday in a major German onslaught. France and Great Britain meet, expected to declare war on Germany in next hours.

6 oktober 1939: Hitler reassures Dutch of his friendship, emphasizes Reich's recognition of existing mutual amity pact with Holland and of Germany's commitment to honor the Netherlands' neutrality stance. Germany and Russia reach agreement on demarcation line partitioning Poland.

Hoofdstuk 0

10 mei 1940. Midnight. The silence was shattered by shouted orders, the roar of the beasts of war, the clang of boots and packs and helmets of troops as they jumped onto trucks and into personnel carriers. The cough of panzer motors wakening, the rattle of the engines of self-propelled canons coming alive, the high-pitched exchange of fears and excitement between tens of thousands of infantry trying to make themselves heard above the cacophony of steel and armor and machine. And in the heavens above, the faint and then rising crescendo of hundreds of aircraft drowning out the turmoil below.

May 10, 1940, zero hour. The Nazi invasion of the Netherlands was on. To the north, the SS Leibstandarte, called Adolf Hitler; to the south, the 207th *divisie,* plus the SS Standarte, called der Führer; in the middle of the line, the 227th *divisie*; all with support in the rear by the *deel* 1st *Cavalerie divisie* to the north and the 526th *divisie* to the south. The attack stretched more than seventy-five kilometers along the Dutch/German border, from Hardenberg in the north, through Hengelo, Enschede, Groenlo, and Winterswijk to Zevenaar in the south. In the sky above, the 22nd Luchtlandings-divisie and the 7th Vlieger-divisie flew troops to airfields far behind the Dutch defenses, into and around Amsterdam, Utrecht, Den Haag, Rotterdam, and Dordrecht. The Führer had instructed his army to sweep across the open fields of the Netherlands and to cross onto the coastal plain of Belgium. It must be done, he ordered, within twenty-four hours.

Midnight. First Lieutenant C. F. ter Weele moved amongst his troops dug in on Grebbe Mountain, quieting their fears, confirming that the invasion was on, urging them to get some sleep, reminding them that they were prepared and ready for the attack, and that German troops would not be in sight for some hours yet. Sleep, he said. He would alert them well before the fighting began.

The Lieutenant's wife, Margery, with their three children—sons Jan,

five years old, and Alex, almost two; and their infant daughter, Margy—
were asleep at home in Eindhoven.

Sleep, my children. An easy sleep will not be yours in the months to
come.

Hoofdstuk 1

30 november 1939: Russian troops invade Finland, Red Army sweeps across Finnish frontier in Karelian sector. Planes drop bombs on Helsinki airfield.

Margy lay on my breast, suckling occasionally, resting peacefully. I dozed, suspended between the joy of her arrival and the anxiety of Carl's coming departure. Margy was born hardly ten days ago, November 21. She had been screaming. It was, of course, the same screams uttered by Jan and Alex at their births, but Margy's screams seemed to me to presage the coming war. Before I left the hospital, Carl had received new orders. He would be posted to Rhenen on December 6, the day after Sinterklaas, to assume his command there. As a reserve officer, he had been called up in August for intermittent training, briefings, and assistance with defense planning. He had been back and forth these past two months between Utrecht and his job here in Eindhoven with Philips. The Netherlands had begun to mobilize despite Hitler's assurances of his kinship with the Dutch, his affirmations of the Reich's recognition of the Dutch declaration of neutrality, and his assertions that Germany would honor the joint noninvasion pact guaranteeing both countries' sovereignty.

No one in Holland believed him.

Carl and I had worried about it. In June he suggested that I should flee with the two boys back to my family in the States, so I trekked to the American consulate in Den Haag to renew my American passport. It had expired some two years earlier. Since 1933 I had traveled on the Dutch passport issued to me upon my marriage to Carl. At the consulate I filled in and signed the required forms. The Consul suggested that he wait and issue the passport right after the birth of my coming child. That way he could include all three children on the passport. Just yesterday I sent him Margy's birth certificate and a photo of myself with the three children. He expected he would have the passport to me in just a few days.

Back in June when Carl and I had talked about my leaving, no one had been certain that war would come. As the weeks progressed and it seemed ever more inevitable, I was increasingly coming to term. How could I travel eight or nine months pregnant? Carl was committed to staying. He would be called up. He would serve. Given that he was determined to serve, there was no question. I would stay and support him, and so here I was.

This morning was the first time since leaving the hospital that I had gone shopping. I had left the boys with Rita, our maid, had taken Margy in my arms, and had gone out for a few small toys and some candy. Two toy airplanes: a replica Fokker Eindecker for Jan and a Junker for Alex, both World War I vintage. Two panzers, two tiny jeeps. The boys were endlessly playing with soldiers and personnel carriers, tanks, and guns. They would love these additions to their toy box. And candy, of course. Licorice. Van Houten chocolate. Peppermint sticks. Two oranges. On December 5, Carl's colleagues would offer him a somber office lunch. It would be his last day at Philips. That evening Jan and Alex would put out their wooden shoes. On the sixth we would fete Sinterklaas. And then Carl would be gone.

How was all this happening? Were we truly being swept into war? How could we, a bourgeois couple with three young children, living a quiet life in peaceful, pastoral Holland, become enmeshed in such a mess? How could I, born and raised in Westwood, Massachusetts, get caught up in all this? Or were we all overly pessimistic? There really was no reason in the world for Hitler to bother with Holland. We posed no danger to him. Carl quieted me with this rationale. Still, he would take up his command post in Rhenen. He would probably be back and forth initially between Rhenen and Utrecht for briefings. With luck he would be home on leave for a few days at Christmas. Maybe all this would blow over. Maybe Hitler was just venting steam. Maybe, as Neville Chamberlain said, he was a perfectly reasonable gentleman.

Margy whimpered a satisfied coo, the nipple still between her lips. She was warm on my breast, her tiny eyes screwed tightly shut. The background banter of Jan and Alex playing at war in their room hung in the distant air. Rita puttered in the kitchen, radio on, no doubt drinking tea as she pared potatoes for dinner. Carl would be parking his bicycle in the front hall soon, home from work.

I drifted away, dreaming that the sun was warm on my face. I was lying on the dock, wavelets lapping at the spiles of the wooden pier. The lake slept in summer silence. Little Squam was virgin but for the rustic cabins where the other Girl Scouts and I bunked. The soft dark hemlocks came right to the shore. Mixed in with them were sugar maples, some oak, and stands of white pine with their distinct aroma, the aroma of wild woods, of serenity, of twinkling stars, the aroma I always associated with New Hampshire, with silence, with crystal clear starry nights, with campfire smoke, with happiness. An aroma I captured in a carefully made sachet at the end of each summer and stored all winter long at home in the drawer with my handkerchiefs. And all winter long the aroma led to dreams of New Hampshire's forests. Little Squam enraptured me. It was a world away from the world. A world made for the deer and the moose and the woodpeckers that wakened us each morning with their staccato thrumming. A world made for the loons, whose eerie night wailing made the hair stand up on the nape of my neck and thrilled me to the tips of my toes. A world we could not own, a world that owned us, a world we could visit only briefly before we had to depart. A world wherein beauty caressed us, a world we could love, a world that slipped away as nights lengthened and summer died.

I started awake. An explosion! My heart leaped into my throat. The war had started! But, no, it was only a crash. A moment later Rita tapped on the door. She was in tears. She had dropped the glass dish full of freshly pared potatoes soaking in water. The dish had smashed into smithereens on the black and white tiles of the kitchen floor. She and I cleaned up the mess together, careful to sweep up all the shards. We were even able to rinse the potatoes and save them for our dinner. No harm done.

In the background, the radio was abuzz with last week's Russian invasion of Finland. The American Secretary of State, Cordell Hull, was attempting a diplomatic intervention that Russia and Germany were rejecting. After all, the Finns had massed troops on their side of the border with Russia. In light of such flagrant provocation, the Russians, so said Stalin, had every right to invade. The Russians were demanding a new Finnish government, one more conciliatory to Russia.

It was increasingly hard to deny: our world was coming apart. It was no longer the crash of a breaking dish that upset my reverie. It was the cacophony of a war rushing to engulf Carl and me, to engulf the peace of our six years of marriage, to engulf pastoral Holland. Indeed, to engulf the whole of Europe. A rag and a broom had cleaned the kitchen floor.

We would need more than that to deal with the blood and mangled steel of war. A tremor of foreboding shook me.

Margy had awakened upstairs. As I sat on the bed cradling her, Jan and Alex rushed in to join us. The two of them bounced and giggled on the bed as I held Margy, trying to protect her from their exuberance. The two boys started tickling each other. I smiled and shared their fun. This, so simple, so profound, no more than joy and laughter and love, this was our life. Our life to date. And now it was all going to hell.

A few days later Carl called from his headquarters in Rhenen. He was being assigned to defend the Grebbeberg.

Hoofdstuk 2

9 april 1940: German airborne and seaborne troops invade Norway, Denmark, occupy Norwegian ports from Oslo to Narvik, capture airfields in Oslo and Stavanger, occupy Copenhagen.

Waiting, waiting. Two weeks now, or was it three? The rumor mill had churned out the news: Hitler had set the date for the invasion. The Germans were about to attack! The news had spread like wildfire amongst the men. The Germans were massing. They would invade on the first sunny day. Hitler would be giving the order any day now. They would attack on April 1. And then the false alarms—German troops had crossed the border, last night the Germans had taken Enschede, Almelo was surrounded. They were coming, they were on their way. Again and again, it was a false alarm.

It put the troops on edge. Fights broke out, soldiers argued with one another, there were complaints about the food. I spent as much time as possible amongst them, checking gun emplacements; improving camouflage; adding sandbags; reviewing notes with each of the artillery teams to clarify gun coordinates for the targets we had sighted in; clearing lines of sight for our lanes of fire; discussing once again the trails we would use to bring ammunition in from the arms depot behind the lines in Rhenen, and clarifying on which trails we would use the horses and on which we would use the trucks. And all the time I talked with them, encouraged them, exchanged views on what we might expect, when the attack might begin, where we might expect to see the first German troops, how we would need to react.

We were all frightened. None of us had ever been under enemy fire, none of us knew how we would respond. All of us uneasy, not so much scared of the coming fight as scared that we wouldn't have the courage to stand our ground, that we were cowards, that we would break and run, that we would panic and lose control. I reminded them that the German troops would be equally scared, that we had the advantage of fighting on

9

terrain that we knew inside and out, that the attackers didn't know the lay of the land and wouldn't know where we were. And I reminded them that we were prepared.

We'd been here on the Grebbeberg, the Grebbe Mountain, off and on for the past six months. Me, 1st Lieutenant C. F. ter Weele; they, the men of the First Division, Eighth Regiment of the Royal Mounted Artillery. We had scared up our own cannons, found them in museums, town squares, garages, and sheds. In the backyards of the pubs where World War I vets met for a Heineken on the first Monday of each month. We had even been supplied—glory be!—with two cannons by our command structure. We had torn the guns down, repaired and replaced and oiled and greased each part, and put them back together.

For every two or three cannons we found, we were able to construct one that worked. They were mostly World War I pieces, some older than that, nothing fancy, but they could fire and were surprisingly accurate. When they hit their target, that target—be it a gun emplacement, a house sheltering snipers, a truck, a train, a troop carrier, a machine gun nest, or a panzer—was destroyed. We knew these artillery pieces didn't have the reach of those the Germans would be using. But we had seen the craters where our shells exploded. We had seen the destruction they wrought. So, while we knew we would be outgunned by the Germans, we had a certain confidence that if they came within range, our resistance would not be futile. We were particularly fond of the cannons we called the 6 Velds. They weighed tons. They were huge, clunky, impossible to move. They were mastodons, creatures of another era, yet we loved them. Outdated they might be, but they were accurate as rifles, and where their shells landed, whatever had been there a moment before simply vanished, as if it had never existed.

None of these troops had ever been in the army. All of them had received five and one-half months of basic training at some point over the past twenty years, when they had reached seventeen or eighteen years of age. The obligatory five and one-half months of military service had become law in 1922. We had all been mobilized six months earlier when our country became convinced that the Third Reich was going to invade. How did we know that Hitler would invade when Belgium and France and England didn't? Hadn't we declared neutrality? Hadn't we signed a treaty of friendship with Germany in 1937? Hadn't our friend Hitler repeated his commitment to our neutrality in August of 1939, and then again two months later on October 6 of that year?

So how did we as a country know that Hitler was going to invade? Was it perhaps because he had annexed Austria? Or his announcement in Munich that Czechoslovakia was now a German protectorate? Or his attack on Poland? Or the German buildup of its war machinery over the past decade? Or the recent movement of German troops from eastern Germany toward its western border with Luxembourg, Belgium, and the Netherlands? Or that Germany had invaded us earlier in this century? Or was it something in the Dutch psyche that gave us greater insight into the intentions of the Germanic mind? Or, simply, that politicians in other countries were cowering in denial?

Whatever the reason, we had mobilized, and I had wasted no time in using these past months to ensure that the troops under my command would be as prepared as we could be when—not if—the onslaught exploded. On paper the Eighth Regiment was comprised of its officer staff, medicos, communications personnel, a pastor, and three groups of three batteries. Each of the nine batteries was to consist of four cannons, for a total of thirty-six cannons. While we had dug in thirty-six emplacements, we were lucky on any given day if more than thirty of the thirty-six cannons were in working order.

On paper, each cannon was manned by four troops. That meant we should have had 144 men to man the guns. The hundred or so troops we actually had were adequate for training and would be adequate during the first hours of an attack. Two men could manage the aiming and firing of any of the artillery pieces, including the gigantic 6 Velds. But even discounting deaths and injuries, a sustained attack would leave us short of manpower as troops succumbed to fatigue and the need for sleep. When the fighting began, the three group officers and the nine battery sergeants would need to do more than give orders, but even then it was clear that sleep would be a luxury no one would be able to afford.

The first part of these past months had been devoted to sighting our field pieces. The 6 Velds needed a short mound behind them for the gun to "run up" after it was fired. They had no recoil mechanism; the mound absorbed the horrendous recoil force of these dinosaurs. Each of the guns needed the protection of sandbags, wooden beams, a partial roof, and camouflage. Ditches or sandbag bulwarks were built, connecting the emplacements to one another and to my command post. Trees were felled, opening lines of sight. The trunks were used to further protect our

11

emplacements, and the branches enhanced our camouflage. Hundreds of meters of telephone cable were laid like a spider web connecting the emplacements to one another, to my command post, and to our central command in the Villa Santa Barbara in Rhenen. Communications were thus barbaric. They worked well enough if the cables were intact, but the moment a cable was severed, all communication ceased until the break could be found and repaired. And breaks occurred daily as someone tripped over a wire, or a wire caught on a truck or an ammunition cart, or as a horse stamped on it in passing.

Once our gun emplacements had been constructed, we began the never-ending task of sighting in potential targets. The summit of the Grebbeberg was some fifty-five meters high. Not much, certainly not a mountain as the name implied, but our view over an otherwise flat-as-a-pancake landscape was open as far as the eye could see. Germany lay to our east. We considered that our front side. Behind us, to our west, just at the foot of the Grebbeberg, lay Rhenen. I was housed in the annex of the Hotel de Grebbeberg there. Our headquarters was a block away in the Villa Santa Barbara. During the initial month of our buildup, I slept in the hotel almost every night. Comfortable, even luxurious. As my troops increased in numbers and the pace of the buildup became more frenzied, I set up a cot in the large hole in the ground that was my command post. That is, I slept outdoors with my men. They needed to see me, to know that their life was mine, that I ate what they ate, that my boots were muddied by the same mud that dirtied theirs, and that I would be there with them when the battle began.

While my compatriot artillery regiments were on the eastern and northern flanks of the Grebbe, the view for my artillery pieces lay primarily to the east and the south. The Dutch/German border was seventy-five kilometers to our east via Arnhem, thirty kilometers to our east-southeast via Nijmegen. No obstructions blocked our view of the road that ran easterly from Rhenen to Wageningen, and then on to the border through either Arnhem or Nijmegen. This easterly view comprised a land that was pastoral: a small village or two, each with a clearly visible church steeple, black and white cows grazing peacefully in vividly green, flat pastures, orchards of apple and pear and cherry trees laid out in neat squares. The line of the road was discernible to the naked eye as far as the church steeple in Wageningen; although where the road wended through the orchards, traffic moving along it was invisible to us.

We had requested permission to clear the landscape of trees and other obstacles, to deny cover to attacking troops. Permission denied. The government did not have the means to indemnify farmers for damage done to their farms.

To the south, our view was across the Rhine. Five kilometers beyond it, across the Waal and farther south, out of our view, was the Maas River. Although the three rivers arrived here from a mostly southerly direction, as they approached the Grebbe, they turned and flowed roughly parallel to one another in an east-west direction. Train tracks ran along the far side of the Rhine, coming from Germany. They turned north and crossed the river on the Rijnbrug Bridge just behind our position, ran through Rhenen right at the foot of the Grebbe, and continued on in a northerly direction. The train tracks thus separated our positions on the Grebbe from our headquarters in downtown Rhenen. Whereas the tracks were built above ground level on a dike where they followed the Rhine, they lay in a depression—a big ditch, if you will—through the town of Rhenen. The Rhenen to Wageningen road crossed the railroad tracks on a bridge as it left Rhenen, and then passed below our guns on its way to Wageningen in the east. To the south, across the Rhine and the Waal, the countryside was dotted with small towns: Ochten, Druten, Tiel, Kesteren, Dodewaard, Opheusden, Markplas, Lede, Oudewaard, and numerous others. The two rivers were alive with commercial traffic, their banks scattered with docks and small businesses. Canal boats chugged upriver with sand and oil and manufactured goods to Germany, Belgium, and Switzerland; and floated coal and vegetables and logs and other produce downriver to Utrecht, Dordrecht, and Rotterdam. Here along the banks of these two great rivers lived the burghers of the Netherlands, hard at work.

The pastoral landscape to our east and the busy industrial areas along the two rivers to our south lay in peaceful unawareness. Soon, how soon? How soon, I wondered, would they become the killing fields? All of us assumed the German thrust would be launched from the east, from the direction of Wageningen. It would be accompanied, one supposed, by a flanking attack from the north. Our supposition was based on the lay of the land. An attack from the south would require transit across the Maas, Waal, and Rhine, three formidable water barriers. An attack from the south would be like a housebreaker choosing to break in through a heavy iron gate locked with chains, guarding an equally impregnable massive oaken front door. On the other hand, an attack from the east or north would be a housebreaker strolling across a clipped lawn to a pleasant garden patio and on into the home through open French doors.

From the east, the German attack would roll along roads and railroad lines, across flat land unencumbered by hills and rivers, all the way from the German border through either Arnhem or Tilburg, and on here to Wageningen and our defensive installations. A thrust from the north would be a touch more difficult—the distance was longer and the IJssel River would need to be crossed. But the Germans would certainly know that the Dutch defenses along the IJssel were stretched thin.

Our nation's overall defense plan comprised four components, a front line and three lines of defense. Our front line, right along our border with Germany, was no more than a long string of outposts manned by one or two soldiers each. They were our watchdogs. The soldiers stationed there would sound the alarm as soon as the German troops set foot on our soil, and then they would flee to help defend the IJssel-Linie, our first line of defense. The second line of defense was the Grebbe-Linie, with the Grebbeberg as its key defensive component. The third line of defense was the Nieuwe Hollandse Waterlinie. Each line of defense was shorter than the previous line, and the defenses of each subsequent line were increasingly formidable. The ultimate defensive line, the Waterlinie, was the historic line, a line that had withstood attacks over the centuries. Here the line of defense would be shortest of all and sheltered by broad rivers, wide canals, small lakes, and thousands upon thousands of hectares of flooded fields. However, it would protect only two provinces, North and South Holland. It would cede the remaining eleven provinces to the enemy.

On the Grebbeberg, we had our principal line of defense at the front of the Grebbe, in front of our artillery installations, and a fallback line directly behind the mountain at the railroad tracks that separated the mountain from the town of Rhenen. We intended to hold our ground. If we retreated, it would mean abandoning our artillery installations. But if we did retreat to the railroad tracks, and then needed to retreat farther, our orders were to fall back to help with the defense of the Waterlinie.

My attention and that of my troops was focused on the semicircle assigned to us. Running in a clockwise direction, it started from Wageningen in the east; southward to the banks of the Rhine and the Waal; west along the Rhine to the railroad bridge; across the Rhine on the railroad bridge north into Rhenen, where our headquarters lay in the shadow of the Grebbeberg, behind our lines to our west. So the gunners and I devoted ourselves to identifying the exact coordinates of every potential target in this semicircle.

We could dismiss those areas that were flooded. South of us and far out of the range of our guns, along the rivers headed to Germany and Belgium, much of the pastureland already stood under water in preparation for the expected onslaught. Much of the land in those areas was below the level of the water in the rivers, and could be flooded by the simple expedient of opening the dikes. While the pastures already stood underwater, more of the dikes would be opened to flood roads, orchards, and even villages as soon as our front outposts sounded the alarm that Hitler's troops had crossed the border. At the Grebbe, most of the land was above the level of the rivers. Nonetheless, much could be flooded by pumping water into areas surrounded by dikes—except that the government had not provided us with the requested pumps. Insufficient funds, we had been told. Nonetheless, we had flooded those low areas near the rivers that could be flooded by merely pulling the plugs in the dikes. Directly below our guns to the south, we had flooded the land bounded by the railroad dike to the north and the town of Ochten on the banks of the Waal to the south, creating a water barrier some two kilometers wide by six kilometers long. That effectively squeezed the passage between the Rhine and the Waal from four kilometers to less than one kilometer in width. To the north of the Grebbe, the regiment in charge of defending the other side of the mountain had been able to flood a seven-kilometer-long portion of our front line. The troops positioned there were pleased, but wished that the water could have been deeper. In some places it came hardly to one's knees.

Our troops had spent the first weeks selecting sites for our guns, digging the emplacements, and then dragging the artillery pieces to their places with the help of our horses. I had been skeptical about the horses. Of what value were they when up against motorized tanks and troop carriers? Mounted artillery? Wasn't that of another day and age? But dragging heavy artillery pieces up a hillside of rocks and trees and brush could not have been done by trucks; and the troops were pleased not to have to wrestle the guns—especially those monster 6 Velds—into place with ropes and great teams of men. The horses also lightened the work of pulling carts of ammunition from the railroad station in Rhenen up to our emplacements. Moreover, the horses provided a sense of normality for many of the men who used them on a daily basis at home on their farms. They enjoyed the everyday routine of feeding and watering and talking to them. I did not ride my stallion Klaas much. I preferred to walk amongst the men so that I could speak to them man-to-man, clap them on the shoulder, and stand—or more precisely, crouch—in the holes we called emplacements that had become the homes of the gunners. But Klaas was important for ceremonial purposes. He lent an air of dignity to me, and thereby to the men, when he was washed and curried and decked out in his best harness; and I sat astride him in my best dress uniform to greet Major Landzaat, whom I liked, or General Harberts, whom I didn't like, or the officer who impressed me the most, General Van Voorst tot Voorst, headquartered up north in Zeist.

Day after day I kept the men busy, expanding our list of targets with their coordinates, sighting in our guns on those coordinates, and shooting at those that were safe to shoot at with dummy shells to further refine our precision. To the east, we sighted in the tower of the church in Wageningen. The men boasted they would be able to hit it with their first shot if the time came. Every ten meters along the road from Wageningen to Rhenen had been measured and sighted in. On this, we spent hours. We were certain that this would be the route of a major German attack. Across the broad plain that the road bisected, we sighted in on every farmhouse, on sheds, on haystacks, on conspicuous trees, on farm tracks through the orchards, on any recognizable object that we could use as identification for our ever-lengthening list of coordinates. To the south we focused on the space between the foot of the Grebbe and the Rhine, on the east-west passage between the Rhine and the Waal, and on objects along the far bank of the Waal. We had coordinates for the roads, for every road junction, for town squares and town halls, for churches, for warehouses, for machine-tool shops, for docks, for jetties, for factories, for cafés, for hotels, for flagpoles, for monuments. We focused particularly on the dike that carried the railroad line. With the space on the far side of the railroad dike flooded—between the tracks and the Waal—the tracks on the dike and the narrow corridor between them and the Rhine would be the space the Germans would need to use in any attempt to break through our lines. The railroad bridge, the Rijnbrug, just behind us was another obvious target. Indeed, we had distinct coordinates for each of the three spans of the bridge and for the four sets

16

of pylons on which the bridge sat.

I had made a game of it, a competition, with my gunners. We created a schedule of alternate weeks. One week would be spent developing a list of new identifiable targets with their coordinates, while the next week would be spent sighting in each gun on the new targets. At the end of the first week in each cycle, each gun emplacement submitted its entire list of identifiable objects with their coordinates. The officers would check coordinates for accuracy, ensuring that there were no errors. Then a list would be tallied for each of the thirty-six gun emplacements, for each of the nine batteries (four guns in each battery), and for each of our three groups (three batteries in each group, thus twelve guns per group). In this way, we could award a prize to the gun emplacement that had tallied the most sets of coordinates during the week, to the battery that had tallied the most sets of coordinates, and to the group that had tallied the most overall. On the judgment of the officers, some targets (such as farmer van der Winden's brown plow horse, or the fair-haired maiden who milked cows each morning over toward Ochten, or the old drunk lying in the ditch on the side of the road last Friday night, or the Sunday afternoon tourist boat floating down the Rhine with a tuba blaring) would be expunged from the list. On Monday mornings, with all troops present, the winners would be announced. As each prize was awarded, there would be great cheers from the winners and catcalls and boos from the losers. The regiment-wide list would be compiled; and we'd go on with a week of sighting in each gun to the newly identified targets and rehearsing sightings on older targets.

March turned to April. We were all hoping that good weather would come. We'd had nothing but rain these past months. A cold rain with a chilling mist broken occasionally by a downpour. A typically dreary Dutch winter and early spring. The last weeks had brought a few clear days with sun and blue sky. The sun lifted our spirits, and brought blossoms to the orchards and green to the poplars lining the fields. The guns were in place, the troops ready for battle, every inch of our killing field had been sighted in. I had been granting a week of leave each month to one-fourth of my troops, to keep their spirits up. There had been less leave for my officer staff, although I had sent one home for a few days when his wife gave birth, and another when his young son had been hit by a truck while he was riding his bike. We had been able to squeeze in an occasional three-day weekend for the officers, and once every three months I had tried to grant them a week off. Now it was my turn. I requested a week of leave. I wanted to surprise Margery. April 8 was our seventh wedding anniversary.

Hoofdstuk 3

At first I had surged ahead every few minutes and then slowed to let Mama catch up. After a half hour, I had settled next to her side at the steady pace she had set. I liked showing how fast I could go. I would crouch over the handlebars, imitating Theo Middlekamp. Theo was the Dutch National Road Race Champion and winner of two stages in the Tour de France, one in 1936 and one in 1938. He was awesome. Whenever there was a race in Eindhoven, I would join the crowd on the sidewalk and shout support as the bicycles whizzed by.

I was impressed that Mama could ride a bike without her hands on the handlebars. She sat up very straight, quiet, almost dreaming. By shifting her weight ever so slightly, she kept the bike going in the middle of the bike path, as if the bicycle were steering itself. Most people in Holland did this without even thinking about it. In the early morning rush hour in Eindhoven, many of the businessmen going to the Philips factory would read a newspaper while biking to work. I asked Mama when she had learned to ride. In Westwood, she said, in Massachusetts where she was born. When she was a little girl. But she had really started to bike a lot in Groningen, when she and Vader had first married. She would use the bike every day, to shop, to go to the tennis courts or to the field-hockey fields, or to meet Vader at the station when he returned from a trip out of town. Just as we do here in Eindhoven, she said. It was in Groningen that she learned to use the bicycle every day.

You mean you didn't use your bike every day in Westwood? I asked. No, she replied. In the States we don't use bicycles every day. We just use them for play.

And for racing? I asked. She told me that there weren't any bike races in the States. No bike races? I thought. Wow! I guessed they just raced on horses with the Indians on the Great Plains. Can you imagine a country without bike races? Wow!

It was the first week of April 1940. The sun was bright, and in the fields we passed, black and white cows grazed in pastures flat and smooth as a football pitch. Brick farmhouses with low thatched roofs clustered under poplar trees. The bike path we were on was sandwiched between a canal on one side and a road on the other. Every hundred or two hundred meters, a ditch at right angles to the canal divided the flat fields into separate pastures. It always astonished me that the cows confined themselves so placidly to a single pasture and apparently made no attempt to cross the ditches.

Holland was like that. Placid, sedate, groomed, organized. *Boring.* I preferred the cowboys, the Indians, the wild prairies, and the jagged mountains of the movies Mama took me to on Saturday afternoons. Just as I liked it when she read to me from *Little House on the Prairie.* Today Mama had suggested a bike ride for just the two of us. Rita, our maid, was watching my baby sister Margy and my little brother Alex.

As we were parking our bicycles at the house, our car pulled up to the curb. Papa! He was home from training for the invasion! He looked splendid in his riding uniform, with his trousers tucked into his boots. A big man with blond hair and laughing eyes the color of my favorite translucent blue marble, he picked me up and put me onto his shoulders. He was my horse, he said. He was in the mounted artillery. Yes, he had a horse, he told me. Black. Klaas. Huge, he said, strong and courageous. And then, with me still on his shoulders, he galloped up and down the sidewalk in front of our townhouse. He was my horse, and I was charging at Hitler's army. He stopped and kissed Mama. Then he picked up Alex, and with me still on his shoulders and carrying Alex, he galloped some more. I laughed and he laughed louder. Alex was a little scared, but then he laughed and so did Mama. With the sun on my face and bouncing on Papa's shoulders, I could believe I was on horseback, riding the Oregon Trail.

As we entered our house, the phone rang. No sooner had Papa answered it than the laughter in those great blue eyes went into hiding. His army voice boomed. *"Ja, Meneer. Ja. Meteen?"* Mama stood frozen, watching him. *"Twee uur?"* he asked. Looking at his watch, he replied, *"Ja, dat gaat wel."* He was standing at attention, ramrod straight, his head up, his chin tucked in. He scared me. *"Ja, Meneer."* And again. *"Ja, Meneer."* He hung up the phone.

Mama looked at him questioningly. "It's coming," he said, putting his arms around her. "I must be back at the Grebbe by two o'clock."

They clung to each other for a long moment. Mama was trying not to cry, trying to suppress a sob.

"And our anniversary?" she asked. Papa shook his head sadly, pulled her closer. "How soon?" she asked.

"Soon," he replied. "A day or two. A week maybe. Nobody knows for sure. But if they're ordering me back, they don't think it will be long." He kissed her on the forehead. "Why don't you wake Margy? I'd like to kiss her good-bye."

We were on the sidewalk then. Mama held Margy in her arms. She was almost five months old. Papa picked up Alex and me. "Jan," he said to me, "take care of Mama." He kissed us all and he was gone.

The next four weeks were horrible. Mama and our neighbors, Loeky and Lou Blok, spent hours listening to the radio. Radio Hilversum in Dutch. The BBC in English. Mama had learned Dutch early in her marriage, in Groningen. English was, of course, her mother tongue. She always spoke English with Alex and me when we were alone with her. When the three of us were with Rita or Papa or anyone else, we spoke Dutch. She also spoke French and Italian, and she told me learning Dutch had been easy. She was quick at languages, she said, and with a Dutch husband and living in a Dutch town, she had mastered the language in a matter of months.

At first the broadcasts were full of speculation. Would the Germans invade France? When? Would neutral countries such as Holland and Belgium be invaded? When?

On the morning of May 10, Loeky and Mama were drinking coffee in our kitchen. Loeky was smoking. She was always smoking. Margy was lying on a small blanket that Mama had spread on the floor, squeaking happily. Alex and I had our troops lined up in battle formation, also on the floor. Alex wanted to fly my Eindecker. No, I told him. You can't handle it. The Eindecker is too fast for you. *Fast.* It's awesome. Dominant. Faster than any plane in the world! You fly the Junker. I'll bomb the troops with the Eindecker.

"Eindecker, Eindecker," Alex whined.

"Fast, fast. It's dominant!" I convinced him that I could handle the speed better than he could. Finally, he flew the Junker. Between the two of us we bombed the enemy troops to smithereens.

I looked up from our battle and realized that Mama and Loeky weren't talking anymore. They seemed in a trance. Steam was rising from their two coffee cups on the table, smoke was drifting upward from Loeky's cigarette, and out the window the late morning dampness mimicked the steam and smoke in the kitchen. Mama's face was ashen. Loeky was equally shocked. They held each other's hands tightly as they stared at the radio. Because of their silence, I listened too. The German invasion had exploded across the border during the night. Tanks and troops had swept westerly into Holland. Paratroopers had landed outside Den Haag, Rotterdam, and Dordrecht, seizing bridges across the Rhine.

Loeky looked at Mama. "En Carl?"

Papa's zone of defense, the Grebbeberg, was only fifty kilometers from the German border. Dordrecht, Rotterdam, and Den Haag lay way behind the Grebbe. Papa's troops had probably already come under attack.

"He called last night," Mama said to Loeky. "He told me not to leave home today." She stared out the window. "He said he wanted to hear my voice." She paused. "He must have known it was coming." There was a catch in her voice. More to herself than to Loeky, she murmured, "He said that he was sorry, so sorry, that he had been unable to be here for our anniversary. He would have given anything, he said—" She stopped in midsentence. Loeky put her hand on Mama's arm.

I slipped over to Mama. She put an arm around me protectively. Margy was still giggling and cooing, lying on her back on the blanket. Alex had captured my Eindecker and was making buzzing sounds as he waved the plane through the air and squealed, "Fast! Fast! Dominant!" Loeky's cigarette lay in the ashtray on the table, smoke rising lazily. Beyond the smoke, out the window, I could see the top of the lone tree in our backyard, and beyond that the two-story building that housed a line of connected townhouses just like ours.

"Mama," I asked, "will Papa be all right?" But I knew he would be. He had guns and soldiers with him. I could picture Papa riding Klaas and shooting at the Germans. They were no match for him.

"Of course," she reassured me, her arm around me, hugging me tightly. "Of course." She kissed me on the forehead. "You know how big and strong he is."

Loeky looked away, her eyes filled with tears. Her husband Lou was a research engineer at Philips. He had not been called up.

22

Hoofdstuk 4

`10 mei 1940:` Hitler invades Netherlands, Belgium, Luxembourg by land and air. Dikes opened. Allies rush to aid.

Rumors, rumors. This time they had the sound of truth. Our command was swirling with a story that our military attaché in Berlin, Major Sas, had telexed, "The swine has left for the western front. The die is cast." We commanders on the Grebbe were called from our positions on the mountain to the Villa Santa Barbara in Rhenen. It was the shortest meeting we had ever attended. We were told that General Winkelman was reporting that our forward outposts on the German border had noticed unusual troop movements. We were instructed to return immediately to our stations and to be on the alert.

Margery! I rushed to the Hotel de Grebbeberg and asked the desk to put me through to her in Eindhoven. Stay home, I told her. I wasn't permitted to tell her that we had been put on alert. Stay in Eindhoven these next days. I did not need to say much. I knew the alarm in my voice was obvious. Eindhoven was undefended. If the Germans attacked, they would roll into and through the city without firing a shot. It would be safer for Margery and the children to stay there than to seek shelter somewhere else. Take care of the children, I said. I love you.

Her adieu was inaudible. Lost, I knew, in a suppressed sob. A moment later I was on my bicycle along with the other officers, headed back to our guns. My instructions were to alert my troops. As is often the case in a bureaucracy, the instructions were irrelevant. What with all the rumors flying about, my troops were already on alert. Hyperalert. My job, then, was not to alert them but to steady them, to calm them, to encourage them, to focus them on the job at hand. To redirect them from the wild swirl of uncertainty and fear onto the concrete plan of methodical actions we had practiced over and over.

I walked among the emplacements, chatting casually. It appeared that the attack was coming, I said. There would be plenty of warning. Our outposts would inform us immediately when the Nazis crossed the border. We would then learn of the fighting when the Germans reached our defenses on the IJssel-Linie. If they breached that line, we would learn of it from our retreating troops and we would have time for final preparations. Get some sleep, I told them. I'll keep you informed as events unfold. I tried to project calm and confidence. It was surprisingly easy. We had drilled and drilled and drilled. All of us knew exactly what we needed to do. I suspected that like me, the men were less worried about themselves than about their wives and children.

Midnight came and went. May 10 had arrived. I was tossing on the cot in my command bunker. The horror began shortly before 0200 hours. At first, a distant drone. An airplane. The drone built steadily, louder and louder, until it filled the whole sky. It was above us and above that. It reached out beyond our world. We could hear it coming from Germany and going toward Rotterdam and Dordrecht and Delft and Den Haag and Utrecht. It filled space, permeated our bodies. We could not imagine how many planes there were. The noise meant that they were there, hundreds of them. They were all around us. Everywhere. Yet in the darkness, we could see nothing. The roar was disembodied. A lion prowling in the night, both near and far. And like the lion's roar, even when one has never heard a lion roar before and doesn't know what the sound was, it made the hairs on the back of our necks rise in fear, a primordial fear.

Immediately, I made the round of my gun emplacements. The regiment was awake, adrenaline pumping. Nothing to worry about yet, I told them. Check your guns again. Check your ammo. Go back to sleep. Yes, the invasion had started. Our action could come later today if the Germans broke the IJssel-Linie immediately. More probably tomorrow or the next day. Or maybe not at all if the first line of defense can resist. Sleep while you can.

Sleep. It was good advice, but not a one of us slept. Tales swirled in the dark. A German patrol had been caught in Didam. They were in Dutch uniforms, but were unmasked when they couldn't pronounce *Scheveningse Scherpschutters*. Our border posts in Kloosterhaar and Langeven had been attacked. Germans were said to be streaming through the town of Groenlo on the Beltrumschestraat. Blood was pouring out of a panzer train that had backed into the railroad station in Westervoort. Two motorcyclists had been captured near the café De Groene Jager in

Bronkhorst. Parachutists had landed behind our lines at the airports of Waalhaven and Ockenburg and were attacking Rotterdam and Den Haag.

Light crept over the landscape. Cows in the pastures below us grazed lazily. The steeple of the church in Wageningen could now be distinguished. One could believe that all was at peace, except that Hitler could be heard on the radio announcing with pride to his citizenry that his 227th Division, Adolf Hitler, and his 207th Division, der Führer, had been sent during the night into the Netherlands to save the Dutch from the imminent invasion and occupation of their country by the British. He was pleased that his troops had been received with open arms as saviors of Dutch independence.

Almost all of our troops could speak German. Dutch was a Germanic language, so the two languages were similar, and six years of German was a requirement in our school system. We all listened in disbelief to Hitler's audacious distortion of events. I made the rounds of our gun emplacements, trying to appear no more than a nonchalant wanderer. Yes, I told the questioners, we would be seeing action soon. Later that afternoon perhaps? During the night or tomorrow? In the meantime, enjoy today's good weather and nap if you can.

The good news was that the field telephone in my bunker, which had been down twice during the night, was working again. Commands and information came to me over this phone, and were also sent in written form by messenger. In my case, the messenger was one of my attachés, Piet Steen, who bicycled back and forth between my command bunker and our headquarters in the Villa Santa Barbara in Rhenen. The round trip usually took him an hour; although in times of distress and if he didn't dally at headquarters, he could probably cut that to half an hour, perhaps twenty minutes if pushed.

As the morning progressed headquarters tried to keep us informed. While all was placid and peaceful on the pastoral canvas spread below our guns, the horror of the waves of invisible airplanes during the night still resounded in our heads. The snippets of news conveyed through headquarters confirmed that the scene below us would not remain serene for long. The German 207th Division had crossed, or had been repulsed, or was perhaps still attempting to cross, the IJssel at Westervoort. German troops had taken Arnhem. Zutphen was under artillery assault. All of that was to our northeast in front of our Grebbe-Linie of defense.

Behind our lines, the parachutists had landed during the night at airfields in Valkenburg, Ypenburg, and Ockenburg, near Den Haag. Dutch troops had those airfields under counterattack. Equally intense action was ongoing at the Moerdijk Bridges to the south of Rotterdam, to beat back the Nazi parachutists who had landed there. Later in the day, a roar of approval sounded from our emplacements as we learned that our troops had retaken the airfields at Den Haag. As nightfall approached, the troops roared again when General Winkelman came on the radio to announce that Her Majesty the Queen had instructed him to inform her troops of her satisfaction with their defense against those who had violated the Dutch declaration of neutrality.

At dark, though, the optimism of the troops waned. Perhaps fittingly, my telephone line with headquarters went down, the third time in the past hours. After a scramble of half an hour, our radioman found the break in our cable and had it spliced. Communications were restored. We learned that the IJssel-Linie had been breached—the German thrust at Westervoort had succeeded in crossing the IJssel River. Zutphen had been taken. And later, the news that the Germans had succeeded in crossing the IJssel at a second point at Klatterstraat. The Germans were moving past Arnhem. They were on a direct line toward the Grebbe.

I moved amongst my troops in the dark. Midnight had come and gone. Yes, we would probably be under attack before morning. It appeared that the IJssel-Linie had been broken. Yes, catnaps were fine as long as one man in each emplacement maintained vigil. Yes, steady as she goes. When the shooting starts, hunker down. Do not return fire until specific targets are identified and the order is given, not before. Careful in the dark, some of the troops approaching may be our compatriots retreating from their positions on the first line of defense. Do we all remember the password? The troops were on edge, but to my satisfaction more focused than frightened.

It was about to begin. We had hardly learned that the troops on the IJssel-Linie had been given the order to withdraw when a squadron of men—half on horses, half on bicycles—appeared on the road from Wageningen. Behind and around them, small groups of men and individuals emerged from the dark, calling out in Dutch and answering to the password. The first groups were moving at a quick pace but under control. Increasingly, those that arrived were in turmoil, panicked and disheveled, often without their arms, running and calling out that the

Germans were coming. Our men quieted them, directed them behind our lines to the road into Rhenen. Fortunately for the morale of our regiment, only a few of the men were wounded. Unfortunately, the numbers retreating increased, streaming through our positions, some wailing, some crying, some swearing at the Germans, others angry that the order to retreat had been given too quickly. They had not even been given the chance to fight. Those last encouraged my men to give the Germans hell when they arrived. I quietly echoed the theme. Let's give them hell. Revenge. Let's get revenge.

The scream of an incoming artillery shell interrupted all conversation and thought. I glanced at my watch. 0200 hours. I picked up my phone. I knew that my announcement, that we were under bombardment, would not be news to Headquarters. They had ears as well. But I was under orders to keep them informed. Their reply was also redundant: hold your fire until you have clear identification of a target.

Again, I passed through the emplacements. Hunker down. Hang in there. Note the location of flashes. Try to identify their coordinates. Don't shoot yet.

It was an eternity before we heard the second incoming. And then it was the opening of the gates of hell. No longer a single incoming, it was now a full-scale barrage. The fireworks finale on the Queen's birthday was a baby's giggle in comparison. The Germans had to have a minimum of a hundred cannons, I thought, to keep up a salvo with such a tempo. More, probably two or three times that. After a minute or two, it became apparent that none of the guns were aimed at our emplacements. The explosions were all in front of us, below us, on the eastern flat, and at the foot of the Grebbe.

Yes, I said to the gunners as I reached each emplacement. The firing is from Wageningen. They're focused on hitting the Grebbe's front line of defenders, our infantry, the machine-gun nests. They're softening us up in advance of an infantry assault. Do you have a good line on the flashes? We should be able to do substantial damage. Their firepower seems to be massed in three distinct positions. Get your guns ready. I'll be giving the order to fire shortly on the most southerly of those flashes. Our two brother regiments will take care of the more northerly flashes. And keep your heads down once we start. The German guns will turn on our position once we open fire.

All three of our artillery regiments confirmed to headquarters that we had identified three distinct German installations firing at our front line from the direction of Wageningen. As light crept over the countryside, those installations went silent. It would be wrong to assume that the German assault had been halted. The nighttime firing on our front line at the foot of the Grebbe had been to soften up our opposition to an infantry attack. The infantry attack would be launched at first light; the German guns had gone silent to avoid killing their own infantry as they approached us. But the morning came and went in eerie silence. Nothing. Tension built in the early afternoon as we saw troops moving on the pastures and in the orchards below us. And then the rat-a-tat of machine gun fire. As the silence broke below us, we received the command from Headquarters to commence firing. It was 1600 hours. Our regiment's first target, as I had already prepped my men, would be the southernmost group of cannons. Once those were silenced, we would reduce our firing range to destroy infantry attackers moving toward the Grebbe.

Our troops relished the opportunity to take action. On the exact moment of the order, we began the barrage. The cacophony of our thirty-six guns blended into the roar from our two adjoining regiments. For a few minutes the fight was one-sided. We fired and reloaded and fired and reloaded and fired again without response from the Germans. Our men whooped with pent-up excitement as each shell exploded in the distance. Finally we were in the fray, we were released, we were doing something! It was no surprise, though, once the Germans had sighted in on the flashes from our guns, that we in turn became targets. The whine of incoming shells, the earsplitting whoosh and kaboom, the dirt flying into our positions, the smoke, the fire, the screams of men who had been hit, the thrashing and fear of frantic horses. It was real. War had exploded upon us. And now it was my turn. Put aside my fears. Keep my men focused. Deal with death, with destruction. Keep it organized. Manage panic, direct it at revenge, at fighting. This was what I was paid to do. Now it was time to deliver.

As if I had no care in the world, ignoring the turmoil around me, I left my command bunker to begin the same measured round of inspection of our emplacements, as I had been doing for weeks. Take your time to aim before firing. Careful not to overheat the cannon. Drink some fluids. Keep your head down when you hear an incoming. Try to get a hit each time you fire. Don't fire blindly. Watch your store of ammo. Send for shells well before you run out. That's the way! Sock it to those bastards. Drive 'em back. After each pep talk, I strolled on to the next emplacement, pretending to all the world that I was oblivious to the scream of incoming shells, to the destruction of explosions, to craters not there a moment before, to flying dirt and debris, to the bedlam and ear-shattering clamor that drowned my words as I chatted as leisurely as one might on the steps of church on a sunny Sunday morning.

Hoofdstuk 5

20 juli 1940: Mass air raids on London by Nazis beaten back by British. Royal Air Force retaliates, bombs German bases. Australians sink Italian cruiser in Mediterranean.

Pushing and shoving my bicycle, I tried to get to the station. Riding it in this crowd was impossible. Being big and strong helped. My six-foot-four-inch frame and 240 pounds gave me an advantage. On the football field, when I had been young and fast, others had had trouble matching the length of my stride and my speed. And I had been lethal in the air with my head. How many of my goals had been on headers when Jan Klijnstra had served me up the corners? And why? Because I had muscled away defenders and stood half a head above everyone. I became a striker to be reckoned with. And at the end of my career, when I could no longer run and played keeper, the spread of my arms in front of the goal, my ability to punch away balls over everyone's head, and the fear I inspired in strikers as I rushed them like a bull about to trample a novice torero, made me a legend again, this time at the defensive end of the field.

Big. Muscled. Strong. There were a lot of Dutchman like me. Blue-eyed, blond, fair-skinned. And big. In this crowd, in front of the railroad station, there were few if any as big as I, and I made use of my size to move to the *stallings*—the parking shed for bicycles directly in front of the station.

A crowd during the morning rush hour was to be expected, but trains were few and irregular now. This was not just a crowd but a seething cauldron of humanity. The German military commandeered most trains to carry provisions to the fronts in Belgium and France. The few remaining trains were packed with Dutch civilians and German troops. On the corner of the *stationplaats*, a panzer squatted next to a pillbox constructed of sandbags. The machine guns menaced. The paving stones laid in the form of interlocking fans were hidden by the crowd, but were

31

slippery underfoot from the intermittent drizzle hanging in the air. A Scotch mist? The Dutch are less sophisticated, I thought. Just *mot regen* in a lowering sky.

I kept my distance from the pillbox. My name was on the German blacklist. The Dutch had surrendered two months ago. The Germans were trying to round up the top officers. With their hands full, what with fighting a war, their search inside Holland had been perfunctory. The borders of Holland, however, were sealed tight. Of my four best friends in the mounted cavalry, one had been shot on the beaches of Hoek van Holland in fleeing to England; two had been shot crossing a farm near the Belgian border on their way to Bruges. And one, Hendrik van der Heijden, had escaped. He had taken a ship from Amsterdam to Kiel, gone overboard off the coast of Sweden, and had swum to Helsingborg. A good plan, I thought. A superb plan. But how to do that with a wife, two young boys, and an infant daughter?

At the *stalling*, I hung my bicycle up by the front wheel and collected a ticket from an attendant. Then I stood in line at the counter to pay for the train.

"*Enkel, meneer?*"

"*Retour, graag. Den Haag.*"

On the platform I read the yellow schedule. Eindhoven-Utrecht and then a ten-minute wait for Utrecht-Den Haag. I'd be there by two if the trains were on time.

And if I wasn't caught. There were Germans everywhere, but the soldiers mostly seemed to be on their way home for leave or reassignment. Only a few were watching the crowd, and their concern was desultory. If I kept my distance and my head down, the chance of being picked up in the melee was slim.

I boarded the train, found a corner seat, and slumped into it. Being tall might be an advantage on a corner kick, but it was a downright handicap when being hunted. On this trip, however, I felt protected. In my pocket was a letter from Herr Gunter Von Bremmen, Under Secretary to the German Ambassador in Den Haag, affirming an appointment for 4:00 p.m. that afternoon. If I was questioned on this trip, the letter would deflect even the most fervent German soldier. The letterhead and seals alone would be enough to trigger the automatic clicking of the heels, the Nazi salute, and the cry of "Heil Hitler," ingrained in any German trained to instant obeisance to higher

32

authority.

In Utrecht I changed trains. The platforms were even more crowded. Soldiers everywhere. Utrecht was the hub of the Dutch railway system. Every German soldier headed to the front or headed back to Germany from the front funneled through Utrecht. The green and black train headed for Den Haag stood waiting on the perron. Despite the war, the train was on time. All that had changed was that the bulk of the passengers were no longer Dutch burghers headed for work or to shop, but German soldiers. I stepped onto the train and found a seat. Ten minutes out of Utrecht I watched out the right-hand windows. My sister Ge lived in Linschoten, a tiny *dorp* of two dozen houses, a mile or two off to my left. Linchoten would be invisible from the train, but I would be able to spot the church *toren* in Woerden, the town where Ge shopped every Wednesday at the weekly farmers market. I wondered how she was taking the war. Perhaps I would have time to stop to see her on the way back. I dozed off. I would be in Den Haag in a half hour.

The tram tracks converged from the side streets into the *stationplein*, like Hitler's troops surrounding and assaulting the Grebbeberg. I boarded tram number 10. What would I say to Herr Gunter? Margery's father, Joshua Crane, had sent her a letter suggesting she contact Gunter. That Gunter might be of help. That Gunter was a "good" German. Joshua had made friends with friends of Gunter's while playing bridge in Italy. Perhaps Gunter could help? Then again, perhaps he would check "Carl Frits ter Weele" against the German blacklist, wave to an embassy guard, and have me arrested. Marching right into the German embassy … Was it crazy? It certainly felt crazy. My stomach rolled over at the thought. But I could think of no better way—indeed no way at all—to escape Holland with Margery and the three kids.

I stepped out of the tram one stop shy of the embassy. I needed the short walk down the street to collect my thoughts. To steel myself. The houses here were Dutch, brick with ivy, orange tiles, wrought iron fences and gates, yards shaded by great trees, manicured flower beds. One in every two or three houses had a great brass plate reading "Ambassade de France" or "Embassy of Luxembourg." Some of these had a guardhouse at the entrance. Embassy row. Farther along I spotted the black, yellow, and red of the German flag and a pillbox next to the guardhouse. At the image of a black swastika on a red background, the muscles of my abdomen tightened. Sweat dampened my brow. The noise of battle crashed in my ears. The sight of armored vehicles racing toward my position with the swastika flying welled up in my mind.

I stopped for a moment. Breathed deeply. Collected myself. Straightened my back, tucked in my chin, raised myself to my full height, and walked confidently toward the guardhouse. As I passed the pillbox, I nodded to the soldiers as an aloof German officer would, hardly acknowledging the existence of a life as low as that of a private first class.

"Herr Gunter Von Bremmen, bitte." I spoke past the armed guard to the soldier sitting behind him in the guardhouse. I replied to his questions with my name and 1600 hours, the time of the meeting.

"*Papieren,* Herr ter Weele."

I reached into my vest pocket. My passport was in the right vest pocket, and Margery's passport with the children on it was in the left. I handed over my passport and Herr Gunter's letter setting up the meeting. The guard glanced at the passport. Spent a moment reading the letter. He reached for his phone, dialed, spoke to, I assumed, Herr Gunter's secretary. There was a brief exchange, the guard opened the gate, and I was waved up the brick walk to the embassy.

So far, so good. I was behind enemy lines. No shots had been fired. I had crossed the Rubicon. My fate was now in Gunter's hands.

I was ushered into a small waiting room, furnished comfortably in French antiques. I glanced at my watch. The appointment was for four o' clock, and I was properly early: three forty-five. The morning mist mixed with rain had turned to a dim afternoon sun. It filtered weakly through the trees, casting a dull glow on the Louis Quatorze chairs and marble-topped table. My reflection in the gold framed mirror looked confident and in command. My insides were in turmoil, though. Had I won? Or lost? I was in the enemy's lair. Was this victory? Defeat?

A soldier, young and blond, stepped into the room. He was all spit and polish. Eighteen years old? Twenty at the most. He clicked his heels, raised his arm upward, stiffened to attention, and startled me with a furious "Heil Hitler!" I pulled myself out of the chair and followed him into the hall.

Hitler Jeugd, I thought. *Fanatic.* Do not anger them, but accord them no status. Assume they are loyal, well-trained, and insignificant. Treat them poorly and they might erupt. Treat them as significant and they might believe they are.

Herr Gunter rose from his chair as we entered his office. He stood patiently behind the desk while the young soldier saluted with another "Heil Hitler" and then announced, "Herr ter Weele."

Gunter said nothing. He did not move. His face was impassive. It was only when the youngster had closed the door that Gunter smiled. He walked around the desk, and we shook hands.

Gunter smiled again, obliquely. "Ach, the young ones," he said in English. "They know how to behave." After a moment, he added, "Yes, how to behave, and how to follow. And how to obey."

He watched to see if I understood English. I did, but I replied in German. Dutch was, of course, my mother tongue. To be more exact, the language of my youth. I had been born and raised in Enschede, smack on the German border. But my mother was German and her "tongue" was German. Married to a Dutchman and living in Holland, she was careful to always speak Dutch on the street or when we had visitors at home. My father also spoke German flawlessly. Many of his bakery's customers lived across the border. Without the stigma of being born in Germany, he could speak German whenever it suited him. Having gone to secondary school, the HBS, I had studied German for six years. Gunter seemed pleased that my German was both flawless and without accent.

He was tall, almost as tall as me, but thin as a reed. He wore his uniform well. A solemn face, thin hair combed straight back, he held himself high, yet relaxed rather than rigid. Obviously well-educated. Heidelberg perhaps. A career soldier in his late fifties, perhaps sixty. He probably had little in common with today's young recruits. The corners of his mouth turned down slightly. He seemed to carry a permanent sardonic smile, as if the foolishness of life amused him.

After greeting me, he waved me to a chair and returned to behind his desk. He rummaged in a drawer, found a pipe and tobacco and a pack of Camels. He offered me a cigarette and spent a minute or two filling the pipe. The room was all dark wood with a leather couch and chairs, also dark brown. The high windows looked out onto a pleasant garden encompassed by a high brick wall. The sun, which had appeared briefly, was gone, and a light rain was helping the coming evening darken the world. The embassy was quiet. Since my host neither moved nor spoke, I also remained silent. I knew he was studying me. Wondering. And I was studying him. Would he help me? Could he? Could I trust him?

After he had lit the pipe, he spoke again, in German. About the weather, a book he was reading. Making small talk. After a bit we settled on football; he had played keeper. We reminisced about international matches we had seen. We smiled when we realized we had both been in Rome three years earlier to watch a Germany-Italy match. A good match, played hard. The Germans—solid, physical. The Italians—creative, mercurial. An especially good match from Gunter's perspective. The German side had won.

It had been forty-five minutes now. Where were we going? I wondered. Outside it was dark. A knock, the door opened, and a young lady tilted her head through the opening. She was going home, she said. His secretary, I supposed. He wished her a good evening, and she left.

He turned to me and shifted to speaking English. "Speaking of Rome," he said, "I get there off and on. I understand that your father-in-law is there even now?"

So, I thought, Joshua's friend in Rome had contacted him, as Joshua had said he would. "Yes," I replied. I weighed my words. "He is an accomplished sportsman. But football? No. He calls it soccer."

He laughed. "But he also plays bridge?"

"Passionately."

"And he has invented a revolutionary bidding system? The Crane System?"

"Yes." I inferred that Gunter had not only been contacted by Klaus Ulmann, my father-in-law's bridge partner, but that the letter had been a long one. "Do you play?" I asked.

He took a slim volume off the bookshelf behind him. "I am a student of the game," he replied. He showed me the book. It was titled *The Crane System of Contract Bidding*. I knew my father-in-law had had his system published. I had played it with him, but I had never seen a copy of the book. "This is a breakthrough," Gunter said enthusiastically. "An entirely new approach. It makes Culbertson look cumbersome." He smiled sardonically at his pun.

"I understand that a friend of yours, Herr Klaus Ulmann, is one of Mr. Crane's bridge partners in Rome," I said. "Do they play the Crane System together?"

"At least three times per week. He tells me that Mr. Crane is a world-class player. And a gentleman."

He toyed with his pipe. Tamped it. Relit it. Before he could take a puff, there was a loud knock on the door. The door sprang open, and the young soldier who had shown me in, the Hitler Jeugd, marched two steps into the office. Saluted and stood fiercely at attention. I tensed. Had I been lulled into letting my guard down? Was Gunter setting me up? Was this my arrest?

Gunter looked at his watch, and I glanced quickly at mine. 1730. Gunter saluted from his chair. It was the end of his duty, the guard reported. He would not return in the morning. Tomorrow he would not be in. He would be at headquarters for training. But there would be a replacement. *Gut?* Gunter saluted again and dismissed him.

I relaxed, although my heart was still throbbing. I had let myself forget. That must not happen again. Gunter, so nice, but a snap of his fingers and I could be shot sitting in my chair.

After the soldier left, Gunter took two or three puffs on his pipe. Then he leaned forward, toward me, and again spoke in English, softly. His voice was hardly audible.

"Klaus has suggested to me that perhaps I could help you. What do you have in mind?"

I paused, took a deep breath. The moment of truth. How much could I tell him? How far could I trust him? That he had apparently waited for his secretary and personal guard to leave before broaching any delicate subject was a good sign. And yet ...

"You know I have an American wife?" I asked. "And two young sons?" He nodded. "And a daughter, nine months old?" This time he raised his eyebrows. My father-in-law hadn't yet known about our third child when he spoke to Klaus Ulmann. Or he had forgotten.

Gunter waited for me to continue. The room was quiet. The embassy was empty but for the two of us and perhaps a handful of others. The only sound was a black rain in the black night.

Should I trust him? Could I? Were there any other options if Margery, the children, and I were to escape? The Nazis were hunting for all of the Dutch officer corps. They had begun at the top. I mentally ticked off those that I knew had already been arrested. Hendricks. Jan Bosma. Oudewater. Van der Heijden. Pieters. And on and on. So many others.

Gunter puffed quietly as I leaned toward him to speak. He also leaned forward.

"I would like to leave Holland with my wife and children. Could you help us?"

"How?" he asked.

"Can you get me visas? To England, perhaps?"

He started to reply, then put up a finger to silence me. He paused for no more than a moment, and then pulled a pack of cards from his desk drawer and deftly dealt four bridge hands.

"Lay the hands out," he ordered. In German, in a conversational voice.

"Good," he said when the hands were spread before us. "Let us say you were the dealer. Explain to me what you would bid if you were bidding Crane."

I looked at him curiously. What was he up to? Still in German, still in a conversational tone, he went on. "Would you open a spade or a diamond?"

I had five spades, queen high, in the hand he had dealt me. And four diamonds: ace, queen, jack, ten.

As I studied the cards, I suddenly realized why Gunter had pulled them out. Someone was in the hall outside the door. The hairs on the nape of my neck rose. I dared not look over my shoulder. Was that someone already in the room? Was there a pistol pointed at me?

"One spade," I said. Had the words come out without betraying me? Did I sound casual, oblivious to danger?

"But the diamonds count as three tricks in Culbertson," Gunter said.

"Yes, but in Crane, the goal is to reach game in a major suit. As quickly as possible." My ears heard nothing, but my brain was screaming hysterically. Someone was in the room, right behind me. Or in the hall, listening. "The probability of scoring a game is greater in a major suit, because one need only bid to the four level, than in diamonds or clubs. In Crane, one is obliged to open a five-card major if one has twelve points in high cards."

"Ach. And how do you count to twelve points? In Culbertson, your hand comes to five tricks."

My senses strained. In the room? Not yet. The door had been closed, and I hadn't heard it open. Someone must be listening in the hall.

"Yes," I said. "In Culbertson, an ace counts as one trick. In Crane, an ace is awarded four points. A king three points, a queen two, and a jack one."

Gunter appeared relaxed. He puffed again. Looking at his own hand, nearer to him, he put on steel-rimmed reading glasses. "And what would

I reply to your bid of one spade?"

He seemed genuinely interested, without a concern in the world. Was I wrong? The finger he had lifted to silence me when I spoke—had I dreamed that?

"Your hand would demand a response in spades," I said.

"Why?"

"You have nine points with the king of spades, ace of hearts, and queen of clubs." I pointed to the three spades. "More significantly you have three spades. That is, three of the major suit I bid. So you must raise me in spades."

I was beginning to relax. Gunter's calm suggested that my fears were misplaced.

"Must raise you in spades?" he asked. "Shouldn't I show my other suits, or my distribution?"

"Remember, the goal in Crane is to reach game as quickly as possible, to shut out bidding opportunity for the opponents, and to reveal as little information as possible to them in order to complicate their defense."

I must have been wrong. I had imagined Gunter's sign to me. He was genuinely interested in the Crane System.

"But one additional matter. Note the singleton diamond you have." I placed my finger on the card. "In Crane, once the partnership has agreed on its suit, one accumulates extra points for some distributions."

Gunter nodded. "Ja. Extra length, voids?"

"Yes," I said. "A singleton is valued at three points. Thus, your total count is the nine for high cards plus three for distribution."

As I finished the sentence, there was a knock on the door and the door was pushed open. Gunter stood up.

"Your Excellency. Good evening." He smiled and turned to me as I stood as well. "I have the honor to present Herr Weele. Herr Weele, his Excellency, the Ambassador."

The two of us shook hands. I greeted him in German.

The Ambassador looked puzzled. "You are Dutch, *nein?*" I nodded. "You are friends?"

I swallowed as he looked at Gunter accusingly.

Gunter chuckled. "Yes," he said. "Close friends." Then he added, "Actually, I am spying on Herr Weele." The Ambassador's mouth opened in surprise. "Herr Weele plays a new and novel bidding system. A foreign system." He dragged out the word *foreign* and then he chuckled.

"I am trying to break the system code."

The Ambassador turned to the four bridge hands lying face up on the desk. "Ach. Bridge." Turning to me, he added, "If you are instructing Herr Von Bremmen in bridge, you must love the game as he does."

When he had entered the room, he had been suspicious of me. Now he dismissed me as irrelevant. Bridge was not his interest. His attitude made it clear that bridge was a silly game.

Turning back to Gunter, he said he would not be in the next morning and that there was an appointment on his calendar for 10:30 a.m. Would Gunter handle it?

Gunter assured him he would, and the Ambassador said good night, turned on his heel, and left.

Gunter and I stood for a moment after he closed the door. We could hear his steps down the hall, hear the front door open and close. Neither Gunter nor I raised the matter, but both of us knew he had been listening for some time to our conversation. What had we said before Gunter realized he was there? Nothing incriminating, I thought. But it left me uneasy. Gunter had also been uneasy. *Herr Weele*, he had said, not *Herr ter Weele*. He had purposefully given the Ambassador a wrong name. To provide camouflage if the Ambassador searched my background?

Gunter turned again to the cards on the table. It took only a moment for us to finish bidding the hands, and then he pulled the cards toward him, riffled them into a deck, boxed them, and returned them to his drawer. His interest in the cards had been feigned. In boxing them, he boxed even the semblance of curiosity.

We sat silently, mulling the intrusion of the Ambassador. I listened to the silence of the embassy, closed for the night. Rain dripped from the eaves onto the outside windowsill. A branch flittered against the pane.

Gunter leaned forward and spoke softly, again in English.

"To leave Holland for England, you need a British visa from the British Consulate that you could quite certainly obtain from the British Consul. His offices are adjacent to the British Embassy two blocks from here." He shook his head slowly. "The difficult part is to obtain permission to leave Holland. You need a letter of free transit out of the country."

I waited. Could he help in that regard?

He went on, "Such permission could be issued by our military upon request by the Ambassador." He shook his head, hearing the question I had not asked. "No. I cannot help in that regard. Were I to even suggest it to the Ambassador, he would find out that you were a Dutch officer on the blacklist." He paused. My throat tightened up. Gunter had searched my background, knew I was being hunted. "He would have me arrested and you shot." Another pause. "No." He shook his head. "There is no way to help you there."

I thought a moment. I had asked about the visa to Britain, which had to be issued, of course, by the country to which one wished to travel.

"Does the embassy"—I gestured to indicate our surroundings—"issue visas for visits to Germany?"

"Of course," Gunter replied. "That is one of our functions." He smiled wryly. "But the Dutch no longer ask to visit *Deutschland*." Even speaking in English, he referred to Germany in German.

"Could you obtain visas to Germany for me?" I asked.

He chuckled. "You would wish to go to Germany?"

I shrugged. "Perhaps. Could you obtain visas for me?"

"Too dangerous for me," he answered. "That would lead to instant arrest and it would mean my death."

I had decided in these last minutes that Gunter liked me and truly wished he could help me. "Who in the embassy issues visas?" I asked.

"The Consul and two or three of his staff. The building next door." He paused. "And the Ambassador. He occasionally issues visas for senior visiting officials."

"Where are the visa stamps?"

"In the right-hand top drawer in the Ambassador's office. At the end of the hall."

He thought a bit, and then he took a ring of keys from his pocket and deliberately placed them on the corner of his desk. "This is the key to the Ambassador's office," he said, indicating one of them. "This one"—he pointed to a small brass key—"is the key to the visa drawer."

We sat for a while. The silence in the embassy suffocated me. Wasn't silence said to be liberating? I found it hard to breathe.

"Look," Gunter said. "You are ..." He paused. Searched. "Stupid. Crazy. Why would you go to Germany? Your wife? Your children?"

He looked at me. It had not yet become clear to me why I would want to go to Germany. But Gunter could not help me go in any other direction. Going to Germany was indeed crazy. Dangerous. But the only help Gunter could give was to get me to Germany. And while it would be crazy to go there, it would be insane to remain in Holland. At any rate, getting visas would be my first step. It didn't mean I had to go to Germany. It just provided me an option.

I shook my head, unable to answer his question. "Can you stamp my passport?" I reached into my pocket for my passport and Margery's. Hers included the names and photos of our three children.

He pushed his chair backward, distancing himself from me. "No. Were I caught helping you, that would be the end. If I went to the Ambassador's office now, the guard would stop me, arrest me."

He glanced at his watch. He studied the ceiling and then looked back at me. He pondered, leaned forward.

"The guards make one or two rounds each night. They unlock every office, check it, then lock it again." He pointed behind me. "Were you to spend the night in that closet, you could do what you wish. If you are caught, you are dead." His smile was thin. "If you say you are here with my permission, I am dead too.

"In the morning, when I arrive, do not leave the closet until I open it and let you out. Neither tonight's guards nor the Ambassador will be here in the morning. If you join me at 10:00 for a cup of coffee, it is probable that you could leave at 10:30 or 11:00 and no one would be the wiser."

"Your secretary?" I asked.

He shrugged. "We shall see."

I nodded. A night in the embassy. With guards. Could I do this? Could I get to the Ambassador's office? Find the visa stamps? And not get caught?

"Remember," Gunter said. "Do not exit the closet in the morning unless I open it. It would not do to come out if someone is here with me. And I will not let you out until the day is underway. It would be too obvious if you leave early."

We studied each other. I thanked him. I was gambling that he would not have me arrested. But even with his complicity, this was risky. There were the guards, and even Gunter, well-meaning now, might get cold feet and a change of heart at midnight.

He nodded toward the closet. "I will close up."

The closet was small. I sat in the corner under three coats. I could hear him put papers in his briefcase, turn off the lights, close and lock the door. He was gone. When would the guards make their round? I settled down. I would not leave the closet until the guards had made their first round. After that, I would sneak to the Ambassador's office, stamp visas onto the two passports, and return. Difficult? No. Safe? No.

I listened for a long time. Not a sound. Gunter had been the last to leave the building. I dozed off once or twice and awoke each time with a start.

Then I heard steps in the hall. The guard. Noises at a door, the snap of light switches, the sound of two or three steps, and then again the snap of light switches and a key in the lock.

The same noises a second time. My breathing was shallow and fast, my heart throbbed. And then the noises at Gunter's door. The snap of the switch, and light glowed under the closet door. Five seconds, ten. I dared not breathe. Then the light went out, the door closed, the lock turned.

I listened as the guard went through the ritual across the hall. Then I heard him going up the stairs.

I settled myself. In my mind, I traveled to the marsh outside Enschede, hunkered in a blind. My father was in a blind farther along the edge of the shadowy bog. Mallards, quacking in the dark. Quacking. Talking. A stone's throw from me, but so dark I couldn't see them. I was hardly twelve. My first time hunting with my father. My heart pounded with excitement. I couldn't move or the ducks would fly. I couldn't shoot because it was too dark. I settled myself. A deep breath. Quiet. Slow. Control. Wait.

The sounds of the guard were gone. Wait for his next visit? Go now? Earlier I had decided to go after his first round, and that still seemed wise. Who knew if he would really make a second round?

Cautiously, slowly, I pushed open the closet door. It was dark, but light filtered in from a streetlight. I made my way to Gunter's door, opened it. No one in the hall. I left the door ajar, thinking it might lock behind me if I closed it.

Quickly down the hall. Fumbled with the keys in the half light. Shh! Careful! No noise. The door opened with a snap. Careful, careful. Sound could kill. Through the secretary's office to the Ambassador's door. The key didn't turn the lock. My heart jumped. Calm. Calm. Wrong key. The other one turned in the lock. Let's not make that noise this time. I was in the office. Visas. Which was the visa drawer? In the desk? The credenza? I noticed a second desk with drawers along the sides and above the writing surface. A cabinet. I tried the key on a small door—no good—and then on a drawer. Yes! It opened. There were a number of rubber stamps. I found my lighter, listened. Nothing, so I lit the flame. It provided enough light for me to see the stamp. It had little wheels: the date stamp. I found another stamp: visa for German Reich. I took the two passports out of my pocket, opened them to a blank page. Moistened the visa stamp on an ink pad, stamped both passports. Twirled the wheels on the date stamp to 27/07/1940, wet the stamp on the pad, and stamped next week's date next to the visa in each passport. Done. I could fill in the required validity dates in pen later, at my leisure.

A noise? I cocked my head. Closed the drawer, locked it, stepped silently to the door. Listened, listened. Nothing.

I was about to exit the Ambassador's office, but turned back to his desk. I opened the middle drawer and lit my lighter again. Pens, a daily agenda of meetings. I opened the top right-hand drawer. An address book filled with lots of addresses along with the names of German officials, other ambassadors. What more? A sheet of letter paper folded in the address book caught my attention. I unfolded it.

It was handwritten. The handwriting was distinctive but hard to decipher. I could make out "In the event you might need them, here are my contacts." Underneath were three telephone numbers labeled in pen: "office/secretary," "control command/always knows my whereabouts," and "personal/use only in the event of emergency." I could not make out the signature. I read the official letterhead embossed in gold at the top. German Reich. Gestapo Headquarters.

I stepped back. My God. I could now make out the signature— *Heinrich Himmler*. There was his signature, and above was his name in the gold lettering of the letterhead. I started to replace the sheet, then changed my mind, refolded it, slipped it in my pocket. Closed the drawers.

Out through the Ambassador's door with a soft click. Paused at his secretary's door. Listened. Nothing. Out I went into the hall, closed and locked the door behind me. I started down the hall. Steps! Steps on the landing! Quickly, quickly, down the hall, slipped through Gunter's door, thankful I had left it open. In. Quick. No time to lock it before hiding in the closet.

The steps came closer, stopping at each door. Not opening them, just testing the lock. One office. A second office. And then he tested Gunter's door. The handle turned and the door opened. I heard the guard swear, come into the office. He turned on the light and took two more steps. And then another. One more. He swore again and walked back to the door. Closed it, locked it, mumbled to himself.

I let out my breath, suddenly realizing I hadn't been breathing. As I breathed again, I smiled ruefully. The guard had supposed he had left the door unlocked on his last round. If not, he would have searched more carefully and I would now be dead. For a moment, I rejoiced. But no, not yet, not yet. I am still in the embassy, still in danger. Don't relax your guard.

The closet floor was hard and the space cramped. I tried to stay awake but dozed off from time to time. At daybreak, a sliver of light limned the bottom edge of the door. For a third time I heard the night guard make his rounds, trying each door to test that it was locked. I heard him grunt in satisfaction that he had properly locked Gunter's office this time. I had been lucky. A more intelligent guard, a more careful one—I didn't finish the thought.

I dared not snap my lighter to read the time on my watch. An hour or two later the front door opened and closed. Within a minute or two the opening and closing was a constant. The staff was arriving. Voices grunted good mornings. Office doors were unlocked, light switches snapped on. I was still sitting, crouched under the coats with my back against the wall. Uncomfortable. Painful. A frame of six foot four inches was not made to sit on a hard floor in a small space.

Another hour, perhaps more, passed, and the door to Gunter's office opened. Someone came in and turned on the lights. The sound of steps, the squeak of the desk chair. A long silence but for the occasional squeak of the chair and shuffling of papers. Gunter, I supposed.

A tap on the office door, a woman's voice. Gunter's secretary. She greeted him and apparently sat down. They exchanged comments about the day's work. The voice was definitely Gunter's. He dictated a short reply to a letter. Told her politely to decline a request in another letter. The exchange continued for a half hour, perhaps longer. I dared not move. Breathed carefully. *Verdomme,* it was uncomfortable!

They finished going through the mail, chatted for a few minutes about her mother, who apparently was ill in Dusseldorf. She reminded Gunter that he was to handle the meeting scheduled for 10:30. It would be in the Ambassador's office. She apparently handed him a file regarding the meeting, and then she was gone. Or so I supposed, though I hadn't heard her leave.

When would Gunter let me out of this solitary confinement? I hadn't moved a muscle in almost three hours. My spine was killing me. The old coats hanging around my shoulders didn't help.

Another twenty or thirty minutes, and I heard Gunter get up. He took a few steps and then seemed to be gone. In the glimmer of light through the crack in the closet door I could make out my watch. 10:25. He must be headed to his meeting in the Ambassador's office. When would he be back? I hadn't heard him close his door. Someone could just walk in, or could even already be in the office, waiting for Gunter's return. I steadied my breathing. No noise, I told myself.

More time passed before someone came into the office. Who? Gunter returning from his meeting? Almost immediately I heard a light tap on his office door, followed by the secretary's voice and Gunter's in response. She was bringing him more papers, I supposed. She pointed out a couple of issues in the pages she had apparently typed and asked for guidance on how to handle another matter. He replied briefly to her questions.

I relaxed my guard. It seemed that only Gunter was in the office. Why hadn't he come to the closet earlier? Even just to whisper to me to stay in hiding? He must be frightened, I thought. Frightened for his own life. I smiled wryly. Worried, perhaps, for my life, but frightened to death for his own.

I began to doze. An image of Marge came to my mind. She standing on the dock in Marseille with my brother Hendrik and a strange man who, I was to learn later, was her older brother Alex. She in a summer skirt and blouse. She took me by storm, I thought. My, my, what a figure. Bare shoulders, brown from the sun of the Riviera, jet-black hair, eyes that sparkled with excitement and teasing, the shapely legs of an athlete. That came, I also learned later, from playing golf with her father. A delightful rump. Was she truly that attractive? I had wondered. Or was it due to my seven years in the Dutch East Indies? Seven years without seeing a *blanke vrouw*. Seven years, plus three weeks by ship to Marseille.

Voices shook me awake. Careful! Stay alert! It was Gunter's secretary asking if he needed anything else. She was heading out for lunch. A few steps and she was gone.

Five minutes. Ten. And then Gunter was at the closet door.

"Herr ter Weele. Are you there?"

I crawled from under the coats, not an easy task at my size and stiff from a night and half a day sitting on a hard floor.

I shook myself. Gunter smiled wryly, knowing it had been a painful night.

He sat at his desk, I across from him. We chatted only briefly. He asked me nothing about the night. No question of, "Did you succeed?" Then he ushered me to his door. He wanted me out during the lunch break. Fewer people to see me go. Fewer people who might be surprised that they hadn't seen me come in during the morning. And I had to be out before his secretary returned. I felt his fear, and my heart rate jumped in response.

He left me in the hall. He had done his good deed. He wanted no further risk. I opened the front door, walked at a modest pace to the gateway. I gave no notice to the guards but for a perfunctory nod. Down the block, around the corner. The embassy was out of sight. For the first time in twenty-four hours, I breathed deeply, enjoyed the sun on my face and the bit of breeze stirring the trees.

I had done it. Gunter was no Nazi, just a human being. Joshua Crane had been right in sending me to him. I patted my pocket. The two passports were there. Stamped. As I boarded the tram, I smiled for a moment. A smile of victory, of relief, but then I grimaced. What, after all, did I have? Visas out of Holland, yes, but to where? Germany. Berlin. Hell. And from there? Would going to Germany be better than hiding in Holland?

I pondered the next steps on the train back to Eindhoven. There would be no stroll in the park, no sprinkling of rose petals, no red carpet to the exit. *And were a carpet to magically appear,* I thought, chuckling ruefully, *it would be blood red.*

Hoofdstuk 6

30 juli 1940: Timing of Nazi drive on Britain discussed in Berlin. Royal Air Force repels air raids on Dover, bombs oil installations in Cherbourg. Rail traffic between Occupied and Unoccupied France halted. Vichy government explains German military has taken control of French transport system.

I gathered Jan and Alex into my arms. Margy was asleep. I had just finished nursing her. The boys had been in our tiny backyard playing with toy soldiers. Imagine, more soldiers. We were surrounded by them. Soldiers in the pillbox in the Petrusdonderstraat right in front of our home. Groups of soldiers at almost every corner, some in pillboxes, others standing next to a tank or a personnel carrier. Soldiers guarding the hospital where Margy had been born just nine months earlier. Soldiers in front of the municipal buildings. Why would the boys want to play at war? Weren't the soldiers in the street enough for them? I smiled wryly. Boys would be boys, I guess.

We had moved here to the Petrusdonderstaat, number 19, from Brussels in June of 1938. I was seven months pregnant with Alex at the time. We'd had good times here, Carl and I. A pleasant row house, *nieuwbouw*. The neighbors were all friendly, and Loeky Blok—our next door neighbor—and I had become fast friends. Carl and her husband, Lou, enjoyed each other as well. The latter was a little toad of a man next to my Carl, with his small eyes, bald head, steel-rimmed glasses, and scientific mind, but each of them had a joie de vivre—which Lou called, in his Dutch-accented English, his love for wine, women, and song. And in many ways Loeky and I were opposites as well, joined in part however by our commitment to our men. She couldn't have children, yet she shared my joy in my three young ones.

I was far from my roots, far from Girl Scout camp on Little Squam in New Hampshire and Miss Winsor's School for young ladies in Boston; far from my father's gentleman's dairy farm in Westwood,

Massachusetts; from my cousins' summer house on Cape Cod and my father's No Man's Land island off Martha's Vineyard. Carl was my first man. He fulfilled me. My three children were my life. My house girl Rita, young and naive as she was, had also become a dear friend. I had learned Dutch. I had learned to please my husband, and he to please me. I had learned to love Holland.

And now this war. Who would have thought it would come to this? Carl had survived the German onslaught. In that we were lucky. So far the Germans had not come knocking on the door, but both he and I knew time was running out. The Germans were clamping down. Their anti-Jewish campaign, initially invisible, was now hideously overt. More and more of Carl's fellow officers were being caught and killed. Hardly a week ago he came home from the meeting with my father's friend-of-a-friend in the German embassy to announce that we would leave for Berlin—yes, Berlin—next week.

Would I, the little Boston girl, have the wherewithal to pull this trip off with him? Would these two boys, snuggled here in my arms, survive? Would my little Margy? Would I? And Carl? I knew he was frightened, but strong and optimistic too. He was certain we could pull it off. Confident in me—far more confident that I was. But even if we had shared our fears at 2 a.m. last night, for neither of us had been able to sleep, we both knew the German juggernaut was closing in on us. Loeky had heard from a friend in the town hall that an inquiry regarding Carl's whereabouts had been received last week. The Burgemeester had sent a response that many of his records had been burned when the Germans overran Eindhoven, and that he had no record of a Carl Frits ter Weele, Lieutenant in the Treasonous Dutch Forces here in Eindhoven. An inquiry of that sort by the Gestapo could be but days, perhaps hours, away from an arrest, heralded by a midnight knock on our door. Not only was Carl a wanted Dutch officer, Loeky's friend reported, but the Nazi inquiry reported that Carl and some of his staff were implicated in a plot to murder the Führer. How that rumor started we had no idea, though it was true that Carl and his staff, and perhaps half the Dutch military, had at some time or other spoken over a beer about their desire to murder Hitler. Or had the Gestapo somehow learned that Carl had acquired a German visa?

To flee or not to flee. The question that had confronted us these past weeks had answered itself. The only question remaining was, Where? To where should we flee? Well, yes, first stop Berlin. And then? And how soon should we leave? Carl and I had talked half the night. So much to do, but we had decided on early next week.

I pulled the boys closer. They were hungry from playing at war. I should feed them. Even if the turmoil in my innards made it impossible for me to eat, I must feed these two. They would need the strength for the trip.

Again my thoughts circled around to what we had to do. Flee? Yes, we must. But Germany? Insane! I had been to Spain with my brother Alex seven years ago, a short while before I had met Carl, and we had watched a bullfight, watched those big bulls charge into the ring. They had frightened me. To flee from them, would I run into the ring, into the sunlight, in full view? No, no, a thousand times no! The Germans were like those bulls. Big, black, indomitable. So we should go to Berlin? My instincts revolted at the thought.

Carl remained convinced, though, that it was our only chance. He had been told by those who had seen copies of the German blacklist that he was on it. The soldiers guarding Holland's borders were on alert, looking for anyone who might try to flee. Only the border to Germany was open to traffic. And now Carl had visas, valid visas, for us to travel there. If we got into Germany, we had a chance, perhaps even a good chance. Or would a family of five, a husband, wife, and three children, raise suspicions? And after Berlin, then what? A boat to Sweden? A train across occupied Poland to Lithuania? Austria? Neutral Switzerland? France? Carl wasn't sure yet. But then, if we were arrested before reaching Berlin, that part of our plan would be irrelevant. Irrelevant in capital letters, with exclamation marks. The soldiers' orders for those on the blacklist were clear: immediate detention. In the event of resistance, shoot to kill. And the Germans preferred a man whom they could bury over one they had to imprison.

I could hear Carl at the front door. He leaned down and kissed me, and I looked at him questioningly. He had been out trying to beg, borrow, or steal German Marks. He nodded at the boys. He didn't want to talk in front of them, didn't want to frighten them.

"Eten?" he suggested. *"Zullen we wat eten?"*

I had already made lunch for the four of us, soup and a bit of pork. Food was expensive, but generally there was enough to eat if one could beg, borrow, or steal the necessary ration coupons. Formula for Margy, however, was largely unavailable. I could only hope that my milk kept flowing.

Carl was edgy. He wanted lunch to be over. At his insistence, I trundled the boys to their bedroom for an afternoon nap. Jan resisted halfheartedly. At his age he normally didn't take a nap anymore.

When I returned from the bedroom, Carl caught me around the waist and pulled me onto his lap.

"What?" I asked. "What is it?"

He kissed me. And kissed me again. "Jan van der Landen."

"Who?"

"Jan van der Landen. One of my *onder-officieren*. He lives on the Multatulistraat." He swallowed. "They picked him up this morning."

I put my hand over my mouth. I didn't know the officer, but Multatulistraat was only a stone's throw away from us.

Carl held me close. "How soon can we be ready to leave? In an hour?" He looked at his watch. It was 2:30. "I would like you and the children out of here at 3:30." He saw my look of bewilderment. "I know. Not next week as we had planned. Not next week, not tomorrow. Now."

"One hour!" I protested.

"Yes. They picked up Jan this morning. He was charged in a plot to kill Hitler. He knows our address. He knows the address of all four of us." He was referring to himself and three officers who lived nearby and who had also been stationed at Grebbeberg.

I must have looked stunned.

"By now Jan has told them," he said. "They could be here at any moment." He touched my cheek to reassure me. "Get Loeky to help you. You can start her on the packing. Then you and the children can leave. She can finish the packing for you and bring the bags to Centraal Station."

I was still trying to take in all he was saying.

"There's a 6:00 p.m. train for Berlin, via Utrecht. You'll be early. Take the boys and Margy to the park and meet Loeky and Lou on the perron at 5:45. They can go there earlier, buy your tickets for you. But you get there as late as possible. Give the Germans as little time as possible to see you in case they are looking."

He paused, thought for a moment. "Tell Loeky that if the soldiers come and question her, she should tell them we're in Maastricht with friends for a few days. That she expects us back tomorrow afternoon."

And then, as an afterthought, he added, "And if the soldiers come to her house, she should not bring our bags to the station. She and Lou must not come either. They might be followed by the Germans. We will simply leave without luggage."

"And you?" I asked.

"They are not really after you and the kids. They won't bother you until they have me." He kissed me quickly. "I've got to leave now. I'll waste some time and board the train at the very last moment. *Geluk, liefje.*" He slipped out the back door and was gone.

My God! Carl's life was truly in danger! We'd known that for weeks but hadn't really worried much. With Jan van der Landen in Nazi hands, they would be after Carl in no time. I wanted to sit down. I wanted to sit down and cry. But I had no time for that.

I walked outside and rang at Loeky's door. No more than a meter separated our two walkways and doors.

"*Eventjes.*" Loeky called from inside. A few seconds later she opened the door, took one look at me, and threw her arms around me. "*Wat is het,* Margery?"

I burst out crying.

"Do they have Carl?" Her voice rose in panic, alight with fear.

"No. No. But they have picked up one of his officers on the Multatulistraat, and he fears they will be after him any moment." I pulled back from her. "We are leaving. Oh, Loeky, we are leaving."

She put a finger to my lips. "Don't tell me," she commanded. "Don't tell me where you are going." She hugged me again. "They can't force me to tell them what I don't know."

I pulled her out of her doorway and into our house. "Can you help, Loeky?"

"Of course! Anything. What do you need?"

"Carl wants me and the children out of the house in a half hour. Could you pack some things for Carl and the children? Two bags, no more."

"*Ach, kind.* I can't get what the five of you need in two bags!" She saw the despair, the fright, on my face. "I'll do what I can, Margery." She pronounced Margery with a lilt in her Dutch-accented English.

We rushed up the stairs. I found two suitcases, some clothes, bathroom supplies, shoes. Quick, quick, quick. Loeky packed for the boys. I packed in my bedroom for Carl, little Margy, and myself. Ten minutes. Quick, quick. Loeky carried one suitcase, I carried the other. Down the stairs to the door. No one outside. Out our door and into Loeky's house.

"If you are interrogated," I told her, "Carl said that you should tell them we are in Maastricht for a day or two visiting friends." We hugged. "And tell them you expect us back tomorrow or the next day."

"Ach, *kind*." She was almost in tears. "It is not fair! To leave your house, to leave me, all in ten minutes! What has our world come to?"

"I'll go and wake the children. Carl wants me to take them to the park. Bring the luggage to Centraal Station. The 6:00 p.m. train, direction Utrecht. You can go early, buy tickets for us. I'll be there with the children at 5:45."

We hugged again, holding on to each other. She had tried to flee three months ago. Immediately after the Dutch capitulation, Philips had ordered all its researchers to England. Philips had managed to get Loeky and Lou and a half dozen of Lou's colleagues to Rotterdam by minibus only to be blocked at the port. The Nazis had suspended all boat traffic. Now it was my turn to flee.

The boys were quick to wake, excited to go to the park. Margy was half-asleep, and I put her in the stroller. The boys had their football. I wanted to look around, see what we might have forgotten, say good-bye to the nest Carl and I had enjoyed these past two years. But Carl had warned me to leave.

As I opened the front door, I had the shock of my life. Three soldiers coming up the walk! I turned to the children, pretending not to see the uniforms, not to see the men, feigning innocence.

"Don't forget your ball, Jan!" I called, raising my voice loud enough to ensure that the soldiers behind me would hear.

When I had the children outside, on the *stoep*, I closed the door. I was still pretending that I hadn't seen the soldiers behind me. As I turned to start down our sidewalk, they were standing there, casually blocking my way.

I smiled and greeted them with what I thought was an expression of friendliness. "Can I help you, gentlemen?"

I smiled again. I was married, but I was still young, still trim. Carl always teased me that I had naughty eyes. I tried to be naughty now.

"*Mevrouw*," one said. "Sorry to bother you. We need to enter your house."

What might they find? My mind raced. At least it would not be Carl.

"Of course, of course." I smiled again, opened the door. "Come in. Please come in."

In they came. I herded Jan and Alex back in with their ball, and then unbuckled Margy from the stroller and put her on my hip.

Two of the soldiers had already checked the downstairs rooms and started up the stairs. The third, the one in charge, asked where my husband was. "In Maastricht," I said. "With friends."

"Will he be coming back?"

"Yes. Not tomorrow. The next day."

"And where are you going?"

He was polite but brusque. I smiled again. "After their nap, the children and I always go to the park. If the weather is nice."

His two companions came down the stairs and shook their heads when he looked at them questioningly. "Nobody."

All three of them clicked their heels and saluted me. I smiled again. It did not take much to charm them. The one officer thanked me. His Dutch was surprisingly good.

As we all started toward the door together, I asked him where in Germany he was from. "Cologne," he replied.

"You have a beautiful cathedral," I said with as much sweetness as I could. He nodded, smiled, pleased at my appreciation of his city's landmark.

When we were all on the walkway, I closed the door. They stood on the sidewalk while I herded the children toward the park. They would reenter the house, I knew, as soon as I was out of sight. Was there anything there for them to find? Would they lie in wait, hoping to surprise Carl?

I was trembling. I wanted to look back, to see if indeed they would reenter the house. I wanted to see our house one more time to say good-bye. Instead I busied myself with the children. We had been lucky. They had missed Carl by an hour. But would they be watching the trains? Would they catch us tonight at the station? Tomorrow at the border? In Berlin?

When we reached the park, I sat on a bench and held Margy close. The tulips were long gone, but what we called tea roses in Boston were in full bloom. A lyrical day. The boys chased pigeons. A lady a few benches farther on was feeding them from a dry crust of bread, rubbing it with her fingers to make crumbs to sprinkle. The pigeons were dancing around her ankles.

So close, I thought. So very close. What had Carl and I gotten into? He had defended his country as any patriot would. Now he was being hunted. We were running like frightened deer from a pack of wolves. Would we be caught? Would they corner us and tear us to pieces? And what of Jan, Alex, little Margy? The calm and serenity of pastoral Holland, of our life here, had turned into a Gotterdammerung. Carl had urged me to flee with the children before the war broke out. Should I have left for their sakes? No, a thousand times no. I had known that the least we could do, if he was to risk his life at the front, was to stay and support him.

My thoughts turned to my flight from the United States fifteen years earlier. Also a hurried departure, but not one fraught with danger.

Father had taken me aside after school one day. How old was I? Fourteen? He told me that I was to go to school the next day as I normally did. I was to say nothing of what he was about to tell me to anyone. George—he was our handyman—would pick me up after school and drive me to Boston Harbor. My father and mother would be waiting aboard ship. We would leave with the evening tide to sail to London. It was only later that I learned why we were making this escape. Congress had instituted the income tax ten years earlier. My father thought it unconstitutional and refused to pay any taxes. Ten years later, the government was pursuing him for restitution, with penalties, possibly incarceration. So he fled. He swore that he would be damned if he'd pay a tax that was unconstitutional.

It led to a wonderland for me. England and Scotland in the summers; at a lycee in Paris during the school year; the Riviera for Christmas. Two years later, the winter months were at finishing school in Florence. I traveled everywhere with my mother. She spoke no languages other than English, so I was her guide in French and Italian. Actually, she was my stepmother, since my biological mother had died during my infancy. But she loved me dearly, as I did her.

My father played polo in England and France, instructed and played golf with the Prince of Wales (later to become Edward the Eighth and to abdicate the throne), and taught me golf as well. We played all the famous British courses together. St. Andrews the most because Father played there with the Prince, but also those less well-known: Turnberry with its salty sea breezes; quirky Prestwick; Royal Lytham & St. Annes; Deal, which brought back memories of Cape Cod. And the three that I liked the most because they reminded me of No Man's Land—Royal Portrush, Royal Troon, and Royal St. Georges.

Yes, our flight from Boston had been hurried, just as this flight was hurried. But it had been a joyful, exciting, magical voyage. This flight would be a flight to hell, not a trip to merry old England and the land of l'amour.

I called to the boys, and they broke off their game of football reluctantly. I had decided we would take a taxi to the station. If I was being followed, it would be harder to follow a taxi than if we were to board a tram. It would take less than ten minutes to get to the station in a cab. It was nearly 5:15.

The park was quiet. Other mothers and their children had left for their homes to prepare dinner, but the late afternoon sun was still bright. Dutch parks were gardens of Eden. Trimmed and weeded, green with grass, bright with flowers. Beauty and serenity here—while in our house sat a soldier waiting to waylay Carl.

A taxicab saw me, pulled over. I asked to go to Centraal Station. The driver stepped out and helped me with the stroller. I had been watching my surroundings while in the park and did not think we were being followed. Still, I kept watch out the window and over my shoulder.

At the station, the driver again helped with the stroller. I paid and tipped him. Not quite 5:30. We had fifteen minutes to kill, so I herded the boys away from the station. Margy started to whimper and then to cry. I pulled Jan and Alex to a table at an outdoor café and started to nurse Margy. When a waiter asked what I would have, I told him I didn't want anything. He showed himself to be put out, but his unhappiness was the least of my problems.

When it was time to go, I broke off nursing, put Margy back in the stroller, and started for the station. As we crossed the street, I realized I had forgotten the soldiers. They were, of course, at the railroad station in force. There seemed to be two groups of five; one group on the sidewalk, the other surveying those who entered the doors. If they stopped me, I thought, I would tell them that I was meeting my mother-in-law, arriving from Maastricht. I hurried the children past the soldiers on the sidewalk. They paid us no heed. The soldiers at the door glanced at us, but a mother with three children did not interest them.

Platform five. I knew the station well. Carl and I often visited his sister Ge in Linschoten. A more pastoral hamlet could not be found anywhere in the world. Step out the back door and one was in the canal. Just down the street was the butcher and the baker; their products were manna from heaven. To get to Linschoten we had to go via Utrecht, where we changed trains. So it was platform five.

The station was chaotic, the throng of people a tornado of noise. People were pushing and shoving. Usually the Dutch were so polite, so well-behaved, but their lives had been shattered by the thunder of war. And everywhere the khaki of soldiers, the swastika, the German flag. Normally I abhorred crowds, but this one I loved for the cover it provided. We reached platform five. The train for Utrecht had not yet arrived. It was 5:48 on the platform clock. Carl? Loeky? Who would I find?

No one, no one. And then I spotted Loeky, just as she spotted me. She took Margy in her arms and then she was hugging me, crying inconsolably.

"Margery, Margery. What will become of you all?"

Margy was bathed in her tears. It was all I could do not break down.

"Is Carl still free?" she wondered aloud. "After you left, the Gestapo spent the rest of the afternoon at your house." She gulped, couldn't speak for her terror. "Did they catch Carl? I was so afraid for him."

The train pulled into the station. No Carl. Loeky handed me the tickets. "I only bought them to Utrecht," she said. "I was afraid to buy tickets ..." She dropped her voice to a whisper. "I was afraid to buy tickets to Berlin."

Yes, I'd slipped up, mentioned Berlin to her. I needed to be more careful in the future. Loeky continued in her whisper, "I was afraid it would raise suspicions. That I would be detained."

She hugged me again. "Oh, Margery! What will become of us? What will become of our country? And of you and the children?" She leaned low, gave each boy a peck on the cheek. "Take good care of your mother and baby sister."

She pushed our bags through the door of the train. The boys followed. I took Margy from her. Loeky stepped back as the doors slid shut.

So fast. I felt the tears on my cheeks as I waved through the window. One last glimpse of Loeky before she was gone. And Carl? Was he on the train? Had he made it? Had he been arrested? And Eindhoven was also gone. It was all gone. The house, our daily routine, the park, the bakery, my friends. One minute we lived there; the next, it had been torn from us. So abruptly and so completely. If we were caught, we would never see it back. If we escaped, there would still be the war, and who knows what would become of us, of Eindhoven, of our house, our friends, Loeky and Lou.

And Carl? Where was Carl?

I pulled the boys down the corridor of the car. There were seats to the left and right, unlike international trains, which had doors leading to closed compartments that sat six or eight people. In the middle of the car we found space for three. A Dutchman politely rose and found another seat, making room for the four of us. A seat or two farther along he found another spot for himself. I raised my hand. "*Dank U, Meneer.*"

I settled the children. Loeky had also given me a little bag. I cried when I opened it. Sandwiches for the children, buttered bread with *hagelslag*. The chocolate sprinkles were a favorite with the boys. Usually I wouldn't let them eat such sweets; she knew that, but she also knew that this was not a usual day.

And still I waited for Carl. Waited and hoped.

The boys ate their sandwiches and watched out the window. They were counting the cows as the sandwich and drink cart moved slowly down the aisle toward us. The travelers were buying snacks. Most of the men bought a Heineken or an Oranjeboom. When the cart reached us, I bought two small bottles of chocolate milk. My movements as I paid the vendor and opened the bottles wakened Margy. She fluttered her eyes, still sleepy. I cooed, and her miniature smile in response warmed my heart. I settled her and slipped her my breast. She was hungry. A good sign. *Drink, my love,* I thought. *Make my milk flow. You will need it to survive this trip.*

I was still looking up and down the aisle, hoping to see Carl, praying that he had not been caught.

The boys were falling asleep. They were excited but they were also tired. I shifted Margy to the other breast. As I began to doze too, I recalled my first glimpse of Carl. It was on the dock at Marseille. He was returning from seven years with the Dutch East Indian Tea Company, managing a tea plantation in the Dutch East Indies. I was standing with his brother Hendrik and my brother Alex. Those two were best friends, living in Nice. They had invited me to stay a few weeks with them. Actually, they were broke and needed me to help pay their rent. They were expatriates, eking out an existence by breeding and selling cocker spaniels, giving singing lessons, and eating at high teas offered by the circle of British matrons luxuriating in the south of France. Then Hendrik had learned that Carl was returning from the East Indies and had immediately invited him to Nice. To help, of course, with the rent!

They pointed Carl out to me as he waved from the shipboard. He was easy to spot. Huge compared to the crowd of Frenchmen and the sprinkling of Japanese and other Asians. Huge and blonde. Not only big physically, but a big smile and a big voice. Later I learned to love his sky-blue eyes, to love them and to drown in them.

The train jolted me out of my reverie. We were slowing for Den Bosch.

No! I sat up straight. Almost a half hour into the trip and no Carl! Had he been on the train, he would have found me long before now. He had been caught! I tried to master my panic, to take deep breaths. To think. I couldn't continue on past Utrecht. We had been planning to transfer there to the international train for Berlin. Without Carl, the children and I would never make it. What to do?

I watched out the window as the train approached the station. I could see the tower of Sint Jan's Cathedral. We had stopped there two years earlier, Carl and I. We had walked through the maze made of cobblestones on the square outside the church.

Alex began to cry. He was waking, fussy because he was tired. Margy was whimpering now too, and I was limp with fatigue. Or more probably, with stress. The four of us were disintegrating already. We could not go on.

I mulled it over. We'd continue on to Utrecht, I decided. Once there, rather than go east to Berlin, we'd take the train west toward Den Haag, debark at Woerden, and seek refuge with my sister-in-law in Linschoten. That was only twenty minutes from Utrecht. The kids needed to rest and so did I. If Carl was not yet caught, he would eventually think of Ge. What were the other options? Go to a hotel in Utrecht? But how would Carl find me? Go east and find refuge in Enschede with my other sister-in-law, Annie? The thought of another two hours on the train with the children decided me. Linschoten it would be.

The train squealed to a stop. More soldiers on the platform. They were everywhere. Seeing them, I knew they had gotten Carl. Maybe he had gone back to the house and they had been waiting for him. No. Loeky said she had seen no one but the soldiers. Had they caught him on the way to the station? At the station?

I shifted Margy and gave her my breast, and then tucked Jan against me on the other side. Alex had gone back to sleep.

The train lurched. The conductor blew his whistle. And then I saw him! Carl! He leaped down the last steps onto the platform, took two long strides, and he was on board. He had spied me through the window as he cleared the last step on the stairs, had waved and given me a broad grin. A few seconds later the train was moving and Carl was in our car, making his way toward us.

He picked up Jan and gave him a hug. Despite his fatigue, Jan laughed. And then with a kiss for me, he took Jan's seat and put Jan on his lap. I looked questioningly at him. He was perspiring as if he had run a long way. He shook his head. He didn't want to talk just yet. He was still catching his breath.

After a few minutes he whispered to me what had happened. When he had left me, the streets had been crawling with soldiers. They were searching for him and the others. He didn't dare go to the station. He had decided to go to Den Bosch, thirty kilometers away, to get on the train there. He had already sold our car for German marks, so he had taken his bicycle and raced from Eindhoven to Den Bosch. He'd had more than enough time, but had been delayed twice by convoys of German tanks. He should have reached Den Bosch an hour ago, but it had been close. He had abandoned the bicycle on the steps of the station. He was still panting, but he was smiling like a child who had just scored a goal to win the World Cup.

"I love you." He smiled. "I'm exhausted." Another peck on the cheek. "And you?"

"Better now," I told him. But I admitted that the children and I were exhausted. "Could we go to Ge's?" I asked. "The children need to rest."

We smiled at each other. We had both been frightened that we had lost each other. We hadn't, though. We were together, and for the moment all my concerns melted away. Margy stirred at my breast. She was no longer nursing.

"Let's do it," he said. "Linschoten is the perfect place to hide for a day or two."

Hoofdstuk 7

31 juli 1940: De Gaulle calls on countrymen to resist Nazi occupation, decries German-French armistice signed in Compiegne as traitorous capitulation. Churchill supports de Gaulle's stand.

I woke up before anyone. We had arrived late in the night at Tante Ge's house. I loved it here. The canal ran right along the house on one side, the cobblestone street on the other. "Just remember," Tante Ge told me over and over, "if you are trying to find the house, it's Dorpstraat Tien." I peeked out the window of our second-floor bedroom. Alex was still asleep in the other bed. The canal was directly below me, touching the side of the house. Across the canal, a cobblestone roadway ran along the water. Willow trees hung over the canal. The town hall and the mayor's house fronted the canal right across from me. His house was bigger than the other houses, built of dark red brick, with black iron railings along the steps, dark green shutters, and orange roof tiles just like every other building in the hamlet.

I craned my neck but could see no ducks on the water. Tante Ge would give Alex and me some bread, I knew. We would go to the tiny back garden, stand on the steps—they went right down into the water so that one could step directly into a boat!—and call "Tee-tee-tee-tee-tee." The ducks would rush to our call, and we would throw small pieces of bread to them. As they scrambled for the morsels, the bigger ducks would be mean and peck the other ducks.

I made my way down the narrow, curvy stairs. I had to be careful. The steps were steep, and I had to stay near their right edge. At the left edge, the stairs were mere slivers, far too thin to stand on. Under the steps on the ground floor was the toilet. The door had a funny latch. When one turned the latch from the inside to lock the door, a little sign on the outside that said *Bezet* in red would appear. When the latch was unlocked, the little sign said *Vrij* in green. The toilet smelled, but next to the toilet was a candlestick and matches. Mama didn't let me play with matches, but she told me that the adults lit the candle when they were inside to burn away the nasty odors. Someday I would be able to do that myself.

"Jan," I heard Mama call from upstairs. "Jan."

I flushed the toilet and climbed back up the stairs. They were so steep, I could steady myself with my hands on the steps, like climbing a ladder.

Mama hugged me when I came into her room. "I didn't see you when I woke up." She kissed me. "I didn't know where you were!" And then quietly, "Is Tante Ge awake?"

I shook my head. Last night Mama had been afraid, worried about Papa. Today she was calm. She always loved me, but sometimes she was worried about Papa or Margy and didn't seem to have time for Alex and me.

"Do you think Tante Ge will let us feed the ducks, Mama?" I asked hopefully.

"If she has stale bread, she will."

Papa rolled over. "Hey," he exclaimed. He grabbed me and lifted me onto his chest. I looked down into his eyes, as blue as one of my marbles. He laughed and tickled me. "You did a good job of looking after your mother yesterday," he said. "And so we are here safe and sound."

Alex came running into the room and jumped on Papa with me. Papa encircled us both with his big arms and squashed us against him. It was all we could do to breathe. All three of us were laughing. Mama laughed too.

Tante Ge was making tea in the kitchen when we all came downstairs. Oom Hill was still in bed. In the dining room we had tea, a soft boiled egg in an egg cup with a little knitted cap on the egg to keep it warm, and bread with butter and *muisjes*, crisp bits of sugar in all the colors of the rainbow. The teapot sat like a brooding hen in a padded pillow that snapped shut around it to keep it warm. Oom Hill joined us at the table. He was small and bald and wrinkled, but he liked to tell jokes and play pranks on Alex and me.

After breakfast Alex and I rushed to the yard to feed the ducks. Near the steps that led into the canal was some ivy. A mother duck was hiding there. Tante Ge had told us at breakfast that she was nesting there. We could feed her, but we should not touch her nest or the eggs, or frighten her. Every day Tante Ge took one or two eggs out of the nest. Since it was impossible to buy eggs, the nesting duck was Tante Ge's secret farm.

After breakfast, Papa took Alex and me to visit one of Tante Ge's friends, Hendrik de Goederen. We called him Oom, and he lived down the street from Tante Ge. It was fun to visit him because we were allowed to run around the big piles of lumber behind his house. Papa and Oom Henk went into the office to talk while Alex and I explored around the piles of lumber. Oom Henk imported lumber from France, cut it, stacked and dried it, and resold it. The wood was stacked in neat piles, each one like a log cabin. Alex ran behind one stack of lumber and hid. He was small, so I could run much faster than he. I yelled "Boo!" when I found him. He ran off and hid again, and I counted to ten before running after him. "Boo!" I shouted, and he laughed.

I told him to go hide again, and this time I counted to twenty. I wasn't sure which way he had gone. Deeper into the lumber stacks? Back toward the house? I walked past two or three piles, toward the far side of the lot. I couldn't find him. I stopped and listened. Whenever I couldn't find him, he would usually giggle, and then I would know where he was. I thought I heard him and took a few steps toward another pile of lumber. I listened again. The sound I had heard was louder. I went past one more stack of lumber and listened again. Now I could hear the sound. It came from inside the stack of wood! People whispering? No … voices on a radio.

I tiptoed around the pile and squeezed between some of the stacked wood. I caught my breath. Inside the stack of wood was a small space, like a room. I took another step, and there were Papa and Oom Henk! They were sitting on two small folding chairs listening to the radio. The radio voice was in English. I knew because Mama spoke English to Alex and me when we were alone with her.

I moved again. Papa turned and caught sight of me. He looked startled, almost angry. When he saw that it was me, he lifted his finger to his lips, telling me to be quiet. Then he pulled me to him.

"Where's Alex?"

"We're playing hide and seek. He's hiding."

"Let's go find him." All three of us squeezed out of the little hiding space. We found Alex behind the next pile of wood, and then Papa, Alex, and I headed back to Tante Ge's. We paused to sit next to the canal, and Papa put one arm around Alex, the other around me. He looked very serious.

"Promise me, Jan, that you will not tell anybody about finding the radio hideout."

"Not even Mama?"

"Mama is okay. I will tell her too. But not Tante Ge. Not anyone else. Promise?" He squeezed Alex. "You too?"

Both of us promised, but I wanted to know why Papa and Oom Henk were listening to the radio in a hideout. Papa explained that radios weren't allowed by the Germans. We weren't allowed to listen to them. But Oom Henk listened to the BBC to know what was happening in the war. Also, he sent radio messages to England to tell them how many soldiers and trucks and tanks were going along the roads. It was like playing war! But this was really exciting because this was real war, not play war. And dangerous! Alex and I promised again that we wouldn't tell anyone. We didn't want to make danger for Oom Henk. I was scared, but mostly I was excited. It wasn't every day we could fool the Nazis!

I thought back to a few weeks earlier in Eindhoven. Alex and I had been playing in our backyard. We had caught two crickets and a small toad and put them in a jar. We pretended they were treasure, and we were digging a hole to bury the jar. Three soldiers looked over the fence and saw us digging the hole. They yelled at us, vaulted the fence, grabbed us by our collars, and dragged the two of us to the back door of our house. They banged on the door until Mama came out. They were angry that we were digging a hole. They screamed at Mama. I wanted to kick them. They pulled Alex and Mama and me over to the hole and inspected our jar. When they saw the two crickets and the toad, they stopped yelling. I was livid at them for telling us we couldn't dig in our own backyard. Later Mama told me that they thought we were burying treasure. Well, we were. Not their treasure, perhaps, but they had no right to stop us from doing what we wanted to at our own house! Now I was happy that we were fooling them with Oom Henk's radio. It served them right. And I wouldn't tell any of them about it. I wanted to beat them, to win the war. And we were going to. Oom Henk's radio would help.

That night I listened at the top of the stairs when Papa and Mama were talking to Oom Hill and Tante Ge. Papa and Mama were asking Oom Hill about the trains and Berlin. Oom Hill had been there long before the war. He was worried the Nazis would catch us, and he tried to convince Papa that we should hide on a farm. He suggested the van der Windens', but Papa only said no. The Germans were after him. Even in villages as small as Linschoten, they would find a collaborator—a traitor!—and Papa would be betrayed. That would be the end of us all. And who knew how long the war would be?

Oom Hill thought that as soon as the British joined with the overseas French forces, the war would be over within a matter of weeks. Papa described the might of the German forces as they had attacked Grebbeberg. A matter of weeks? No, no. The Germans had a powerful military. They might win. Probably would win. If they eventually lost, it would be because of a stalemate that gave England the time to build the necessary war machines. There was no way a family of five could hide from the Germans for that long a time. He was certain our only chance was to go to Berlin. The Nazis would not be looking for him in Berlin. It was the only place they would *not* be looking for him.

Oom Hill disagreed. "*Je weet niet wat je doet. En met een vrouw en drie kindjes!*" He seemed angry. "*Moet je echt niet doen.*"

Despite Oom Hill's warning that Papa didn't know what he was doing, Papa remained adamant. I could hear Tante Ge begin to cry, and then Mama. I could tell she was trying not to cry, but when Tante Ge repeated Oom Hill's "And Marge and the children, Carl?", Mama cried, not for herself, but for Alex and Margy and for me. It scared me to hear Mama cry, and I ran into the room.

"Jan!" She hugged me, held me for a minute, and then told me to go back upstairs. I should have been asleep long ago. Tante Ge was still crying. Papa didn't spank me. He didn't even scold me. Instead he lifted me up and kissed me.

"We shall fool them, Jan," he said. "And you will help us."

As I climbed the stairs, I knew he was right. Oom Henk was fooling them with his radio. We could fool them too.

Hoofdstuk 8

1 augustus 1940: Romania willing to cede territory to Hungary and Bulgaria in effort to forestall farther spread of Communism into Balkans. Hitler, Mussolini agree to Russian occupation of Bessarabia and Bukovina, but warn Stalin to halt farther westward expansion.

Oom Henk de Goederen offered to drive us to the station in Woerden. He was the only person in Linschoten who still had a car. His trade in wood was important, perhaps, to the Germans. As we got into the car, Tante Ge hugged Alex and me at the same time. Tears ran down her cheeks, but she pretended they weren't there.

I calmed her. "Don't worry, Tante Ge. Papa can fool them. Alex and I will help." It made her cry even harder. I stood up straight. "And I will help with Alex and Margy." I was, after all, six and a half years old!

The Woerden station was quiet. Almost no one was on the platform. The train to Utrecht was a local and not busy. Utrecht Station, when we got there, was another matter. We had to push our way through the crowds. I held fast to Alex's hand. I didn't want to lose my little brother. Soldiers everywhere, carrying rucksacks, helmets, rifles. Papa explained later that some would have been heading south to the fronts in Belgium and France, while most were heading back to Germany. Mama looked worried and hugged Margy close to her breast. Alex and I just watched the soldiers. Papa had told us not to say a word. The soldiers might be angry or curious that we were Dutch, he said. They might arrest us. But Alex and I were smart. We played war with our toy men and trucks all the time. Military strategy and troop deployment was one of our strengths.

Papa told Mama to buy the train tickets to Berlin. I saw her cringe and I wanted to hug her. But Papa was being smart. Mama was carrying Margy. The soldiers would not suspect her.

The conductor was blowing his whistle as we pushed our suitcases in through the doors. There was just enough room inside the train for the

69

five of us to crowd in. People were standing everywhere. The train lurched, and we were underway. I held Alex's hand again. He was being brave, but he and I could hardly move, jammed against the knees of the other travelers.

It would be a long ride, Papa said. Two hours to the German border. Mama sat on her suitcase holding Margy. Alex and I stood for a long time. When we got tired, we sat on the floor. The smell was horrid. It made me think of the van der Windens' cow barn. Papa walked along the corridor hoping to find seats for us. He returned and shook his head. No places available.

The train slowed after a long time. Papa told Mama that we were approaching the border. Then the train stopped completely, and soldiers in groups of twos and threes stepped into the cars. The train started moving slowly again. Papa said the next stop would be Enschede. The soldiers in our car started walking through it, checking passports and visas. They didn't check the German soldiers at all. As they got nearer to us, I could sense Papa's worry. But like Alex and me, he knew military strategy and troop deployment. He knew how to fool the Germans.

When the soldiers asked for his papers, he passed the two passports to them and spoke to them in German. I could see that Papa had fooled them. They looked at him, but joked with him.

"Ja," I heard him say. "Dutch," but he winked at the soldier as he said it. And then he joked with them in German. They checked our passports, studied the visas, signed and stamped those pages, and returned the passports to him. One of the soldiers smiled at me. I smiled back. A big smile. I wanted to kick him in the shins. Alex saw me smile and smiled a big smile too. He was only two years old, but he was smarter than that German. I was proud of him. He knew how to fool them.

An hour or more later, Mama began to cry a little. She was tired from holding Margy, tired from sitting on her suitcase. Papa and I walked down the corridor to look, once again, for possible free seats. The corridor ran along the windows on one side; sliding doors opened into compartments on the other. We could hardly move through the narrow corridor. Soldiers crowded every possible space, and rucksacks piled on the floor made walking difficult.

There were few civilian passengers. No one wanted to visit Germany. Even I knew that. The soldiers looked at us, probably wondering what we were doing, why we were on the train. All of them were drinking beer. Empty bottles were everywhere. Most of the compartments were jammed with eight or more soldiers. When we moved into the first-class car, the aisle was still jammed, as were most of the compartments. But in one compartment there were only four soldiers, and in the compartment next to them, there were six soldiers. All ten were drinking, sitting comfortably, and talking sociably. None of them appeared to be drunk. I knew that these were officers. The four had insignias everywhere, like some of my toy soldiers, while the six in the other compartment had fewer bars and stripes and medals.

When we reached the end of the train, Papa and I turned and went back. We hadn't found a single empty seat, except for the four in the compartment with the superior officers and the two in the adjoining compartment with the underofficers. The other soldiers, the privates, didn't dare enter and sit down in either of those two compartments. They would be eaten alive, I knew that.

When we reached Mama, she was still crying softly. I could see she was tired. Margy was wailing. A little sister was fun, but not when she pinched her face up and cried.

"I need to nurse her." Mama looked at Papa, then at the German soldiers. "I'm afraid to in front of this crowd."

Papa thought for a moment. "Okay," he said. "Let's go get some seats."

He picked up our bags and gave a small one to me. Alex carried Margy's diaper bag. Mama followed as best she could with Margy. Moving down the corridor with the five of us and our luggage would have been impossible without Papa at the front. I remembered once trying to walk in deep snow when we were in Switzerland. I was small then, and the snow was so deep, I could hardly walk. But Papa walked ahead of me, breaking a trail, and then I could follow. Most of the soldiers laughed with us as we pushed past them and stumbled over bags. Only one or two were nasty. Some of them looked at Mama and raised their eyebrows. Papa turned once or twice to stare them down.

At last we reached the first-class car. I couldn't imagine where Papa was taking us. When we reached the compartment of the four high-level officers, he put down the bags, threw open the compartment door, stepped in, raised his right arm in salute, and roared, "Heil Hitler!"

What, I thought, was he doing? Was he crazy? Then he commanded them with another roar. "Attention!"

The four officers sprang to attention and responded with "Heil Hitler!" as they saluted smartly.

"Attention!" Papa said again. "I am under orders. Secret mission. *Aus!*" He saluted and moved aside to let the four officers get past him, out of the compartment. To my surprise, they smartly returned his salute and pushed by him into the corridor. As Mama with Margy and Alex took their places, the officers opened the door to the next compartment, the one with the six lower-ranking officers. *"Aus,"* they ordered, and they took over the compartment. A moment later, those six officers threw the noncommissioned officers out of the next compartment and took their seats. None of the officers were perturbed in the least. It was the non-coms from the third compartment, now scrunched in the aisle, who grumbled.

Had Papa really planned all that out? I wondered. Just then he winked at me, barely suppressing a smile.

I suddenly remembered Mama reading me a story about a little boy who loved animals. Everybody adored the little boy because he was so sweet with all creatures. The story had a sad ending, though, when the little boy drowned trying to save his dog, which had fallen into a swollen river. I cried, and Mama explained that tragedy was when a person's greatest strength led to his downfall. The little boy's unbounded love for his dog had led to his death. That had made me cry, but now I smiled. The officers' instinct of instant obedience had led to their downfall.

I winked back at Papa as we all settled comfortably into our now private compartment. Alex didn't understand why Papa and I had winked at each other, but when I smiled at him, he smiled back. I smiled because Papa had fooled the Germans. Like Alex and me, he liked fooling the Germans.

Hoofdstuk 9

1 augustus 1940: Four British troops killed, seven
wounded in explosion of ammunition dump on
Gibraltar. Last civilians removed from the rock.
British Sunderland flying-boat-patrol bomber downs
two Fascist fighters while attacking Axis ships off
Italian coast.

I was having trouble staying awake. Carl was holding Margy. She was sleeping, but I didn't know if it was from fatigue or hunger. My milk didn't seem sufficient for her. I dozed off.

I was on the train from Boston to Wolfeboro, New Hampshire. The clickety-clack of the tracks comforted me. And then I was carrying my camping gear from the station to the pier, not a hundred yards away, just across Wolfeboro's main street. There the other campers and I, perhaps fifty girls in all, boarded the Mt. Washington, a gorgeous stern paddle wheel boat. We plied the waters of Lake Winnipesaukee for more than an hour. The water churned behind us, the shoreline a distant forest. Mt. Tecumseh and the Sandwich Range loomed north of us; stately Mt. Chocorua to our northeast; and beyond her, the magnificent Mt. Washington, queen of the north, wearing a sparkling white tiara of snow. It was a glorious June day, the sun warm on our faces, and gentle clouds smiled down at us. How could I not be happy? School was out, and we would be staying in cabins on the shore of Little Squam Lake.

I knew we were approaching Center Harbor when the captain pointed out Six Mile Island. A bit later it was Five Mile Island, and finally Half Mile Island. After Three Mile Island, he also pointed to Black Cat Island, my personal favorite. I always wanted to visit it but never did. Father had black cats in our dairy barn, and I loved playing with their litters of kittens.

We disembarked the Mt. Washington at Center Harbor and clambered aboard big horse-drawn hay carts, empty of hay, with our duffle bags, ten or fifteen of us to a cart. We giggled and sang campground songs as we swayed and bumped the mile or so to Squam

Lake. The wagon ride was even better than the train or paddle wheel ride.

At Squam Lake, rowboats awaited us. We climbed down from the dock, five of us to a boat, three astern and two in the bow, a boatman with his long oars in the middle. The boatman helped each of us in turn, reminding us to step lightly and keep to the middle of the boat so as not to capsize it. Most of us had been to camp before and had learned to paddle a canoe; a sixteen-foot rowboat was far more stable than a canoe.

Silence always settled over us on the lake. It was a long row, first along the shoreline of Squam Lake, then through the pinched waistline between the two lakes and onto Little Squam Lake. And farther to our rustic camp …

I awoke with a start. It was not the loons of Little Squam I heard, but Margy that was wailing. Carl handed her to me and I settled her on my breast. The dream had seemed real, but those summer weeks were long behind me. Would I ever visit Little Squam again? Would we escape Germany?

We would arrive at the Bahnhof in Berlin in another hour or so. Only a few of the German troops were still awake. The aisle was full of snoring bodies. Escape Germany? Our first step was to hide safely in Berlin, then to leave Berlin safely. To where? Carl hadn't yet decided on our next destination. Escaping Germany seemed a remote, insoluble problem. Our focus during our first day in the capital would be to find a haven for the first night. Then we would be in a position to tackle the problem of flight.

My poor little Margy. She was suckling, and I could only hope my milk would not dry out. Finding formula for her might be impossible. I had not thought of that. What if Carl and I and the boys escaped, but Margy died? Did I want that, for me to escape while my baby died? I pushed the thought aside. Focus on Berlin, on finding a bed for the night.

Hoofdstuk 10

2 augustus 1940: The RAF fends off daily raids by Luftwaffe; Wales attacked heavily in the last days. Count of Messerschmitts downed over the English Channel this week nearing one hundred.

Margery was exhausted. The boys were exhausted. Little Margy was no longer wailing, but only because she didn't have the strength to complain. I had figured we would change trains in Berlin and go on immediately. We had been lucky to get this far, and the thought of staying in Berlin made my skin crawl. I had been in the city once, when I was in my late teens and playing for the Dutch youth team. A friendly tournament with Jan Valstar, Frans Nije, Bandi Horvat, Jan Bruin, and Henri … What was his name? Joubert. Henri Joubert. From the Dutch West Indies. Who else? Kees Nije, Chris van den Berg. I couldn't remember them all. We played one game on Friday, two on Saturday, and two on Sunday. Who else was there? The Danes. The Swedes. Poland. Norway? I did remember it was two brackets of four. Ah, the English. Their midfielder had been Gerry Harrison, a tall, blond, blue-eyed Brit. Quick despite his size, smart, a great passer. He dominated midfield. Indeed, he dominated the tournament. The Germans were there, of course. And the eighth team? Scotland? Or had it been Norway?

We won the first group and moved on. In the semis, we faced the Brits. I was playing center forward. At the kickoff, the inside right forward touched the ball to me to begin the game. Just as he did that, the tie on my shorts snapped. I grabbed the shorts with both hands to hold them up. I panicked: I had to get rid of the ball so I could solve the problem of the shorts. Twenty thousand spectators would be rolling in the stands if those shorts dropped around my ankles. So I kicked, hard, at the goal. To my astonishment, the keeper was chatting with one of his backs at the top of the penalty area. He saw my kick too late. He backed up furiously, stumbled as the ball landed in front of him, and it bounded over him into the unprotected goal. We won one-zero.

75

I don't remember much of the tournament except that score and that we lost—badly, if I remember right—to the Germans in the final. In those days, they were the team we always wanted to beat. Always good. Always physical. But though we wanted to beat them, we considered them friends, older cousins so to speak. It was now no longer a friendly rivalry. Nor was it a game. Now it was blood sport. They were looking to kill me.

That weekend, we had visited many cafés. Since it was a friendly tournament, the evenings meant beer and singing. I still remembered the part of the city that had reasonably priced hotels. Margery and the children couldn't go on. We needed a room. We'd head there and see what we could find. Uptown, in the international hotels, I might raise suspicions. Further, we probably couldn't afford them. There were only so many Marks in my pocket.

We arrived at well past midnight, and the Bahnhof was largely empty. Margery was limping, worn to the bone. She held Margy on her hip with one hand, carried a suitcase in the other hand. I put Alex on my shoulders, picked up the two largest bags, and told Jan to hang on to one bag so we wouldn't lose him. Alex hardly stirred, and I worried he would fall off. Jan was walking like a zombie, more asleep than awake. None of us had eaten a real meal since leaving Linschoten.

The cheap hotels weren't far from the station. Two blocks, perhaps three. Their neon lights glowed blue. An occasional red light whispered alluringly. I knew Margery would take them in stride. When we reached the Swan Hotel, I looked back at her questioningly. She didn't care. All she needed was a bed.

The night clerk was dark-haired, unshaven, groggy with sleep, in a rumpled undershirt. Yes, he had a room with two beds. I signed, was asked to pay in advance. High-class, I thought. Others might need a room for only an hour or two; important for the hotel to have its money up front.

We stumbled up the narrow stairs. Margy started to cry. I hit the light button, and we made our way down the hall. Margy began to wail. Ahead of us, a door opened. An elderly lady leaned out her door and berated Margy for her two a.m. wail of exhaustion.

"Silence," she scolded.

Two a.m., I thought. Two children, an infant, ten hours on the train. What can you expect?

Politely, I whispered to her, "You are right, Madame. The baby is definitely impolite." Curlers in what remained of her hair, night cream on her wrinkles, old of face, ugly of character. I went on, even more quietly, conspiratorially, "At your age, your beauty sleep must be particularly important to you."

She slammed her door. We slipped into our room. Children to bed, Margery and I to bed. We held each other. We were exhausted. Worse, we were terrified. Margery clung to me, trying not to cry, not to dissolve into tears. Should we be exuberant that we had made it to Berlin? To the nerve center of the Third Reich? Had we not traveled into the very hell we were trying to escape? Wasn't our situation worse now than two days ago? We pulled close to each other for comfort. What had I done to this woman I loved? She from a life of comfort and ease. Why had I married her? What was I doing to her and the children? Shouldn't she be strolling with a baby carriage on Boston's Common, or on Cape Cod playing on the beach with her children? Into what hell had I thrust her?

"Marge," I whispered. "What have I gotten you into?" We kissed. "Perhaps we should have stayed and hid in Linschoten. Or run for the Belgian border. It was so close." And then I realized my stupidity. "No. I should have left you. Why didn't I leave you?"

She pulled away slightly to look at me in the almost dark of the room. "I wouldn't have let you leave without us." She said that in love. More practically, she went on, "And you know how that would have ended. If they couldn't find you, they would have dragged the children and me off." Another kiss. "This will work. We will make it."

The light from the street was eerie. Shadows and deeper shadows on the black walls of the room.

Almost asleep, she murmured, "It will work, Carl. It will work. If anyone can make it work, you will do it."

I had almost been asleep. Now I was shocked awake. She was counting on me. Could I make it work? I thought back to another time I had asked myself that question, when I was sailing from Rotterdam to Djakarta. I was hardly twenty. I was being sent to a spot two hundred kilometers inland on the island of Sumatra to set up a tea plantation. I would be alone. Then it was the Dutch East Indian Tea Company that had faith in me. I had some gold coins to hire bearers and purchase tools and supplies; and a map to help me find where the plantation was to be and where I was to clear the jungle, prepare the soil, plant the tea. And seven years, alone, alone, to manage the plantation. Not that I was to do the work. I was to hire indigenous labor. But could I do it? I asked myself that over and over during the trip: Could I make it work? The company had taught me the technical skills of planting and harvesting tea, but was I prepared for the weight of the responsibility of hiring and managing 1200 Sumatrans? And would I be capable of living for seven years in solitude? I had been frightened then, but my life had been mine alone. Now my concern was not just for me, but for the lives of Margery and the three children. Could I make it work? I had no choice. I had to make it work.

Margery was asleep. Little Margy whimpered, but she too was asleep. The boys were the most resilient. I felt myself relax, listening to the breathing of the four of them. I had no choice, I thought. It had to work.

Hoofdstuk 11

3 augustus 1940: Vichy government in France further restricts civilian transport, arrests French Resistance fighters, Belgians, and other foreigners attempting to flee Vichy-controlled France. Berlin announces destruction of 200,000 tons of British shipping in last days; claims pace of loss will soon lead to starvation in London, other major cities.

It was sunny and bright when I looked out the window. Berlin! Papa had said that it was the capital of Germany. That made four capitals! I had been to Den Haag, Brussels, and Paris, and now Berlin. I hardly remembered last night. It had been dark, and we had gone straight to bed. I poked Alex. He awoke so quickly, I think he had not really been asleep. "Berlin," I whispered, and dragged him to the window to look.

There was a trashman emptying garbage cans along the sidewalk. He dumped them into a big wagon while his horse clumped along, pulling the wagon so slowly that the man only had to whistle to him to stop if there were five or six trash cans clumped together. We watched two dogs following the cart, competing for tidbits that fell on the street. A lone cat sat on the mound of garbage enjoying the ride, preening itself. The cat was jet black with shiny fur. Garbage made for good food.

"I wonder how Barbara is," Alex murmured.

"Tante Loeky is taking good care of her," I assured him, hoping it was true.

Barbara was a black and white English cocker spaniel that Oom Hendrik, Papa's brother, had given to Mama and Papa as a wedding present. I'd heard lots of stories about her from when they lived in Groningen. She had pooped all over the floor right after I was born. Mama said she had been jealous of me, that Mama had made a mistake when she came back from the hospital right after my birth by not letting Barbara in any room with me. Once she laid me on the floor and let Barbara sniff me and make me a member of the family, Barbara loved me and the pooping stopped. She brought Papa his slippers when he came

79

home from work. She also brought the mail up from the foyer when the postman slipped it through the slot in the door. Once she left a letter on the sidewalk across the street when she went there to pee. Mama had seen her drop it and went to retrieve it herself. It had been a bill from the vet! Mama and Papa had laughed at that. Alex and I loved Barbara, and I didn't want Alex to worry about her.

Mama and Margy were still sleeping, but Papa was gone. When Alex asked where he was, I said he might be getting breakfast for us. I hoped so. I was getting hungry.

We played listlessly on our bed with the two toy trucks and the two planes we had. I let Alex fly the Eindecker to keep him quiet. He smiled and whispered so as not to waken Mama and Margy, "Dominant! Fast, fast, fast!"

Mama stirred, and we both crawled onto her bed and hugged her. She laughed even though she was mostly asleep. Some mothers were grouchy in the morning. We were lucky. Mama was always happy, especially when we squashed her with hugs. We did it now, and she squeezed us in a bear hug, pretending to squeeze us so hard that it would hurt. She wasn't strong enough to hurt us, though. Alex and I were tough. All three of us were still tickling and hugging when the door opened.

We stopped our roughhousing when we saw Papa's serious expression.

"Wat is het, liefje?" Mama asked. She spoke English with Alex and me, but she and Papa almost always spoke Dutch together.

"I listened to the radio in the café," he said. "Here." His arms were full of fresh rolls and cheese, and he had a pitcher of hot chocolate.

We all sat on the bed to eat. We usually did that at home on Sunday mornings. Today we had no choice—there was no other furniture in the room. The bread was still warm. The cheese was good too, but Alex wouldn't eat it. He didn't like cheese. He made a face, and Mama said he didn't have to eat it.

She looked at Papa. "And?"

"The radio was blasting news about the Battle of Britain."

Alex and I listened. We liked to hear about the war. The Battle of Britain was exciting because it was an air war. The German Luftwaffe attacking London, the RAF pilots defending. Alex and I would mimic those battles with our toy planes. When we fought, the RAF always won.

"You never know what to believe," Papa said. "But the announcer was spouting about great damage to the city and the large number of British planes downed." He looked grave. "He made it sound as if England was done for."

He and Mama exchanged a look, their eyebrows raised.

"Yes." Papa nodded. "I thought our problem was to escape Germany so that we could go to England." He shrugged. "The radio was probably just propaganda. Anyway, we can always go to New York if London has fallen."

As he ate, he and Mama talked about what to do next.

"How would you like to go to Sweden?" he asked me. He poked me in the ribs, tickling me.

I laughed. "Good," I said. "That will make six countries!" I had already been to Holland, Belgium, Luxembourg. and France. Germany was my fifth country. Sweden would be six. I jumped on the bed, but Mama stopped me.

"Shh! Margy is still asleep."

Papa explained that there was a noontime train to Stralsund on the north coast. "From there we can get a boat to Malmo."

Alex was even more excited than I was. Neither of us had ever been on a big boat. "A boat. A boat!" he sang. He had a big smile. At first, I laughed at him, but then I saw Mama's face. She wasn't laughing. She was staring at Papa.

"Won't they be looking for us at the border?"

Papa tried to smile. "What do you think, jongens?" He was looking at Alex and me. "Do you think we can steal a boat and sail to Sweden?"

We laughed, but Mama didn't like the joke.

"We have some money left," he said to Mama. "The Swedish coast isn't far. With luck we can pay a local fisherman to take us fishing. All the way to Malmo."

Margy woke with a scream. She had been lying quietly in Mama's arms. Mama rocked her and kissed her, and Margy quieted as Mama began to nurse her. Alex kissed Margy too. He always became terribly sad when Margy cried. I hugged Mama. She had tears in her eyes, and I could see she needed a kiss. The trip to Malmo might be dangerous, but I knew we could do it. Alex and I would help. Papa would know what to do. I held Mama tight. When I hugged her, she always laughed. This time, she hugged me hard and tried to smile, but there were tears in her eyes.

Hoofdstuk 12

4 augustus 1940: Hitler denounces Churchill as warmonger in major speech, warns of need to thwart at all costs British plans to invade France, Belgium, and the Netherlands. Führer praises Luftwaffe for its glorious victories, destruction of Dover, sinking of ships, and the almost total devastation of London.

The train to Stralsund was empty compared to the train from Holland to Berlin. Not a single soldier on board. It was a gorgeous August day—the sun bright, the trees in full leaf, the cows fat and placid as they grazed in lush pastures flat as pool tables. The sun had perked up Jan and Alex; they were bright-eyed and bushy-tailed and full of mischief. Margy was still tired but not complaining. Our departure had been delayed by a day, and Carl was in a good mood now that we were underway. I could see that he was optimistic. We would be in Stralsund in a few hours. Until then, we had no worries. We would keep our fingers crossed that Carl could find a fisherman who would fish us all the way to Malmo, on the southern tip of Sweden, for a few hundred Marks. We could only hope our luck would hold.

I watched Jan and Alex play with the two airplanes they had received from Sinterklaas last year. Alex was begging to fly the Eindecker. Usually Jan was reluctant to share, but he must have felt everyone's stress, for he decided to be generous. Alex flew the plane, zooming it through the air. "Dominant!" he cried.

Jan agreed. He was flying the other plane, moving it slowly because, he explained, the Junker was slow.

Alex laughed and almost yelled, "Dominant! Luftwaffe, Eindecker!"

They were getting too loud. I shushed them and gave them their two metal cars in exchange for the airplanes. They started making roads across the back of the seats and along the armrests, humming the sound of car motors. As they quieted, my thoughts drifted back to my first train ride from London to Edinburgh. My stepmother and I were going to St.

Andrews to join Father for a few weeks of golf. What year was that? 1926? Father had been playing with the Prince of Wales, teaching him golf, although no one used the word "teach" or "instruct." Father was referred to in royal circles as "Joshua Crane, the gentleman from Boston." Father had started me on golf at the Dedham Country Club, and he wanted to continue those lessons with me at St. Andrews. Mother was along to enjoy the fresh air, play bridge, and take tea on the terraces of the Royal and Ancient Club.

Just after Jan was born, the prince had become king when his father died, and he abdicated the same year when he said he would marry Wallis Warfield Simpson, the American divorcée. I smiled at the memory of my mother telling me, well before the Prince of Wales became king, that the seamstress in Paris who sewed my mother's lingerie showed Mother lingerie ordered by Mrs. Simpson with her initials, those of the prince, and the crown of England embroidered onto them. I wondered whether she had discarded the lingerie when the king abdicated.

Those days in England, Scotland, and France with Mother and Father had been idyllic. Golf for me with Father, shopping and teas with Mother and her American friends, and traveling in England and France to watch Father and his team play polo. Even school was exciting: a lycee for girls in Paris for a year to learn French, and a year in Florence at the finishing school to learn Italian and study art. And to win a prize for sculpture!

Margy began to whimper. Which breast? The right one. Carl was rocking to and fro as he walked down the aisle, returning from the WC. Alex was dozing, Jan was reading a Dick and Jane book for the umpteenth time. Outside there was little to see but pastures and cows. The brakes groaned and groaned, the train began to slow, and then it stopped. Carl peered out the windows, first on one side of the train and then on the other. Curious, I thought. Why would we stop way out in the middle of nowhere, in the middle of cow pastures? There must be something on the tracks.

For a few minutes, everyone was looking out the windows. Jan and Alex were standing on their seats, the better to see. First on one side of the train and then on the other, soldiers came into view. They dispersed along the length of the train, on both sides. Then we heard yelling as a captain and a group of soldiers walked through the train. *"Aus! Aus!"* they commanded loudly.

We were herded to the end of the car, told to leave our baggage behind. Germans out the train to the left, foreigners out the train to the right. *"Aus! Aus!"*

There was nothing to do but follow orders. Soon we were standing in a long line in a pasture. Alex and Margy were crying, frightened by the soldiers' bellowing. Jan was angry. I put my hand on his shoulder to quiet him. I knew he wanted to protect his little brother and sister, but I did not want him to scream at a soldier or kick one of them.

Once we were lined up, the captain and two soldiers worked their way down the line, checking passports and interrogating the travelers. On the other side of the train, the German side, they were looking for Jews; on this side they were looking for foreigners who were in the country illegally or were on the blacklist.

As the captain drew nearer to us, a man just beyond us in the line grew increasingly nervous. I could see him fidget, sweat glistening on his face. His right eyebrow twitched. He was watching the small groups of soldiers who, with drawn guns, were overseeing the interrogation operation. The captain was checking the papers of a man and his wife six or eight places ahead of us in the line. The conversation became heated; the woman began to cry. I couldn't understand much, but it was evident the couple was Polish. The captain beckoned to two of the guards. They grabbed the couple and marched them toward the line of trucks parked on the road beyond the pastures. The woman wailed and collapsed. A third soldier hauled her onto his shoulder, and the couple was pulled and carried toward the trucks.

While the melee was going on, the man I had been watching moved furtively down the line, forty or fifty meters farther away from the captain. His movement apparently gained him little except to postpone the inevitable checking of his passport, until I realized it had gotten him near to a line of brush between the fields. Just as the captain took our passports from Carl, the man broke for the brush.

The captain ran in that direction, crying "Halt!" Everyone in line turned to see what was happening. The captain yelled "Halt!" again and fired his pistol. He was still holding our passports in his other hand. The man was running for his life, zigzagging like a rabbit with a fox just a step behind him. Several of the guards now had their rifles up and were firing. The man disappeared into the brush of the hedgerow, four or five soldiers in hot pursuit.

Suddenly I was walking across the brush on No Man's Land, Father shooting at a fleeing hare. I was terrified for the hare. How old was I? Four, five?

I blinked, and as I did, the man broke from the small copse of trees at the end of the hedgerow some two hundred meters away, sprinting across the field. The soldiers nearest him began to fire. For a few seconds he sprinted, then he tumbled forward. The soldiers ceased firing.

"It's not fair!" Jan screamed. No one heard him since everyone was screaming or talking. Jan kept on screaming, "It's not fair! He's unarmed! It's not fair!"

I knelt and put my arms around the two boys, even while I still held Margy. I wanted to protect and comfort them all. Jan was angry. Alex was wide-eyed in disbelief. I was terrified. What would the captain do to us, a Dutch family traveling to Stralsund?

The soldiers had now approached the fallen man. He moved a trifle, and one of the soldiers shot him again, in the head this time. He and the other soldiers standing over the body laughed, and then they looked toward the captain for instructions. He waved his hand in a gesture of dismissal. Two of the men picked the body up and threw it into the brush of the hedgerow.

When the soldiers returned, the captain spoke briefly with them, all of them in good humor. He shook the hand of the soldier who had fired the killing shot, slapped him on the shoulder. The soldier returned the captain's broad smile.

Carl had watched all this without a flicker of emotion or interest. I supposed that he had seen worse on Grebbeberg. As I looked at him, though, I realized it was not that he was inured to such a scene. Rather, he had ignored the incident and used the moment of reprieve to find a way to resolve our dilemma.

As the captain returned to our line, the talking and crying and sobbing stopped as if a switch had been turned off. Faces were frozen. Not one of us moved. The incident had instilled an overwhelming fear in everyone. If we had not been adequately aware of it a few minutes earlier, we all realized with incredible clarity that our lives were in the hands of this officer.

The captain looked at the two passports in his hand. He could not remember to whom they belonged. "Herr ter Weele," he called. Carl signaled, and the captain walked over to us. "Aha, a Dutchman. A fleeing soldier, I suppose." He looked satisfied, as if he'd caught a rabbit in a snare. He leered at me. "With an American wife? Or are you just his mistress?" He sneered at Carl. "And where did you obtain the visas to travel in Germany?"

Politely but matter-of-factly, Carl replied, "At the embassy in Den Haag."

That the visas were all in order puzzled the captain, but they did not deflect his intent to arrest us. "You served in the Dutch forces?" It was an accusation.

Again speaking simply but firmly, Carl said, "Of course. We had no choice."

"As I supposed," replied the captain. "And now you are fleeing to Sweden?" He laughed. He enjoyed his power. For everyone in line to hear, he almost yelled, "Escape to Sweden? Not anymore." He raised his pistol. "You know that you are an enemy of the Reich. Tell me why I should not shoot you!"

Carl leaned forward, and I could hardly hear him as he whispered, "I am on a secret mission."

The captain straightened for a moment, then he collected himself. "Fine story." He looked as if he was ready to pistol-whip Carl.

Carl leaned forward again, still whispering. "Be careful how you treat me. Your superiors will have your neck if you harm me. I am under special orders."

"Fine!" the captain bellowed. "Produce them."

"It is not permitted," Carl said. "I suggest that you take me to your commandant. I will explain the matter to him." He straightened. "And I suggest that you be more respectful. If not, I will report your lack of civility to your commander. Come. Take us to him."

Carl gathered us together. "Have one of your guards come with us so that we can get our belongings from the train. We will wait for you there." He nodded to the row of trucks across the field. "Finish your work here, then you can take us to headquarters."

The captain was hesitant, uncertain. Carl's quiet composure apparently rattled him. Where he had been belligerent, he was now polite. Reluctantly polite. "Fine," he replied. He assigned two guards to us. As he turned to the next person in the line, he looked back and smiled nastily. "I can tell you now that the commander won't believe a word of your story. You are running for the border. You are a Dutch soldier. We will find your name on the blacklist. The commander will have you shot." He lifted his left eyebrow. "I will volunteer to do the shooting." He chuckled. "Yes. And I will do so with pleasure."

I was trembling. Carl had bought us some time, but to what purpose? Did he think we could escape the two guards? Should we try to steal one of the trucks and make a run for it? I wanted to cry; I wanted to scream with fright. I could do neither. I pulled Margy closer to me and took Alex by the hand. Jan held fast to Alex's other hand. We stumbled awkwardly across the pasture to the train. Carl strolled ahead of us, apparently without a care in the world, joking in German with our two guards.

We waited a long time at the trucks with the guards. The captain arrested at least a dozen of our fellow travelers. They were pushed unceremoniously into the rear of a truck with a half dozen armed soldiers. Most of the captives were wailing or calling for help.

The captain turned to us and nodded over his shoulder at the departing truck. "Deserters. Enemy soldiers. Traitors. They will be shot in the morning." He waved us into the backseat of another truck and sat next to the driver. A dozen or more soldiers swarmed into the bed of the truck.

Carl smiled at us. He was serenity personified. He chatted with me and the children, but I couldn't focus on what he was saying.

We drove through a couple of towns, and in the third town we wended our way to the central square. The truck stopped in front of the town hall, an impressive building with matching stairs mounting from the left and the right up to a massive center doorway. The military had taken over the civilian government offices. Soldiers at every door stiffened to attention and saluted as we passed through. Our captain was carefully polite now. He did not want to risk a run-in with his commandant.

The commandant sat behind a great oaken desk in a room that rose three stories above us. Impressive, I thought. And hard to heat. It would be stone cold in winter.

Carl strode toward the commandant's desk. He might have been Julius Caesar ascending toward his own throne. He snapped to attention in front of the desk, saluted sharply, then relaxed into a civilian's manner.

The captain began to explain the situation, but Carl interrupted. "My commandant. We trust you can be of assistance. I am on a special mission and should be in Stralsund at this moment." The commandant raised his eyebrows in question. "Perhaps you could assist us in securing a room for the night?" Carl went on. He nodded at me and the children. "You can see that my family is exhausted. The good captain and his men stopped and searched our train, and we are now running well behind schedule."

The commandant sat pensively.

"Herr ter Weele is Dutch," the captain exclaimed. "He admits to serving in the Royal Dutch forces. He is an enemy of the Reich. He is one of those hoping to escape to Sweden."

The commandant looked questioningly at Carl. "What is this 'special mission' you are on?"

"I am not at liberty to share that information with you, Herr Commandant. I am able to say that it is a mission of grave importance. A mission directed at the highest level of government."

The captain huffed in disbelief. The commandant glanced in his direction, stilling him with an icy glare.

"Come, Herr ter Weele," the commandant said. "Helping you and your family to find a hotel for the night is not a problem. But, the captain and I are charged with halting ..." He paused, seeking the right word. "With halting *leakages* across the border and across the water to Sweden." He looked at the captain. "As you will see if you arrive is Stralsund, we have placed troops there to ensure the enemies of the Reich are arrested. We have many enemies looking to flee to Sweden."

He paused again. I was in a state of frenzy. Carl was on their list of enemies. We were sure of it. How were we going to escape? The commandant turned toward me and pointed at Jan.

"That one. He has dark hair, a narrow face, dark eyes. Not Dutch. Not German." He paused for effect. "One might say he's Jewish."

I wanted to grab Jan, to pull him to me, to protect him, to protest.

"The little boy," he went on, now pointing to Alex. "Handsome. Blonde. The baby. A girl? Blonde. How is that? Are you perhaps smuggling a Jew out of Germany?"

Alex started to cry.

Carl spoke easily and slowly. "My commandant. You and I, we are in this fight together. I can see the problem I am for you. You must follow orders. You must ensure the integrity of the frontiers of the Reich."

How, I asked myself, could he be so calm? Germans everywhere. This commandant could snap his fingers, and we would be dead. And if he didn't, we would be caught and shot in Stralsund.

"As I said," Carl continued, "I am under orders. I am not at liberty to reveal those orders to anyone."

He stepped around the desk. As he did, the captain drew his pistol and shouted, "Halt!"

Carl waved the pistol away, smiling. "Sorry to frighten you, my captain. I have no intention of attacking. I wish to share some information with your commandant." He reached into the pocket of his vest and drew out a paper. I recognized it. The note he had taken from the Ambassador's desk drawer in Den Haag.

"My commandant," Carl said as he spread the single page on the desk. "Since I am unable to tell you my mission, perhaps you could call this number, and my superior officer would be willing to explain why I am here."

The commandant studied the single sheet. I knew what he was looking at. It was signed in pen with only one word—"Heinrich." And then the gold letterhead spelling out "Heinrich Himmler." And again in pen: "You asked for my contacts." Three telephone numbers: "office/secretary" "central command/always knows my whereabouts," and "personal/ only to be used in an emergency." Carl pointed to the bottom of the paper. The personal number, I guessed.

"Ring up this number. He will explain to you why I am here."

The commandant continued to study the paper. I saw his gaze pass from the top to the bottom and back up to the top, to the letterhead. He looked at his phone for a moment, then he folded the sheet of paper carefully and returned it to Carl.

"Captain, please find a comfortable hotel for Herr ter Weele and his family for the night, and arrange to get him to the station tomorrow morning."

The captain saluted, nonplussed. I could see he was angry. No, raging.

Carl thanked the commandant for his hospitality and then snapped to attention, raised his right hand as if pointing to the sky, and roared a staccato, "Heil Hitler!"

At the hotel room all five of us slept in one big bed, together. The other beds were empty. We held one another, all five of us, until the three children were asleep. And then Carl and I clung together. We were exhilarated to be there, holding each other. Happy beyond words. Exhausted. And terrified for our lives.

Hoofdstuk 13

4 augustus 1940: German bombers hammer London, driven off by RAF fighters. U-boats torpedo two British cargo ships in North Atlantic.

I didn't like him. He was ugly, fat, with a head bigger than a football and just as round. He was mean and a liar. In front of his commandant he had been nice to Papa. This morning, he was nasty.

"You have fooled my commandant," he said to Papa when he picked us up at the hotel, "but you don't fool me. I know that you intend to flee to Sweden. I know that boy"—he pointed to me—"is not your son. He is a Jew."

Later, in the truck on the way to the station, he snarled like a dog at Papa. "I have already telexed ahead to my staff at Stralsund. They know you are coming. When you attempt to flee, they will catch you. They will shoot you like a dog. I have instructed them to find an excuse, any excuse, and to execute your wife and children as well." He almost smiled at the thought, and then he spat on me and almost screamed, "And your little Jew boy will be the first they shoot!"

I thought Papa was going to slug him the way Popeye slugged Bruto. But Papa was too smart. He knew the captain would use that as an excuse to shoot him.

By the time we were on the train, my stomach hurt, I was so angry. Papa and Mama were silent. I could see that Papa was thinking, making a plan. Alex was quiet. I kissed him and put my arm around him. I knew the killing he had seen yesterday had frightened him. Margy had screamed all night and was now asleep in Mama's arms.

After a while Papa said, "Marge, let's get off at the next station. We'll take a bus back to Berlin. We won't be able to get to Sweden. They'll be watching us like hawks in Stralsund. We'll have to find another way."

I could see that Papa was worried for us. I wanted to tell him that he shouldn't be worried for me, that I would help him. But Papa was smart. His last plan had been thwarted, but he would turn it into a victory. He would use it as a feint. Alex and I used that tactic all the time with our toy soldiers. Set up a feint, and when the enemy has committed to resist the feint, attack elsewhere. Alex and I had read and studied all of the battles of Alexander the Great. Papa had feinted toward Sweden, so now he would turn and thrust somewhere else. I didn't know where. Perhaps Papa didn't yet know where. But he would find a weak spot in the enemy's lines and throw all his strength at that point. He would win. He and Mama and Margy and Alex and I, we would win.

I wiggled onto Papa's lap. Before I fell asleep, I whispered to him, "It's okay, Papa. It will work. We're going to win."

He put both of his arms around me. I thought of Alexander's victory of Gaugamela. I looked up at Papa to tell him how Alexander had tricked Darius, and a tear fell onto my face as Papa kissed me. A surge of love filled me as I realized Papa did not want the Germans to catch me.

Hoofdstuk 14

5 augustus 1940: RAF bombers reach Berlin, turned back by heavy antiaircraft fire. New Italian bomber sinks cargo ship off Sicilian coast. Mussolini lauds technical superiority of Italian Air Force.

We took a room in a different hotel in Berlin. We felt certain that returning to the same hotel would be dangerous. The reception might suspect us and report us to the police, or the captain and his commandant might search for where we had been before they found us on the train. It had been one thing for the commandant not to dare to call Himmler. It was quite another for the two of them to buy our story and dismiss us.

Carl did not wish to dally in Berlin. He wished to be out of Berlin, out of Germany, before the net tightened further. First thing in the morning, he sent me to the Swiss consulate for visas. As I walked the last block and could see the Swiss flag, the hair on the nape of my neck rose. I was being followed! I could feel it, feel my skin crawl. At first I didn't know who was watching me. I didn't want to be obvious, to stop and look around. I strolled on, pretending nonchalance, and then I noticed him. A small man, about my age. Goatee, glasses, a fedora, carrying a folded newspaper and a walking stick.

I ambled along, not changing my pace. He followed, paying me no attention, keeping near or behind other pedestrians. I continued past the Swiss consulate without changing my pace. A block farther along, the row of embassies and consulates morphed into small, chic stores. I hesitated in front of one of the shop windows. Hats. No one inside. The same for the next boutique, which sold shoes. A bit farther along was women's fashions—dresses, skirts, scarfs. A half dozen shoppers inside, all women. A man would not want to enter here; he'd be out of place. I went inside, held up a skirt or two within sight of the sidewalk. Pretended to consider them for purchase. I worked my way toward the back, slipped into a storage area meant for staff only, and found a door leading into the alley. I tried to hurry without hurrying to a side street, and fled without fleeing. My heart was pounding. After a few blocks I relaxed, caught my breath. So much for the Swiss! I changed plans and headed for the American consulate, watching my back the whole way. As far as I could tell, no one was following me.

The American Consul greeted me with open arms. He knew Dedham, had even played on the course at the Dedham Country Club, and he was pleased to see someone from "home." He saw few Americans now in Berlin, he told me. Not many visitors, not much to do. And yes, it would give him great pleasure to walk my passport and Carl's to his confrere, the Swiss Consul. They were old friends and it was only a few blocks away, just around the corner, an excuse for some fresh air and exercise. He would arrange the visas for us. No trouble at all. A great pleasure.

By late morning, Carl and I and the three children were at the train station purchasing tickets for Basel. Despite my close brush with the Gestapo—Carl was convinced the small man with the walking stick had been Gestapo—I was beginning to be more worried about the children now than about the Germans. Jan was tired, the circles under his eyes as dark as his hair. Alex was more than tired. His usual buoyant smile was gone. He moved slowly, sadly, and he slept poorly, if at all. But the worst was Margy. At nine months she should have been putting on weight, growing with a vengeance. She had been babbling up a storm those last weeks in Eindhoven. Now she was losing weight; every day she was thinner. She was languid, impassive. She coughed steadily, and every cough hurt me physically, in the pit of my stomach. She no longer babbled at me. I was unable to find the cereal I had been giving her, and my milk was insufficient. Bad enough that it was all she had; worse now because my flow was meager. I had never had adequate quantities when I was nursing the boys, but it was so much less now. Too much stress? Too little food for me? Was I exhausted? And her cough! I wanted to take her to the doctor, but contact with any German was a risk we dared not take. Margy reminded me of the daughter of the handyman who worked for Father on the farm in Westwood. The girl immediately fell ill after birth. I was seven years old. I remember only the vacant eyes of the infant, her incessant coughing, and the sobs of the mother when the baby died. I had cried, partly for the baby but mostly for the mother. I wanted now to cry for Margy.

We needed to escape Germany. It was no longer a flight solely from the Nazis. It had become a race against time. Without better nourishment and a doctor's care ... I pulled Margy against me. I couldn't finish the thought, didn't want to think about it.

The train to Basel was crammed with soldiers for the first hours. Sitting, standing, lying on the floors. On the trains toward Berlin, the men had been happy, drinking, making jokes, no doubt looking forward to their homes, their wives, their mothers. These soldiers were headed, I supposed, toward France, to Alsace, toward the front. No one paid us heed. They were bound for battle. Civilians traveling in such a direction could hardly be suspicious.

The land lay peacefully on either side of the tracks—rolling hills, fields of grain readying for harvest, copses of trees in the draws, sun reigning gloriously over it all. I saw few men. Women were the workers in the fields, mixed with small boys and their grandfathers. The men were on this train or on the battlefields. Still, it was all so serene. How could a country that spread thunder and lightning and death so terribly appear so pastoral and peaceful?

And then, somewhere along the French border, all the men left the train. They were somber. They walked quickly along the platform toward some destiny they knew not, could not imagine. Their departure left the train all but empty, silent but for Margy's weak cough. I tried to feed her. She would suckle for a minute and then drop the teat. I tried her on the other breast with the same result. Too weak to suckle? Too little milk? Putting her on my shoulder, I burped her, patted her, caressed her back. She quieted and seemed to sleep.

The boys had watched the soldiers disembark. When they were all gone, Jan jumped gleefully on Carl's lap. Alex, on invitation of his older brother, climbed on his father's lap as well.

"Papa, we are free!" Jan crowed. "The soldiers have left!" Together the boys cried, "Yay!"

Carl hugged them, smiled at them, kissed them. "Just a few hours more," he said.

Over their shoulders, he winked at me. They were happy, and both Carl and I knew that in two or three hours we would be at the Swiss frontier. Unless the train was stopped and searched as it had been going to Stralsund. And then there would be the border crossing. Would they let us across? Arrest us? Execute us? Were they even searching for us? It seemed likely. We were certain we were on the blacklist. But were they checking everyone?

I put the thoughts out of my mind, turned my attention back to the children. The boys needed to eat. Carl went through the almost deserted cars until he found the vendor with the trolley of snacks. He returned with bottles of chocolate milk and four sandwiches. He also had two bottles of beer.

"It will make your milk run," he said, smiling at me as he opened a bottle for me, the other for himself.

The boys did not hesitate. They were famished. I felt guilty eating when Margy was so hungry, but Carl encouraged me.

It would be good for my milk, he said. And then, more quietly, he added, "A few more hours." He stopped and took a deep breath. "A few more hours. And then ..." He hesitated once more. "And then we shall be free. Switzerland or ..."

He couldn't go on. I put my hand on his knee. Yes, I thought. *Switzerland, or ...* I knew what he hadn't been able to say. Switzerland, or we will all be dead. The moment of truth. How many times does such a moment come? For most, never. For us, this would be it. The commandant on the way to Stralsund had backed down; he had not dared to dial Himmler's phone number. Would we be so lucky at the Swiss border?

Hoofdstuk 15

18 augustus 1940: Germans take control of French transport system, clamp down on civilian travel. Vichy government institutes food rationing. RAF hits Cherbourg.

We were there. The boys were pointing out the windows of the train at the mountains ahead of us. Switzerland, a land of peace. Margery was white as a ghost as she stared at the mountains. She had vacationed in Switzerland several years before with PC, her oldest sister. PC had taken her to Geneva on their way to visit their sister-in-law Mary, who was on an archeological dig in Greece. Margery spoke often of that trip: it had been memorable, enjoyable, and full of fun. She had been seventeen. They had taken donkeys into the mountains near Thessaloniki. They had run into snow so deep, the donkeys had floundered. It had been an adventure, a scary adventure, but fun nonetheless.

I looked at her now. This trip was not a fun adventure. She was frightened—frightened for all of us, frightened that we would be caught here. Frightened, I suspected, for little Margy, who was coughing, as pale as her mother, listless, eyes vacant. Margery wanted to cross the border to be free, to be rid of the Germans, but most of all to get Margy to a doctor.

Ever since the German troops had exited at Alsace, the train had been mostly empty. This made for comfort, but we were now exposed. There was no crowd in which to hide. The train would go no farther than the border. End of the line. The conductor announced that in German as he passed through the cars. *Aus.* End of the line. *Aus.* All out. End of the line.

If I had been alone, I would have wandered away from the station and the dozens of border guards, and then sneaked across the border on foot at night. With five of us, with the three children, that was not possible.

We were herded off the platform toward the *douane*, the customs. Tables were set up. Crowds of civilians milled about. Near the tables and the border-control point at the bridge across a ravine to Switzerland, there were more soldiers than civilians. The boys, awake and alert now, were impressed by the uniforms and the weaponry, excited by the mountains. Margery smiled until little Margy went into a fit of coughing. She cooed and quieted our daughter.

"Halt!"

Shots rang out at the entryway to the bridge as two men burst onto the bridge and raced for the far side. One of them had a pistol, and he had shot the two soldiers barring entry onto the bridge. But other soldiers were after them in a flash and caught them before they had gone twenty meters. One of them pushed the man with the pistol to the ground and shot him. The second man cursed and screamed as he was hurried away. Two soldiers carried the body of the downed man to an ambulance parked along the road.

The crowd, boisterous before, was silent. Margery and I exchanged glances. Where she had been white before, she was now ashen with fear.

I looked again at the bridge to Switzerland. There was no crossing here for trains or cars or trucks. Only pedestrians could cross. The bridge was hardly wide enough for three or four persons abreast, and was perhaps a hundred meters long. This side, Nazi Germany. The far side, neutral Switzerland.

The tables were organized by letters of the alphabet. The end table was for *S* through *Z*. It would be here that I would need to show our passports and have them stamped before we could walk onto the bridge and cross. We had the visas we needed for Germany and for Switzerland. Our papers, our documents, were legal. All would depend on whether they were looking for me.

I sent Margery and the children to the toilets a hundred meters down a village street. They needed a break. While they were gone, I studied the action at the tables. The "customs officers" sitting at each table were all military, all men. Most of those who presented themselves with their passports were couples. A few were single men; very few were women alone. And some were families like ours. The single women seemed to be the least scrutinized. Often the douaniers would smile and joke with them. The single men, in contrast, suffered the most. Often insulted, every second or third was sent off, pulled and pushed and manhandled by two or three guards, for interrogation. Heaven knows how that went. The elderly couples fared a bit better. The younger couples seemed to be treated more civilly when the lady was cute and outgoing and the man was more reticent.

The most aggressive of the douaniers was the one at the *S* through *Z* table. He affronted everyone, checked and rechecked papers, called time and again for his supervisor, and condemned person after person to further interrogation by the guards. He was young, a true Nazi. A formidable graduate of the Hitler Jeugd. Nasty.

I turned down the street where I had sent Margery and the children. I didn't want to deal with that bastard. When Margery returned with the children, I suggested lunch. We walked to the edge of town and ate under an awning. Jan and Alex picked up pebbles from those scattered around the trees edging the street. They set up a miniature fort with walls made of leaves and twigs and rolled the pebbles at them. Cannon fire! They flew their airplanes, Jan with his super-fast Eindecker, Alex grudgingly with his slower Junker, and dropped pebbles. Aerial bombardment!

Margery nursed Margy. I wanted a beer but settled for coffee. I would need my wits about me when we presented out passports. I had already decided to wait for the next shift of douaniers. We needed, at all costs, to avoid that son-of-a-bitch I'd been watching.

Margery was studying my face. "What are you thinking, Carl? Are we going to give it a try?"

Putting it off wouldn't help. "Of course." I tried to sound nonchalant, confident. "We'll make it."

She couldn't manage a smile. I knew she wasn't worried for herself. She was worried a bit for me, but mostly she was worried for the children. I was worried as well. If Margery and I were shot, what then for Jan, Alex, and Margy? I put the thought aside.

"Look," I said. "Take time after lunch to pretty up a bit. Do you have your tennis shorts?" She nodded. "Put them on. And a pretty blouse." I gestured down my chest.

"Cleavage?" she asked.

I nodded. "Not too much, but yes."

"I don't have much with me," she said.

"And brush your hair." I smiled at her. "You know how to do it. "

"Lipstick? Rouge?"

I nodded. "Tasteful, of course, but yes." I winked. "These are all guys. A pretty gal …" I shrugged, laughed. "You caught me that way." After a pause, I added, "And clean up the boys too. A bright smile from them might help as well."

I paid as she and the children returned to the toilets. I walked once more to the bridge to watch the douaniers. There was a new watch. Still all soldiers, of course. The *S-Z* table had an older man. More senior, serious. Serious about checking papers. He processed two or three couples as I watched. He stamped their passports and waved them past the guards at the head of the bridge.

The next couple, both with swarthy skin, was clearly not German. Polish, I thought. Jewish, maybe? Gypsies? He asked questions, checked their passports against his lists, called over two guards. The couple protested, raised their voices, and the douanier signaled for two additional soldiers. The four of them dragged the couple off. The crowd around the tables quieted as the couple was pushed and prodded along. No one dared to intervene. I watched for a few minutes more as he processed another couple; vigorously questioned a middle-aged man and sent him off for more scrutiny; smiled broadly as he stamped the passport of a young mother, blond and carrying a tow-headed tot, and winked as he waved her on; stamped the papers of an elderly German-speaking couple, he supporting himself on a cane, with hardly a second glance.

I turned and walked back to the café where I had told Margery to meet me when she was done cleaning up. Would it work for us? I wondered. They seemed to be letting Germans through. The foreigners were the ones under scrutiny. And men of military age were almost all dragged off.

We had half of what we needed. Our passports and visas were in order, but we were foreigners. And the real issue, the constant question— was I or wasn't I on their list?

The boys were in a good mood, laughing and pushing each other. Margery was low key but stunning nonetheless in shorts and a blouse, her hair loose under a bright red hairband. If I were checking her passport, I would let her through. She laughed when she saw my look of approval.

Good, I thought. Better to appear happy and confident than dark and suspicious.

"Let's go," I said gaily. And to the boys, "March!"

We dragged our bags and approached the back of the line leading to the douaniers. Still, I wondered. Should we wait or go for it? Ten years earlier, when Margery and I first met in Nice, our mutual brothers,

Hendrik and Alex, had dragged us to Monte Carlo. Somewhere near the start of our visit to the roulette tables, Henk urged me to buy a few chips. He had not a cent of his own, couldn't find even ten cents with which to bet, but he egged me on. I winked at Margery and gave her a stack of chips. She leaned over and placed them, all of them, on number sixteen. She winked back at me. We had met only a week earlier and were still in the early stage of flirting. Hendrik, living off the combined rent both she and I were paying him and Alex, was appalled. He didn't want her to risk such a large sum on thirty-six to one odds. Margery had played sixteen because June 16 was my birthday, and she knew sixteen was my lucky number. Hendrik reached across the roulette table to take back the stack of chips, but couldn't get them before the croupier cut him off with *"Les jeux sont faits."* Henk's face darkened with annoyance. Thirty seconds later when sixteen came up, he was quick enough to pick up the original $500 bet and the $18,000 in winnings. He ran with the chips to the nearest teller and cashed them in, then he ordered us all home. Would we be so lucky this time? Margery's smile made me confident that we would prevail.

As we stood in line at the *S-Z* table, my initial confidence ebbed. And yes, the first question from the douanier as he inspected my passport was, "Dutch?" I nodded. "Military?" I nodded again. "Did you resist the Fatherland?" Again, I nodded. "Where?"

"The Grebbeberg." This was not going well. But for a thirty-seven-year-old Dutchman not to have been part of the Dutch resistance to the German invasion would be unbelievable. Better to be candid.

"You are a traitor." The sentence was an accusation.

I snapped to attention. "A traitor to the cause of the Fatherland, my Commandant." He looked up at me in surprise. Then I added, "But a patriot to the cause of the House of Orange."

"Here you answer to the Fatherland," he said coldly. He waved to two guards. They arrived, stood behind me. I waited for them to take my arms and march me off, but the douanier gave them no further instruction. They stood closely behind me, waiting. The douanier picked up Margery's passport. Studied it, looked up at Margery, smiled. And shifted to English. Was he testing her as well, or was he old school, gallant to the ladies?

"Married to an American, I see?"

He spoke fluently. His English was better than mine, and had a pronounced British accent. He must have spent time in England, perhaps had studied there.

He looked at me. He continued speaking in English, but his smile had disappeared and his British accent seemed more formal. "And that one?" He pointed at the picture of Jan in the passport and then at Jan himself. "A Jew, *nein?*"

The question—no, it was more an accusation than a question—angered me, as it had when other officers asked it. A Jew? Jan? But I realized his perception was more important than the facts. I calmed myself, did my best to speak easily.

"My oldest son. Five years old."

Margery smiled as she stepped up next to me. "He's more me." She shook her head to draw attention to her dark hair. Her dark eyes sparkled with her smile. "And this one"—she proudly pulled Alex forward—"is more his father."

The douanier didn't smile, but I could see he appreciated Margery's style. He looked from Margery to Jan and back, and seemed to nod.

Standing beside Margery, Alex pointed at the medal on the douanier's breast. "Luftwasse," he exclaimed in awe. "I have a Junker. Did you fly one?"

The douanier was obviously amused that a tot would recognize his medal and knew about German planes.

"No, not a Junker. An Eindecker."

"Eindecker! Fast! They dominated!"

The corners of the officer's mouth twitched ever so slightly. He suppressed the smile, returned to the passports. He studied the visas, particularly the visa to Germany.

"It is not possible for a Dutch soldier to have a German visa." Again an accusation.

I shrugged nonchalantly. "As you can see, the Ambassador himself issued it."

The douanier didn't buy it. "What was your unit?"

Before I could reply, Jan chimed the response. Proudly. "He was in the Mounted Artillery."

Not to be outdone, Alex added, "His horse was Klaas." And then, sadly, "He died."

The douanier raised his eyebrows at me for confirmation. I nodded. "Mounted Artillery. As I said, Grebbeberg."

"The Dutch made a gallant stand at the Grebbe," he said, a reluctant acknowledgment.

I snapped to attention. *"Danke, mein Commandant."*

He continued darkly, "Many of the Führer's best troops were lost in that attack."

He turned to the two guards. Before I could move, each of them had a tight grip on one of my arms. Margery paled. We each sensed the tide turning against us.

Alex stepped forward again. "Can I go up in an Eindecker?" he asked.

"How old are you?" asked the douanier, apparently surprised that such a young boy spoke so well.

"Two! My birthday is tomorrow." And then, for emphasis, "Tomorrow!"

The officer checked Margery's passport and looked back at Alex. "Ach, yes, you will have two years on August 25. Not tomorrow. Next week." Alex smiled broadly. The officer looked up at Margery. "He could be German."

Yes, I thought. *Blond, almost white hair; a quick smile. But no, Meneer, he is Dutch.* I held my tongue.

"My first grandson was just two when he and my daughter, his mother, died in ..." The douanier paused, thinking. "In 1918. Almost the end of the War. Saarbrucken. An artillery shell ..." His voice trailed off. He was speaking, of course, of the last war.

Margery's sorrowful expression conveyed her genuine sympathy for him.

The moment passed. The douanier leafed through the pages next to him. Page after page of names. The list. I swallowed hard. Realizing I was holding my breath, I forced myself to regular breathing. He held my passport in one hand as he flipped pages. Was my name there? My heart pounded. Margery's face went white.

He reached the *W*s. Upside down I could read Wargerink, Warmolts, Warnaars, Weerd, Weise, Westenberg, Wevers. My name wasn't there! Since it was spelled ter Weele, both in Holland as well as in Germany it would be alphabetized by its first upper-case letter, the *W*. The douanier knew that. But it wasn't there!

He flipped backward. His finger ran down Straten, Stroeve, Stroink, Tatersall, TerWeele, Thomasson, Tichler. The finger stopped and ran back up to TerWeele. Paused, ran down farther, past Tonis, Traast,

Tromp, all the *T*s, to Unitis, Verbeek. Then back to TerWeele. He coughed, picked up the passport. He had us! We were caught!

My chest exploded as if I'd been hit by a mortar shell. I put my hands on the table for support. I thought I was going to fall. He held the passport up next to the list. The passport read Carl Frits ter Weele. The list read Carl Frits TerWeele. Next to my name on the list was the date 16-06-1903. My date of birth, the same as in my passport. Holding the passport up to the list, he looked at me.

"You?"

My breathing stopped. My heart seemed to stop as well. I couldn't speak. I moved my mouth, but nothing came out. Still he looked at me. Slowly, very slowly, I shook my head.

He looked again at the list. He had me. "Sixteen June 1903?"

From a box on the table he took a rubber stamp and inked it. He pressed the stamp onto the page in Margery's passport with the German visa, wrote something in pen. I couldn't read the upside-down script. He did the same with my passport, closed the two passports, and signaled the guard standing to my right. Still holding my arm, the guard stepped forward. As he did so, the douanier handed the two passports to him.

A moment passed. Another. Then he said, "Help this gentleman and his family with their luggage." He nodded toward the bridge.

The four of us and the two guards walked to the bridge. I was confused. Why to the bridge? He had recognized my name and date of birth. Wasn't he going to arrest us? The four guards at the bridge stopped us, looked to our douanier for instructions. He waved to them to indicate that they should let us pass. The two guards who were helping with our luggage handed the bags to us. We were free to cross? For a moment I couldn't believe it. The douanier had identified me. He had found my name on the list. What was happening?

A shudder ran through me. Perhaps they would let us start to cross and then they would shoot us. They would claim we were trying to escape. Easier to bury five bodies than to imprison five persons.

As we started to walk, I said to Margery and the boys in English so the guards wouldn't understand, "Don't turn. Don't look back." I repeated "Don't look back." Turning and looking back might appear to be a sign of guilt. Also, I did not want anyone to turn and see guns leveled at us. If the boys were shot in the back, they would be dead without knowing it. I did not want their last moment to be one of terror.

106

A hundred meters of bridge to Switzerland. The spot between my shoulder blades hurt, burned as if seared by a red-hot branding iron. It was the spot where a bullet would hit if the guards fired.

Twenty-five meters behind us. Another twenty-five and we would be at the midpoint of the bridge. That would be the moment the guards would fire. I wanted to encourage Margery, to stem her fear. I turned my head ever so slightly to see her. Her face was still white, and I had never seen her so concentrated. She clutched little Margy tight. Even Jan was holding his breath. None of us dared speak. Alex, young as he was, sensed the terror.

Fifty yards. I listened for the clack-clack of ammunition being pumped into the chamber. Still nothing. Seventy-five yards. We were being let free! I took one full breath, and the Swiss guards were checking our passports. We were there! Then Margery was in my arms, Jan and Alex clasping us around the knees, little Margy pressed between us. Margery was in tears, smiling, laughing. Tears spilled down her cheeks onto little Margy. We had done it!

"He knew," Margery whispered. "He knew." We hugged harder. "He knew."

Her body was shaking. As her legs went limp, I clasped her to me, held her erect for a long while until I felt her recover.

Switzerland! We were in Switzerland!

Hoofdstuk 16

24 augustus 1940: Prince Filippo Andrea to be jailed for anti-Fascist activities, Mussolini warns. Hitler vows to devastate London as RAF bombs French coast, German manufacturing. Vichy government imprisons hundreds of foreigners accused as Allied sympathizers.

The bears were below us in a great walled enclosure. Honey-colored and huge. Alex pointed at the bears, pretending to shoot them with a pistol. I heard Jan explain that with brown bears of this size, like grizzlies, a pistol wouldn't do. Grandfather Crane, he told Alex, had hunted grizzlies in Alaska. Grandfather had used a lever-action Winchester, a 45-70. It looked just like the lever-action guns that the cowboys in the movies carried. Alex nodded and put up his two arms as if he were firing a rifle. After each shot, he pretended to eject the used shell casing and to lever a fresh shell into the chamber. I had seen the boys play like this hundreds of times. Already they knew war too well.

Still, I was pleased to see them enjoying themselves as only children can, without a care in the world. These past days it had been playing in the park, shooting Germans, riding Klaas into battle. Carl and I alternately laughed and cried and made love, the stress of the trip stripped from us as if we had shed a heavy backpack and peeled off layers of winter coats.

We hadn't stayed long in Basel, only long enough to recuperate from the strain of the trek through Germany. As a border town, Basel was acutely aware of the war pounding on its door. From there we had taken the train to Berne. Berne was Paradise, the city humming with a delicious humdrum of daily routine, oblivious to the roar of the inferno of war, of the flames lapping at the foothills surrounding the mountains of Switzerland. We scoured the daily papers for real news, not the propaganda fed to us the last weeks by the German press. Austria was occupied. Poland had been invaded. Holland and Belgium overrun. Northern France was German. The Vichy government ruled southern France at Hitler's bidding. The utter devastation of Rotterdam, of which we had learned while in Holland, was perhaps, and thankfully, not quite so complete as we had believed. Mussolini and Hitler had become fast friends. Switzerland was an island in the stream—peaceful, untouched, and awash in serenity. Carl read the German language newspapers; I read those in English, French, and Italian. I wondered about my father in Rome. All the while, the boys played in the park.

Best of all, I had found an American doctor. She treated Margy, gave me new formula, and with Gerber cereal and baby foods available in the stores, Margy began to put on weight and smile. Yes, Switzerland was a paradise!

We would have liked to stay, but Carl had concluded we should flee immediately. The money from the sale of the car was dwindling. The Vichy regime's hold on southern France was increasing daily. The ten days here had been idyllic, but we needed to escape Europe. Carl was anxious to join the Dutch forces being reassembled in Canada.

The American Consul had been marvelous. He knew the Consuls for France, Spain, and Portugal personally, and he took our passports to each of them for the needed visas. And he stamped Carl's passport with an American visa. Carl smiled broadly at the US visa. He had never been in the United States, and he was excited at the prospect of going there. I was excited to return. I had been away now for, what, thirteen years? Fourteen? Before marrying, I had traveled with my parents; and my sister PC and brother Alex had both visited with me in Europe. My brothers Josh and Emery had died while I was away, and I hadn't seen my sister CC in all these years. But much as I loved Europe and Carl's Holland, America was still home for me. I was as excited as Carl. I couldn't wait to return.

With Margy asleep on my breast, I turned my attention back to the boys. Alex was resisting Jan's suggestion that he take the part of a German soldier so that Jan, as a Dutch soldier, could shoot at him. Jan soon conceded, and the two of them joined forces and shot at German troops concealed in the park's flower gardens. The sun on my face was bliss. Peace. The cacophony of Berne's cars and trucks and Europe's turmoil dissolved into a background hum. The fear of the last weeks melted away.

Carl was arranging our trip to Lisbon. We had considered traveling to Rome. My father was there and would be able to help us financially, but we had concluded that Italy was too dangerous. France would be our best route. Not entirely safe for Carl, but not too dangerous if we made our run now.

Carl had found that Thomas Cooke was operating busses through France to Madrid and then onward to Lisbon. Of course, we were not the only ones fleeing Europe. He was at the Thomas Cooke office now purchasing tickets for us. He had asked at both the Dutch and American consulates for help with boat tickets from Lisbon to the US, but so far to no avail. All scheduled departures were fully booked, and the steamship lines were canceling their voyages from the United States to Europe. Too dangerous. German U-boats were sinking ships daily. Soon there would be no more boats arriving in Europe, and thus no more boats sailing for the US. Carl was optimistic that something would come up, but it was imperative that we reach Lisbon as soon as possible.

When I returned to the hotel with the children, Carl was in the room. The boys clambered over him for hugs and kisses. Alex was blabbing about how he and Jan had been shooting soldiers hiding in the bushes. Margy was trying to touch his nose. I had been showing her the parts of the face—nose, eyes, mouth, tongue, ears, hair, teeth. Carl alternately grimaced and laughed as she touched and pulled at his nose, ears, and hair.

That afternoon, he told me, we would take the train to Geneva. The Thomas Cooke bus to Lisbon was scheduled for a seven a.m. departure tomorrow from Geneva. I packed for the train trip, and in Geneva we had a quick supper and went to bed early. Thomas Cooke had reserved two seats on one side of the aisle for Jan and Alex, and two seats across the aisle for Carl and me. Margy would be on our laps. There was a crowd at the station, and the bus was chockablock full, every seat taken, the hold below the bus crammed with suitcases and trunks, the bins above our heads overflowing with parcels, boxes, loose clothing, food, drink. All of us were fleeing the war and determined to take, it seemed, every bit of our prewar lives with us.

Although it was crowded and early, we were all in good spirits. Everyone shared stories about where they had come from and where they were going. We all reveled in our good fortune to have a ticket and to be on our way. As far as I could make out, there was not a single Swiss on board. Austrians, Brits, Italians, French. Lots of French. One couple, he a German, she an American, was also headed for New York. I didn't ask, but they were almost certainly Jewish. He was quiet, as if in hiding. I supposed that in a way he was.

No sooner had we started than we were at the French border. The boys and Margy were already asleep. The Swiss douaniers came on board, checking and stamping our passports without fanfare. We were of no interest to them. They were happy to be rid of us. We represented an unwelcome detritus of the war that seethed at their borders.

A few hundred yards farther, it was a different matter. The French military—the Vichy military, I should say—directed the bus to park, and we were all instructed to debark with our packages and personal effects. Suitcases and trunks were disgorged from the hold. Carrying our goods and possessions, we entered the custom hall and stood in line. We had been on the bus hardly ten minutes, and we spent about three hours clearing French customs.

First it was a check of our passports. Many people didn't seem to have their papers in order and were turned away. We had no problem, although my American passport with the children on it raised an inordinate amount of scrutiny. Then they checked our luggage. Everything had to be opened. Everything taken out, unfolded, refolded. Having already been on the road a month, we were carrying far less than those who had started their journey in Geneva. Carl had two cartons of Camels in his bag. He slipped a Swiss Franc note between the cartons as the douanier checked them. He lost the note and one carton of cigarettes, but he was pleased that one carton was returned to him. I had two pairs of silk stockings. Without comment, those disappeared into the agent's pocket. Some of the travelers tried to resist the pilfering. One particularly boisterous man was ushered out by soldiers without any of his possessions. The douaniers simply seized whatever they wanted. Resisting was not a wise strategy. Carl had simply smiled and nodded at the agent fumbling through our suitcases as the cigarettes and his one Franc note vanished. When the silk stockings disappeared too, he had winked knowingly and said in French, *"J'espere qu'elle va les aimer"*—I hope that she will appreciate them—with an emphasis on the *she*. The douanier smiled broadly. He seemed already to be looking forward to the evening to come.

It was noon by the time we were back on the bus and underway. The children were cantankerous. Too much standing, too much noise. Carl handed down the snack bag, and I fed them. That helped. Seven of the seats on the bus were now empty. Not all of our fellow passengers had made it into France. The German with the American wife, despite that they looked Jewish, were still on board. We'd hardly gone five miles, but for us at least, so far, so good.

The two seventeen-hour days of travel from Geneva to Sete in southern France were a nightmare. The roads were jammed with lorries, buses, cars, carts pulled by horses, and crowds of pedestrians. The bus seemed to stand more than drive. We saw a family with a horse-drawn cart three or four times. They would pass us moving slowly along the berm of the road. An hour later we would pass them, only to run into another traffic jam and have them pass us again. If the French military, whether a single vehicle or a convoy, came along, all traffic had to move to the side of the road and halt to let them pass. Sometimes for a few minutes, sometimes for two or three hours.

For the adults on the bus, the trip was awful. For the children, it was disastrous. Not only was the ride itself horrible, organization in Vichy France was zero. No butter, soap, or flour. Sugar restricted to 500 grams per month for those lucky enough to have coupons. We could barely obtain milk for Margy. People were surviving on bread, fruit, and wine, and the bread was awful. I could hardly imagine what might happen to the population during the coming winter. True or not, we heard that the German zone was far better organized.

From Sete east to the Spanish frontier, the bus moved along more regularly. But at the border, half of our contingent was refused entry into Spain. The border was closed to anyone wishing to go on to Portugal. Spain was cooperating with Hitler. Anyone suspected of "fleeing" would be blocked entry to and transit across Spain. Half of us stood on the sidewalk with our possessions scattered around us, watching our Thomas Cooke bus pull away. I wanted to cry. More than a month of travel and tension and all for naught? What now?

Carl commandeered a taxi and back we went to Perpignan, France, to find a hotel. The boys turned their exhaustion into anger. Everyone between the border and Perpignan was transformed into a nasty German soldier, and they spent the whole ride shooting them all. With some of them it was a single *bang*. With groups, it was a constant *rat-a-tat*. After a while Carl and I and the cab driver began to laugh. Soon we were all helping with the shooting, and by the time we reached the hotel we were in stitches. We had killed half the population of France. Better to laugh than to cry.

Hoofdstuk 17

29 augustus 1940: Hitler congratulates German Navy for spate of sinkings in North Atlantic. Vows not one Allied cargo, passenger, or naval vessel will reach British shores, that Churchill and cronies will die from starvation by Christmas.

It was not yet eight in the morning when I reached the Spanish consulate. Already fifty or so people waited in line. The sign on the door informed us that the hours were ten to noon and two to four on Tuesdays, Wednesdays, and Thursdays. I shrugged to myself. Spanish hours. Nothing to do but wait.

It appeared that most of us were in the same predicament: refused entry at the border to Spain and trying to find a way to get across. The man in front of me was Portuguese, he said. He spoke no English and of course I spoke no Portuguese, but we managed in French, although his French was sprinkled with Portuguese. He lived near Lisbon. His wife and children were there. He sold corks for wine bottles and came regularly to France on business. This was the first time he had incurred difficulty at the border. He had tried to convince the douanier that he was not fleeing from anywhere to anywhere. He was just a businessman on a business trip trying to return home. The douaniers had stood firm: no one with a transit visa through Spain would be allowed entry. He shrugged.

A few minutes after ten, the door opened. By now the line had lengthened. I estimated we were upward of two hundred persons in the queue, perhaps more. Every few minutes someone who had been in line in front of us came out of the building, disconsolate. We would crowd around. What happened? Each one gave the same story. No entry into Spain. Some had been told it was because they were not Spanish; others because their transit visa was no longer valid.

The line had moved enough so that the cork salesman and I had entered the building and closed to within a few feet of the window with a clerk on the other side who was answering everyone's queries. Only six or eight people stood between us and the clerk. The tiny waiting room was empty of furniture but for a decrepit couch, chair, and desk. While we waited, the Portuguese cork salesman—he had now become Antoine and I had become Carl—flirted with the cute blond secretary at the desk. The two of us took her to be Swedish, perhaps Swiss. No, she laughed. Spanish! The three of us were speaking French. She poked fun at Antoine's Portugo-French. When we reached the counter, the cork salesmen showed his Portuguese passport with his multitransit visa and explained that he had used it many times without a problem. The man behind the window concurred but shrugged. That was before. This was now. Transit visas were no longer valid. No. Not valid. Sorry.

How could he get back to Lisbon? Antoine asked.

A shrug, nothing more.

Then it was my turn. My Dutch passport raised the clerk's interest. Margery's American passport increased his interest further. He inspected them both carefully. French, Spanish, German, Italian, he said he saw frequently. Even Swiss. Dutch and American? Almost never. He turned to the visas. Invalid, he proclaimed. I pointed out the date: issued just a week ago. That was before. No longer valid. Sorry. And no, no, we no longer issue transit visas. Not valid.

He handed the passports back, and the cork salesmen and I turned away. To the others in the line behind us, we reiterated what they had already heard over and over. Existing transit visas were invalid. New transit visas were not being issued.

Some toward the end of the line walked away. They would not get to the window by noon, so they were going to lunch. Others stayed doggedly in line. Antoine and I exchanged the names of our hotels, and he gave me his Lisbon address. Maybe we could help each other?

Margery and I exchanged views on our predicament back at our hotel. She had already learned there was neither an American nor Dutch Consul in Perpignan. While she took the children to a nearby park, I spent the afternoon at the hotel switchboard trying to reach the American Consul in Berne. The hotel operator was patient but could not get through to the Consul. She could not even get through to an operator in Switzerland. Two hours more the next morning proved equally futile. Our hotel operator was being terribly nice—I brought her some flowers, which earned me a smile—but it was clear that her patience with my dilemma was wearing thin.

Margery and I talked, and we decided we would try to reach her father in Rome. So armed with a few French francs, a pot of coffee, a pack of cigarettes, and a smile—all for the hotel operator—she and I spent the next morning trying to get through to Rome. The cigarettes and French francs helped the operator's mood, but the result was the same. She could not get through to Italy.

That afternoon I went to the cork salesmen's hotel. He was there, and we sat outside the hotel at a table the size of a plate, jammed on a sliver of cobblestone sidewalk, and had a beer. He had had no luck either. He had contacted clients at local vineyards with no success. One of his clients had called his lawyer for advice. Everyone agreed: transit visas were no longer being issued. The lawyer did explain that there was always a way to get around a law in Spain. That was to obtain a letter of exception from a high official with an appropriately impressive letterhead, official seals, and signature. He did not suggest who such officials with appropriate authority might be. Antoine and I wondered who might fit that description. The mayor? No. Wrong nationality, no authority.

The salesman had begun to explore where he might be able to sneak across the border. Not at the checkpoint, obviously, but at a farm or hiking trail. Perhaps through a vineyard that straddled the frontier. Once in Spain, he thought, he would have no trouble reaching the Portuguese border, but there—without a valid Spanish visa showing legal entry into Spain—he would once again need to sneak across the frontier, this time into Portugal. It was risky, but he knew his way around and he thought he could make it work. We talked about my joining him, but he was skeptical. First, the children would encumber two illicit border crossings; and second, an obviously non-Spanish family (light-skinned children, two of them blonds; a six-foot-four father with blue eyes) would hardly be able to travel across Spain unnoticed, unchallenged by authorities. I suspected he was right.

Margery was holding up with the children, but she and I were becoming increasingly tense, the boys were eating poorly—there was little more than bread available and they didn't like that—and we were all losing patience. Should we strike out for Bordeaux? Try to find a boat there? Retrace our tracks and try the Italian border, heading for her father in Rome? Was he even still there?

At ten to noon the next morning, I waited outside the consulate. The line was just as long this day as it had been when I had been there before. Soon the doors closed. Noontime. Still I waited. Most of those in line had disappeared, off to eat lunch.

A few minutes after the door closed, it opened and the secretary with whom the cork salesman and I had flirted slipped out on her lunch break. I joined her on the sidewalk. Walking along with her, I told her that she had become the love of my life, that I had not slept a wink since I had seen her, that she was beautiful and that she should be a screen actress. She smiled at my effusive flattery. After a block of walking together, with me praising her charms to the skies and beyond, we were both laughing at my ridiculous hyperbole. As we reached the café where she was intending to lunch, I asked if I could treat her. She shrugged. Why not?

I ordered a beer with a baguette, and she a glass of wine and a baguette. No beer, said the waiter. So it was a larger pitcher of wine for the two of us. The wine was an acceptable vin ordinaire. The bread was disgusting.

After a few minutes of chatting, we became Theresa and Carl. I explained our trip, showed her Margery's passport with its picture of Margery and the children, and recounted how we had been turned back at the border crossing. She sympathized and told me about the written order that the Consul had received from Madrid the week before. No transit would be permitted through Spain. We had arrived two days too late. It had become a nightmare for travelers like us.

What to do? I asked. She shrugged, and then turned her palm up and rubbed her first two fingers together. You do what everyone in Spain does when he needs something, she said. You pay.

How? I asked. To whom? What do I need?

She explained that it would not be possible to stamp anything in a passport. We already had a valid transit visa. We would need a visa of exemption—a letter of permission, if you will—instructing the border guards to honor our transit visas on an exceptional basis.

Who could prepare such a letter? I asked.

Smiling, she patted the pendant around her neck and rubbed her thumb and fingers together again. When I asked how much, she shrugged and said, "For you, twenty-five Swiss francs. But I need to type two letters, one for each passport. Fifty francs." She saw my disappointment, and lowered the price to thirty-five francs for the two letters.

And then? I asked. Then she would need the Consul to sign and stamp the letter. But ... Once more she rubbed her thumb and fingers together. The Consul charged fifty Swiss francs for each letter.

"When can this be done?" I asked.

She said the Consul would be in the next day. It took her only a few minutes to type the letters. She had a dozen ready on her desk for his signature. She would add ours to the stack. "If you have the money, you can have the letters by three or three-thirty tomorrow."

The Consul was doing well, I thought. A dozen letters at fifty Swiss francs each. Not bad. The new "no transit visa" rule was like winning the lottery for him. And Theresa wasn't doing so badly either.

I counted out thirty-five Swiss francs for her and added a hundred franc note for the Consul. And she needed the two passports. She could see I was worried, and she assured me that I could trust her. This was everyday business. My payment and passports were safe with her. "The Consul and I are honest folk," she said sincerely.

The next afternoon I was back. This time I did not join the line, but walked to the door of the consulate and into the waiting room. Theresa smiled, winked at me, and handed me the two passports and the letters, snapped together by an elastic band. It was done! The next day at the border, it was like magic. The douanier stamped the letters and the illicit transit visas in the passports and we were on our way. Lisbon, here we come! Theresa had been right. All one had to do was pay.

Hoofdstuk 18

4 september 1940: Luftwaffe bombards London in three raids as Churchill and ministers commemorate first anniversary of war. British air ministry announces twenty-five Nazi planes downed, fifteen RAF fighters lost. Two cargo ships torpedoed off Irish coast.

Lisbon was a wild sea in a tumultuous storm. Even under German siege, Holland hummed like a Swiss watch in contrast to the hubbub and disarray that seethed around me. Buses were crammed to overflowing, and people pushed and shoved to get on board. The Dutch boarded trams politely, calmly. Here, the buses and trucks and taxis and even burros filled the streets, jockeying with one another to move ahead a few meters. I was fortunate to be big: I could see above the others to pick out the path of least resistance, and I was able to push harder than most.

It had taken me the better part of an hour to get to the docks from our hotel. I had spent much of the past two days here on the quay, inquiring at each shipping line, waiting in line at the ticket windows, scouring the timetables posted on bulletin boards. Confusion was rampant, information regarding expected departures ethereal at best. I presumed it would be smarter to inquire about arrivals—there could only be a departure if there was first an arrival. As best as I could determine, inbound ships were nonexistent.

So I had spent six hours the day before in the only line with hope. That was at the Cunard Line's pier. Alongside the pier was moored the only ship in the harbor. Six hours of standing in line got me to the window. No tickets. Fully booked. First class? No, senor, fully booked. All classes fully booked. The departure date? Probably the day after tomorrow. Waiting list? She shrugged, a shrug of futility. Of course, she said, if you insist. I had my name added to the waiting list with our hotel as our point of contact. How many on the list? She riffled through the pages. One thousand? Two thousand?

Steerage available? Fully booked, senor. Other departures? Another shrug.

121

So I had turned away, and the next customer started the same line of inquiry. The queue behind him snaked through the huge terminal, entirely empty but for the line that wound through the massive hall and out onto the street, where I had started six hours earlier.

Before I left, though, I noted the door to the right of the ticket window with a frosted glass pane labeled Accounting. Next to it another door labeled Shipping. Further along a less shabby door labeled Administration. I watched that door for a while. It was only a minute or two when a janitor came along with a trolley of brushes and mops. As he propped open the door with his trolley, I could see a large anteroom with two or three secretaries at desks. Compared to the hubbub at the ticket window, the interior of the anteroom was a haven of serenity. I got close enough to see that behind each secretary was a door: Director of Personnel, Director of Finance, and one or two I couldn't read. At the far end, a low railing enclosed a carpeted area where a particularly attractive secretary sat behind a longer desk and guarded a door labeled Director General.

I smiled to myself, thought wistfully of my days at Philips. Office structures were much the same everywhere. Each layer of administration had a more luxurious office than the one below it, including a larger desk and a more attractive secretary. My friend Lou Blok had always been a bit of a maverick in this regard. He was Vice President for Research at Philips. A technical nerd, but a technical nerd with a joy for life and a wicked sense of humor. He had an office near the President's office as a matter of course, but he spent most of his time in the laboratory, where he installed a desk amidst the electronic equipment being tested and redesigned. He didn't have much patience for the trappings of power.

Walking back to the hotel, I wondered how Loeky and Lou were doing. Was Philips closing? Had it been taken over by the Germans? Were Loeky and Lou all right? And then I worried about our trip. Was there any way to get on the Cunard ship? It was so close, moored right there at the pier. And if we couldn't get on it, what next? Wait for the next boat, a boat that might never come? How else could we get out of Portugal? Travel to France, to Bordeaux or Le Havre? I wouldn't stand a chance. Once in the German zone of France, I would be captured by the Germans in a minute, a hare pursued by a pack of Dobermans. South through Spain and across Gibraltar into Africa?

We were running out of money too. We really didn't have anything left. Two hundred Swiss francs in bills and a pocketful of assorted coins in guilders, Marks, Swiss and French francs, Spanish pesetas, and Portuguese escudos. And we still had to pay our hotel bill here. On settling that, we'd be essentially broke. I thought of the cork salesman. He might be able to help.

The two boys swarmed me at the hotel. I put one on each knee as I sat on the edge of the bed and bounced them as I sang, "This is the way the lady rides … This is the way the gentleman rides … This is the way the farmer rides …" And I jostled them off the horse into a pile onto the floor, all of us laughing.

Margery and I talked, wondering with me what we should do.

"I'll give it one more try," I told her. "Iron my uniform. I'll see what I can do in the morning."

And so here I was, back on the Cunard pier. I was aiming for arriving at 10:30 a.m. Administrators needed an hour or so to deal with any pressing issues they found on their desks in the morning. They tended to be busy and often out of sorts during that time. Once they resolved the immediate problems that developed during the night, they could turn to less immediate concerns and might be in better humor. Lunch, on the other hand, was also a bad time. So I was aiming for 10:30 or 11:00 a.m.

In the big hall of the terminal, the line had not changed one whit. It snaked from the ticket window across the vast space and out the door. I strode across the hall. Some of those waiting in line complained at me, assuming I wished to jump the queue. I continued, unhurried, unfazed, purposefully. I passed the ticket window, and the complaints and catcalls from those in line faded. I continued along to the door marked Administration and entered. The hubbub from the hall vanished as I closed the door behind me. The half-dozen secretaries glanced up at my entrance expectantly, each wondering to which of them I would address myself. I strode along the line of desks and the doors they guarded. Director of Personnel, Director of Finance, Director for Shipping, Deputy Director-General. The farthest secretary was the pretty one I had spied yesterday, her desk inside the railed-in enclosure with the plush rug. I nodded pleasantly at each secretary as I passed their station, and at the few visitors awaiting their appointments with one of the directors.

As I passed the secretary to the Deputy Director-General, the secretary behind the railed enclosure lifted her head inquiringly. Since there were no more secretaries and doors, it was obvious I was headed to her. The railing that enclosed her desk and the plush rug, and which guarded the door to the Director General's office, was hardly knee high. I could see a small gate in the railing, closed. Its lock would be operated, I suspected, by a button at the secretary's desk. She could "buzz" a visitor in by pushing the button.

She looked young, alert, and intelligent. She was also blond, blue-eyed, and fair-skinned. Ah, I thought. The secretaries down the line were Portuguese. This one was British. Of course. The Cunard Line was a British company. The plaque on her desk read Assistant to the Director General. I had saved a broad smile for her.

As I approached the railing, she greeted me in Portuguese. She was inquiring, I supposed, if I had an appointment, knowing full well that I was not on her calendar.

I smiled conspiratorially and held my finger across my lips, as if to hush her. "Carl," I said. And then in English, nodding toward the door behind her and winking, I added, "We're old friends. I just escaped from Holland. He thinks I was killed there in the attack." I gestured at my uniform.

She was pleased and amused at my English. After my eight years of marriage to Margery, I spoke grammatically correct English, but with an obvious Dutch accent. Still, she was in no way prepared to buzz in a stranger without the approval of the Director General. The little gate stayed locked. We exchanged pleasantries as I flirted with her, and when she was about to rise from her chair to go in and speak to her boss, I stopped her, saying no as I stepped over the rail.

"Don't spoil the surprise!" I strode to the inner door and knocked on it. Without pause I opened it and stepped through. I could see Mary— we were already on a first-name basis—halfway from her desk to the door in a flurry of fear. I gently closed the door. I was in. She was too late.

I turned to see the Director General sitting behind an over-sized desk. He eyed me curiously, somewhat bemused. A true English gentleman, white hair thin and combed straight back over his teardrop-shaped head, his large forehead descending into a narrow, pointed chin that sported a trace of a white goatee. Iron-rimmed glasses, black suit, precise French cuffs decorated with gold cuff links.

I excused myself for intruding and for frightening his secretary by striding in unannounced. "I told her two lies," I said. "That you and I were old friends and that you thought I had been killed during the

German attack on Holland. In the first case, I hope that I can correct the lie and that we may become friends. And the second lie … I can only say that I am glad it is not true and that I survived battle."

He chuckled and stepped around the desk, shook my hand firmly, properly. Not too long, not too short. He asked my name.

"Lieutenant Colonel ter Weele of Her Dutch Majesty's Royal Mounted Artillery."

"Ah." He shook my hand again. "Then your first lie is no lie at all. It is a truth before the law." I raised my eyebrows in question. "We have been friends for the many years our two countries have been allies," he said with a smile. He seated me in the chair next to the desk and returned to his own seat behind it. "I served many years in His Majesty's Royal Navy. I continue in that capacity as an Admiral in the Reserves."

This was a good start. It hadn't occurred to me that he had served, but it made sense that a high-ranking Cunard administrator had first been a high-ranking officer in the British Navy. Lady Luck had smiled on me: I had been fortunate to dress in uniform.

We chatted as old friends. He wanted to know about the German attack, the German invasion strategy, its army's equipment, the professionalism of its soldiers and officer corps, whether I thought the turmoil would lead to an invasion of England, how I had escaped the Nazis' grasp after the capitulation.

He rang Mary for morning tea. She served us, obviously relieved not to have been reprimanded for failing to stop an unscheduled visitor. It appeared to her that it was as I had explained, that Sir Oliver and I were fast friends.

Finally Sir Oliver ended the discussion of the war by asking, "And, Lieutenant, to what purpose may I ascribe the honor of your visit?"

I explained that I was with Marge and the three children, and that we needed passage to New York. He listened politely, warily.

"I would love to be able to be of assistance, Lieutenant." He shook his head. "You are certainly aware that the ship"—he nodded through the window toward the quay—"is fully booked. It sails tomorrow. We have no idea when our next ship may arrive. Perhaps never. Departures, world-wide, scheduled to debark here in Lisbon have been suspended." He shrugged, wishing to mollify me. "You have seen the war firsthand. The North Atlantic is simply too dangerous for our ships."

His news did not surprise me. I sipped the tea. What next?

"Nothing scheduled for departure from Bordeaux?" I asked. He shook his head. "Porto?" Again the shake of his head. "Spain?"

"Were there any ships there or elsewhere, I would have suggested it, Lieutenant." He sipped from his cup. "It is as if we are out of business." He thought for a moment. "Indeed, perhaps we are."

It was clear that the ship moored so near was my only hope. So near...

"Sir Oliver." My tone was polite and a touch more formal. I leaned forward a bit. "You understand that I am under orders to join the Dutch free forces in Ottowa. It is imperative that I get there." He was watching me carefully. "Upon reaching New York, it is probable that I will be the first Dutch officer to arrive in the United States." I paused. "The newspapers will be excited to interview me. The escape from the Nazis with my wife and children will make great news." I pulled a picture of Margery and the children from my wallet. "Won't photos like this serve as fodder for war propaganda? Anti-Nazi propaganda?"

He listened, interested. I nodded at the window.

"She is to sail tomorrow?" I asked, more statement than question. He nodded.

"Look. I know that you hold back two or three first-class cabins at every sailing to accommodate VIPs, politicians, statesmen, military brass, cinema stars, and other important passengers who present themselves at the last moment." I could see from his expression that I was correct. "Well, if the ship is sailing tomorrow, this *is* the last moment." I emphasized the "is" in "this is the last moment." "Why not give me and my family one of those still empty cabins?" I paused to let him consider that. "What are the chances that someone else presents themselves in the next twelve hours? Spain has bottled up anyone trying to reach here. I know."

He was silent. I could see that he was thinking. It astonished me how complete the silence was in this office. I hadn't noticed it during the hour we had been talking. I didn't move a muscle, didn't breathe. I watched him thinking. If a brain made any noise when it functioned, I would have heard his right then. After what seemed an eternity, he leaned forward and pushed the call button on his desk. He smiled broadly at me as his secretary entered.

"Mary, could you please arrange to have two additional cots installed in one of the two remaining cabins, and reserve that cabin for Lieutenant ter Weele and his family? And could you provide the Lieutenant with the necessary tickets? They will be two adults, two children, and an infant." He looked at me. "If Lieutenant ter Weele is unable to pay immediately, please arrange to bill him, payable after arrival in New York."

He stood. "Lieutenant." He shook my hand and then stepped back and saluted. I returned the salute.

"Admiral. I will be forever grateful, sir."

"Drive that monster back to Berlin," he ordered. "The whole world will be ever grateful."

Hoofdstuk 19

11 september 1940: Waves of Nazi bombers pound London. Führer vows total destruction of the British capital, demands English replace Churchill with a government willing to accept Nazi rule in Europe. Mussolini bombs Tel Aviv and Palestine, killing 150 civilians. Nazi U-boats score two kills in North Atlantic.

Carl burst into the hotel room, smiling, holding aloft and waving … what?

"The tickets!" he almost yelled. "Pack up! Pack up!"

He started to dance and sing. The boys rushed to him to share his excitement. He grabbed them in his arms and threw them on the bed. They tussled and wrestled and rolled, squealing and laughing. The fun was infectious, and soon, with Margy in my arms, we were all squirming and laughing on the bed together.

When we had all caught our breath, I asked, "When?"

"Eight a.m."

"Tomorrow?" I asked with astonishment.

"Yes. We board at eight, sail at noon. In a first-class cabin!"

The rest of the afternoon was a flurry of glorious activity. Packing, of course. Wash would have to be done on board. I wrote and mailed letters to both our families: Alex in New York, Hendrik in Santa Fe, Father in Rome; Loeky and Lou, the Klaassens, Annie, Ge and Moeder in Holland. Cautious letters to those in Holland to avoid information or subjects that might rouse the curiosity or anger of the censors. And a telex to PC, also in New York, asking her to meet us on arrival.

There was shopping I would have liked to do, but after Carl paid for the hotel room, we counted what remained of our money. The remaining Swiss francs and the change in four or five currencies amounted to $88. So much for the shopping!

Both of us had been worried for days about getting passage. We had also been worried sick about our money running out. But we had made it to Lisbon. We had boat tickets in our hand. We would sail in the morning. Our money had not run out. It was over! The fear of the Germans, the daily worry over travel arrangements, the tension over our lack of money—it was over! Once on board we would have beds and food, and in New York Priscilla would be waiting for us on the dock.

"Carl," I murmured, hugging him. "We did it."

The thought of German submarines dismayed us not at all. Not that they did not exist, just that such danger was beyond our control and thus irrelevant. We had done what had to be done. We had done our part. I cried while he held me. Lady Luck would be in charge of the German submarines. We could dance on board and leave the worries to her. I sobbed on his shoulder, smiled as he kissed me. Margy was gaining weight, the boys were charged with excitement, and this great hulk of a man loved me. What more could I cry for?

Hoofdstuk 20

11 september 1940: RAF strikes Berlin, and bombs hit the Reichstag, the Brandenburg Gate, Unter den Linden, the Via Triumphalis Monument, Wilhelmstrasse. Hitler vows retaliation.

The quay was awash in people. Some were yelling, pushing, carrying loads. Others were laughing or crying as they hugged. Papa had Alex perched on his shoulders so he wouldn't get squashed, and I held tight to Papa's hand. Papa and Mama had outsmarted the Germans! We were going to America!

Stuck in a swirl of adults, I couldn't see much. I could see the funnel that dominated the ship's superstructure, and the "Exeter" on her stern. I searched for the cannons that would be necessary to battle the German Navy and couldn't see them. I asked Papa, and he said there weren't any. That worried me. When Alex and I played with our ships, we always had them properly armed. And that was just play. This was a real war. Who was in charge? What were they thinking?

I pulled hard on Papa's arm. He couldn't hear my question, so he picked me up. Why no cannons? I asked him. Wasn't that dangerous? He explained that the Germans would save their ammunition to shoot at ships of war and supply ships traveling to Europe. Ships leaving Europe and passenger liners were low priority targets. That made sense. Still, I thought, if I were an admiral, all my ships would be armed. It might be possible to sink a German ship if they came too close; and when Alex and I played, we knew how easy it was to wipe out masses of assets if they weren't armed and protected. Unarmed ships? Not if I were in charge.

And then we were on the gangplank. Papa put Alex and me down. Both of us had our backpacks on, mine a bit worn since I had used it in Holland to go to school. Alex's was smaller and newer. Papa carried suitcases, Mama carried Margy and some bags. I warned Alex to be careful. We didn't want to fall between the boat and the pier. Excited, he pointed at the different parts of the ship. Portholes! The hole on the bow

131

where the anchor chain disappeared! Lifeboats! The wheelhouse! The huge thick ropes attached to enormous iron cleats on the pier!

Papa had said that there would be cots for Alex and me in our cabin, but it was better than that. There were two double bunks.

"The top bed is mine!" Alex said.

"Bunk, not bed," I corrected him. I turned to Mama and Papa. "Can I have a top bunk too?"

They laughed. "Top bunks for you. Bottom bunks for the old people."

We climbed up, and Alex and I threw pillows across the sea between us, firing cannons as our ships battled.

And then we were back outside, clinging to the railing as the ship's horn bellowed. Alex put his hands on his ears. He looked scared, so I laughed to make him happy. The people on the quay were waving, pointing to people they knew on board. We waved at everyone even though we didn't know any of them. Papa had his arm around Mama. She kissed Margy, who was crying as the ship's horn bellowed again. It was better than a circus. Flags were flying everywhere, happiness flapping in the wind.

Looking down through the railing, Alex and I could see the strip of water between the boat and the pier widening. Widening. Widening.

"We're sailing!" we both yelled.

Papa picked us up three times. "Hoorah!" he shouted, and we screamed "Hoorah!" with him. The ship's horn bellowed again. I was happy because we were having fun being on a ship. I was especially happy because I could see how happy Papa and Mama were.

The sea made Alex and me sick, but after a day or two the sickness was over. Papa helped us scout the ship. The captain let us visit his wheelhouse with its big steering wheel. The speaker tubes were neat: mechanics way down in the engine room could talk to the captain through them. Alex and I decided that when we built a house, we would have speaker tubes between the kitchen and our bedroom. We'd be able to speak to Rita to tell her what we wanted for breakfast. Except that Rita was in Holland, Alex reminded me. And the Germans wouldn't let her out.

The engine room was awesome, the engine enormous. Alex didn't like the noise, though. Way louder than even a big diesel truck. It was too hot, so we didn't stay long.

Most of the time we spent on deck, near the bow to watch the ship cut through the waves, or astern to admire the boil of the wake. And always we watched for submarines and pretended to roll depth charges overboard to bomb them. I explained to Alex that we had to set each charge to detonate at a different depth. We planned how best to do that. We'd start with charges nearer the surface, because the sub would be near the surface when we first spied it. Then we would try deeper charges, because the sub would be diving to escape. To be sure the sub didn't fool us, we'd include a few deep charges at the start as well and mix in some shallow charges later just to be sure. When we got into our bunks at night, we gathered all the pillows in the cabin and rolled them one by one off the top bunks, count to three or five or whatever depth we had set, and make a big *boom* sound when the depth charge detonated.

Papa and Mama told us to be quieter; they didn't want us to annoy the people in the adjoining cabins. Papa explained that we would hardly hear the explosion of most of the charges anyway because they would be so deep. Most of the time, Alex would count and I would make the explosion. He could only count to six though, so for deeper charges, I would count and he would do the exploding.

Hoofdstuk 21

18 september 1940: St. Paul's Cathedral and St. Mary-le-Bow church saved from fires. Most Londoners now sleep in shelters. Gas and water service impaired. Hitler vows bombing of capital will continue until Britain yields. RAF hammers vital installations in Germany to weaken foe.

I was in heaven. No cooking, no cleaning, no shopping. The steward saw to our laundry, to making the beds, to tidying up the bathroom. Well, to tidying up the head. We signed up for the late breakfast sitting to let the children sleep, and to the early dinner sitting so that we could get them to bed on time. Carl and the children were a little seasick at the start, but it seemed behind them now. I had my sea legs from the start. Father had taught me to sail on Buzzards Bay, and we regularly took the boat across to No Man's from Woods Hole.

Carl played bridge for long hours with three other avid players. They played the Culbertson system, not the newer Goren nor Father's Crane system. One of the men was an American, a Roman Catholic priest who was returning from a seven-year missionary post in Uganda. According to Carl, he was totally incompetent at bridge. Apparently he had taught himself and then a coterie of Ugandans at the missionary station, and had spent seven years playing bridge and persuading himself that he was an expert. Convinced of his prowess, the priest insisted on playing for money. Every three rubbers, the players switched partners. Carl learned quickly to avoid bidding when the priest was his partner, because the priest overbid every hand, played them as the tyro that he was, and regularly went down catastrophically. Carl's strategy when he played with the priest as his partner was to try to lose the rubbers as quickly as possible in order to minimize the loss. Conversely, when playing against the priest, he would taunt him into overbidding, punish him with a double, and string out the rubbers to maximize the priest's loss—and, of course, Carl's gain. Carl was intent on doubling the $88 we boarded with, and apparently was well on the way to his goal.

One afternoon the boys and Margy were in the nursery, and I was dreaming in a deck chair while Carl was at the bridge table. On the leeward side of the deck, there was no breeze and the sun was delightful on my face. Nothing to see but the dancing of the waves and the sparkle of the foam. The slap of water and the thrum of the engines provided background music. I melted into a dream of the sun on me as I lay on the beach at No Man's, the view of the ocean broken only by the smudge of Gay Head's cliffs on the horizon. Alex would row me out to the lobster pots a bit later to collect the half dozen lobsters we would need for dinner. The small ones were the best, tender and tasty. Or would we collect mussels off the rocks? No, the tide was waxing. Lobsters it would be tonight.

I woke from my reverie. Another day and we would see PC. It would be wonderful to be with her again. The last time I'd seen her was when we were living in Brussels. When? Jan was about two, so 1937? Just before we moved to Eindhoven. Our brother Alex had been with her. We spent two days on the beach at Knokke, Jan playing in the sand, Barbara biting at the foam and barking with excitement at the waves. Alex painted a watercolor of us to pass the time.

Loeky was taking care of Barbara now, and loving her, but Barbara would miss playing with the boys. How she adored them! But how jealous she had been of Jan when he was first born. I had been silly, I guess. I didn't want Barbara to infect him, so when I returned home from the hospital after the birth, I kept Barbara in the living room and Jan in the nursery. The first few times I went to change or nurse Jan, Barbara pooped in the middle of the living room floor. Since she had long been housebroken, it was a conspicuous act of spite. Carl and I concluded that Barbara had to be included in the joy of Jan's birth, so I placed Jan on a blanket on the floor and introduced Barbara to him. She sniffed him head to toe, her excitement showing in the rapid beat of her bobbed tail. Thereafter when I nursed Jan, Barbara would lie quietly at my feet; and when the three of us were walking, Barbara would growl protectively at strangers approaching the baby carriage.

That was in another world, another life. A bit more than a month ago, we had left Barbara, Eindhoven, and Holland behind. Not that long ago, and yet an eternity. I had lived one life for my first twenty years, a second with Carl these past ten years, and now, thanks to the Führer, we would embark on a third life. Would we have nine of them? How would this one go? At least its start would be propitious, marked as it would be by PC and Alex waiting for us dockside.

PC was working in New York now as an editor with Simon & Schuster. Alex had been in New York tending an antique store when he and Hendrik were buying furniture in Europe and selling it in New York. But now Alex was married to Mary, working as an artist in Connecticut, and Hendrik had purchased property with John Levert in Santa Fe. Hendrik and John were running the property as a guest ranch.

Aware of the passage of time, I bestirred myself. Time to pick up Margy and the boys at the nursery and get them ready for dinner. Carl's bridge game would be breaking up. He would be in good humor if he had been paired with the priest and lost by only a little, in better humor if he had played against him and won. Those were apparently the only options possible. I was still musing about No Man's Land as I started for the nursery. Would we have a chance to visit the island? No. I remembered that the US Navy had seized it, claiming it was essential to national defense. Apparently German subs had stopped there, used it as a lookout. Heavens, our world had certainly taken a turn.

Hoofdstuk 22

20 september 1940: New York Mayor La Guardia predicts victory for Roosevelt/Wallace ticket, sees third term as essential to continuity during period of war. Willkie in campaign speech opposes bill to delay draft until after November election, emphasizes need for United States to prepare itself for any contingency.

Alex was pointing at the boat approaching us and jumping up and down. "Boat, boat!" he yelled.

"Look," I said. "The tallest one." I pointed at the Empire State Building.

"Skyscrapers. I see skyscrapers!" Again he yelled and jumped up and down.

A small boat came alongside ours. I explained to Alex that this was the pilot boat, and that the man clambering on board the *Exeter* was the harbor master. I pointed out the two tugboats nearing us as well. One placed itself near our bow, the other alongside our stern. I'd read about tugboats and explained to Alex that they were nothing more than floating engines, very small, but very strong.

Alex flexed his arm. "Like me. Small, but real strong." He pushed me, and I almost fell over. I was laughing.

"Boys!" Mama reprimanded us. She was holding Margy; Papa had his arm around her. More and more of the passengers were coming on deck, and we all watched the Manhattan skyline get nearer. I showed Alex the next tallest building and told him it was the Chrysler Building.

Papa nudged Mama. "There it is."

"What?" Alex and I asked.

Papa picked us up. "There." He nodded. "Over there."

I looked. "The Statue of Liberty! Alex, look!"

Mama had read to us how it had been given to the United States by the French as the symbol of American freedom. Alex and I were excited, and so were Mama and Papa. Even Margy cooed. Papa was still holding us; he leaned over to kiss Mama and Margy. He was crying! I had never, ever seen Papa cry.

"Your country," he said to Mama. "I already love it."

We were passing the Statue of Liberty, and Papa was still crying. Alex and I hugged his knees to try to make him happy. Mama was happy, we were happy. I couldn't understand why Papa wasn't happy.

And then it was the Fourth of July! Not really, of course. But two fireboats had neared and were shooting great columns of water into the sky. "Like fire engines," I explained to Alex. "If boats are on fire, the fireboats come and save them." As we watched, I said it was like fireworks.

He laughed. "Waterworks, waterworks!" And then, "Like feathers. Featherworks. Look at the featherworks!"

Behind the shooting streams of water, behind the sparkle of Alex's featherworks, shone the tallest buildings I had ever seen. New York was neat. Mama was right. She'd told me I'd like the United States.

Hoofdstuk 23

22 oktober 1940: Greeks fall back as Italians advance along Epirus coastal plain and capture key bridge in Pindus. De Gaulle and the Free French Forces prepare to attack Vichy forces in Gabon, while Fasciti resist British in attack on Gallabat in Sudan.

Today was my birthday, my twenty-eighth. The last weeks had been a flurry of activity. Alex and PC had met us at the dock in New York and whisked us off to their two houses here on Jinny Hill Road in Cheshire. The Connecticut countryside was peaceful, a treat for both Carl and me. We'd arrived on September 20, a date we'd remember forever. The autumn colors had begun. I'd forgotten how magnificent the New England autumn was! Holland was painted in greens. Dark greens, lighter greens, gray-greens, gay and somber greens, but always greens. New England in the autumn was painted with a palette of glorious yellows and golds, oranges and fire reds, magentas and auburns. The beauty turned me to tears. Autumn had always been my favorite season. It made me homesick to be here. How could I be homesick when I was home? I had missed fifteen years of autumns. In the gray sky, dank mist, and cold rain of Groningen, Brussels, and Eindhoven in October and November, I had never once remembered the glory, the beauty of a New England Indian summer day. I had simply forgotten that such days existed. Now that they were thrust upon me, they engulfed me, overwhelmed me. The beauty brought me to tears.

Carl, too, was in his element. He'd never experienced such a season. Not in Holland, not in the Dutch East Indies, not in the south of France. The colors, the leaves, the nip in the air, sunshine like liquid gold, the ethereal blue of the sky—a combination unique to New England, I thought. And every day, he was in the field with Alex's double-barreled 12 gauge. He had hunted as a youngster in Enschede with his father, and on Sumatra on his tea plantation. Hunting here was a release, an essential release. A chance to recover from the danger and stress of the Grebbeberg and our escape.

The newspapers and magazines had sought him out. The Defense Department had organized a speaking tour for him. Rotary Clubs, Lions Clubs, the Elks, the Veterans of Foreign Wars. Articles in *Time* magazine, a chapter in *We Escaped*, a book rushed into print to entice the United States into a greater war effort in support of Great Britain and the Free French. PTOs and PTAs, garden clubs, bridge clubs, the Connecticut Artists League—they all loved him. The first Dutch officer to escape the German war machine! A survivor of the Nazi Blitzkrieg through the Netherlands! A hero of the Dutch defense of the Grebbeberg! Reporters loved the story. I was pleased that quite a bit of it was true.

It was easy for me to be proud of him. With his big frame, blond hair, and blue eyes, he looked every bit the archetype of a brave Dutch soldier. And his Dutch-accented English captivated his audiences, audiences eager to embrace him and the story of Dutch bravery in the face of Nazi brutality. The applause as he came on stage, before he had spoken a word, evidenced America's horror of Hitler's unprovoked onslaught on the civilized world. It heartened me as a US citizen to witness my country's revulsion to an act of aggression that others might consider as none of their business, as irrelevant to their own lives.

The idyll here in the Connecticut countryside, though, was drawing to an end. Carl was to report to Stratford, Ontario. We would be housed, we were told, at 13 Front Street. I could only wonder what awaited us. We would be in the hands of the military; our lives would be organized for us. Carl would be drawing a paycheck again, although we had few complaints on that account. We had been doing quite well on the honorariums he had been receiving for his speaking engagements. And of course PC was providing our housing. Ontario? Winter would be upon us, and we could expect that to be brutal. On the bright side, we would be about as far as one could get from Hitler's cannons.

Alex organized a quick trip to No Man's at my request. PC would stay in Cheshire to watch over little Alex and Margy. Carl, Jan, my brother Alex, Alex's painter friend Rose Churchill, and I would go over to the island from Woods Hole.

The sea breeze smelled of salt, ocean air, and the marshes at low tide. The captain was a lobsterman; he would drop us at the jetty and return three days later to pick us up. Alex had provisions on board for us for the three days. Because we had arranged to go on short notice, our caretakers, the Woods, did not know we were coming. I had asked Alex about the navy's takeover. The lease of the island to the navy, for one dollar a year, had apparently not yet been signed.

As we pulled out of the harbor, the captain was preoccupied with the rip currents, provoked first by the narrow gap between the mainland and Naushon, and then by the gaps between the string of the other Elizabeth Islands. After Naushon came Pasque, then Nashawena. After we cleared Cuttyhunk and began the long reach to round Gay Head, the wind picked up and waves smoothed from the random chop of offshore water to the more regular rising and dropping of the greater swells of the ocean. Alex and I reveled in the freedom of the wind and the waves, the familiarity of a trip often made together as children, and the limitless space to the horizon. Carl and Rose were also enjoying themselves. Carl's face flickered with an undercurrent of trepidation—fear?—of one who has sailed infrequently on a small craft on open waters. Jan was both mesmerized and uneasy, but seemed to be enjoying the trip. I held his hand to keep him far from the railing. Once out of the rip currents that were nearer the shore, the captain kept up a stream of conversation with Alex. One would believe he had known Alex his whole life long.

The captain steered well clear of Gay Head. He wanted no part of the coastal current. Slowly the cliffs of Gay Head rose to our leeward and then receded, as we approached and then passed the Vineyard.

The breeze stiffened, and the swells increased in size. The aroma of the salt marshes had been left behind, replaced by the taste of salt on my lips from the wind-whipped spray each time the fishing smack dipped into the trough of a wave. I smiled encouragement to Carl. From his wry smile in response, I suspected he would have preferred to be at Grebbeberg waiting for the Nazi invasion. I guessed he was focused on keeping his stomach pacified. A sailor he wasn't.

I stood up and braced myself in the wheelhouse to better watch as the familiar sights of No Man's crept into view. First Spy Glass, the summit of the island; then to our right, the outline of Haulbowline Head, rising gently in swells to the height of Spy Glass. How high was that? Eighty-five feet, PC had told me. PC was working on a map, a sketch, of No Man's. She would share it with me, she had said, when it was finished. Behind Spy Glass the island rolled gently to the South Cliffs, which in turn dropped abruptly into the pounding surf. The cliffs were open to

143

the ocean and took the brunt of nature's constant assault on the island. On this side that we were approaching, the north side, the attack by water and wind was far less savage.

Soon I could make out the houses clustered near the jetty. To our left, the Squibnocket House; to the right, the Gatehouse. In front of that, the Butter House. All small. We often referred to them collectively as the fisherman's shacks. The Woods used the Squibnocket House as their quarters. Behind and above the other houses, I could now make out the main house. Father had named it the Stockade. The other houses had existed when Father bought the island. He had repaired and improved them. Initially the family had lived in them, and then he built the Stockade. He often grumbled at its expense: all the stone, cement, and other materials had to be ferried over from Woods Hole. It was difficult to see the Stockade from this distance, some four hundred yards back from the harbor. Well away from the danger of water and wave, it was built low on the lee of the hillside so it would be sheltered from the worst of the rages of nature's winds. From afar it appeared no more than a low rock outcropping, an integral part of the island.

As we neared I could see the stone jetty, curling like the loving left arm of a mother reaching out to envelop her child. The jetty, too, Father had built; great blocks of stone also brought in from the mainland.

To the left of the harbor, I could now make out the low peninsula of East Point. Its terminus was a spit of loose rocks, most the size of a lobster pot, many the size of a large lobster, others smaller than that. At high tide, this terminus was buried in the waves. At low tide, it was four hundred yards of wet, slippery black stones as smooth as glass. East Point was a living sea creature. It grumbled and growled as the currents rolled its rocks one way with the tide coming in, then rolled them the other way with the tide going out. Not only did it talk, it also moved. The tip would swing toward the harbor if the wind prevailed for some days from the east, and then swing back toward the east with a few days of blow from the west. But always it pointed to the distant cliffs of Gay Head.

As we approached the shore, the captain turned hard to starboard to enter the harbor. In foul weather, this entry was next to impossible. Despite today's relative calm, he had ceased his chatting with Alex to concentrate on slipping into the small space. The jetty protected the boat from wind and wave, but it could stave the bow in an instant with a false move at the helm.

As the captain pulled tight to moorings at the pier, I waved to Mr. Woods as he came from the boathouse barn, pulling a rope hooked to a pulley astride a long line that ran from the barn's peak to a pole on the beach. The line held a number of pulleys which could be used to transport a skiff from the barn to the beach, or to haul cargo from the beach to the barn. I could see Carl explaining its use to Jan, even as the captain was placing our supplies into the large crate hanging below the pulley.

The next two days were a delightful trip back to my youth, with my husband and oldest son sharing my memories. Carl borrowed one of Father's shotguns, and he and Jan shot hares that Mrs. Woods prepared for our dinner. Father had stocked the island with Belgian hares; they had multiplied and become a pest. We walked the island, and I showed Carl the duck blind in the middle of Ben's Pond, the three blinds scattered along the shoreline of Rainbow, and the blind on Sisson's at the far end of the island. End to end, No Man's Island measured three miles in length, two miles in breadth. As a young girl, I had thought it a world unto itself. Hiking with Carl from the jetty out to the Viking Rock off Haulbowline Head, from there to the Air Field behind Spy Glass, and back to the harbor to visit just the western side of the island took us the better part of the morning. About four miles of walking, Carl estimated. Visits to the eastern edge of the island took more time. One had to work around Beach Pond, Long John Silver, Loch Katrina, Rainbow, Sisson's, and Alice Pond. Jan was particularly excited that PC was naming the smallest pond—hardly more than a puddle—Jan's Pond on her map. When he saw it, nestled at the edge of Rainbow, he insisted on taking off his shoes and wading in it. For just a moment.

"Cold!" he yelled, and immediately jumped back out. "My pond is like ice."

Ben's Pond was the largest, about three-quarters of a mile long. Long John Silver and Rainbow were almost as large, but more irregularly shaped. Father had stocked them all with trout. The brookies in Beach Pond had not fared well. Soon after the stocking, there had been a nor'easter, and the surf had rolled right over the shingle into the pond. The saltwater had apparently killed them all. The rainbow trout in Rainbow— Had Father named the lake after he stocked it with rainbows or simply matched the trout to its name? Jan asked me. I told him I didn't know. He'd have to ask his grandfather. Anyway, these trout had done the best. The brook trout in Ben's Pond had also fared well. The other bodies of water had apparently been less friendly.

After two days on the island, Carl and I were exhausted, a delightful physical exhaustion. While we had walked everywhere, Mr. Woods traveled the island on an old gentle mare. One of his tasks was to tend the sheep, not that they needed much care, but he rode regularly out to West Shelter, to the two sheep sheds near Haulbowline Head, to the shed near the beach north of Rainbow, and to the East Barn and the West Barn. He also patrolled those parts of the shoreline where the sheep gathered to eat the kelp, which gave them such high quality wool. Father thought it was the iodine in the kelp. More regularly, Mr. Woods, at his wife's bidding, rode out to the spring house. It was on the other side of Ben's Pond where ice cold water bubbled up and kept our perishables fresh.

Our last day Carl, Jan, and I spent time on the beach. It lay just west of the jetty, the only sandy shoreline on the whole island. The water was far too cold at this time of the year to even dream of swimming, but the fifty yards or so of sand was an irresistible playground. I had spent whole days there as a girl. To watch my son build forts where I had built castles lapped me in a wash of warm nostalgia. From here, in today's clear weather, Gay Head was distinct despite the distance, and I imagined that I could see a smudge on the horizon far to the left that was Cuttyhunk.

While the days on No Man's were a respite from the travails of our trip and from the coming move to Stratford, our return to Cheshire brought me brusquely back to reality. A message awaited us at Woods Hole. The Harbor Master had received a call from PC. Little Alex had been injured. We were not to be frightened by his appearance when we reached Cheshire. The injury was less serious than it appeared. Alex was fine. That was all the Harbor Master could tell us.

While we understood that the message was meant to relieve us of anxiety, its effect was just the opposite. It filled me with trepidation. What was the injury? How had it happened? How serious was it? The Harbor Master didn't have any details. He could only repeat the same message. The five-hour drive to Jinny Hill Road was so anxiety filled, it might as well have been five days. At last we pulled into the drive. PC came out with Margy in her arms. Alex was holding her hand. His head was swaddled in gauze. He looked like a mummy!

He ran to me and clambered into my lap before I could get out of the car. His bandages looked terrifying; they enveloped all of his head except for the eyes. It was frightening, but he was laughing. Carl and I had to laugh with him.

PC quickly told us what had happened. She had brought a load of firewood to the house in her Plymouth and was unloading it. Wanting to help, Alex had lifted himself up onto the rear bumper and begun to crawl toward the wood, when the solid-steel trunk lid fell. It pinned his head between the lock on one side and the clasp on the other. His face was lacerated, and the crown of his head had split open. There had been a lot of blood, which had terrified PC. But the doctors had cleaned up the wounds at the hospital, stitched up his crown, and pronounced him fine. She had been relieved then, and was even more relieved now to see Carl and me laughing with Alex. It clearly did look worse than it was.

Yes, the trip to No Man's had been a pleasant escape for a few days for both Carl and me. What we hadn't known, however, was that Alex would bear scars on the crown of his head for the rest of his days. Nor had we known that the family's patriotic lease of No Man's to the navy for one dollar a year for "the duration of the war" would lead to the government's expropriation of the island after the war. We would never again sojourn like this; No Man's would never again be ours. Never again would we live or vacation on our island. The navy would destroy the houses, destroy the roads, destroy the barns and sheep sheds and pastures, destroy the jetty, the harbor, and the pier. It would take the island from us against our will in return for our patriotic gesture of the one-dollar-a-year lease. The taking would destroy our family heritage, our memories, a portion of our lives. The family would fight tooth and nail, but the juggernaut of government would quash us as easily as the Nazi war machine had quashed Holland. And the government would have a measure of remorse equal to that of the Nazis. No, the government would have less remorse. We had met a few Germans who did not approve of Hitler.

Hoofdstuk 24

16 december 1940: Hitler reviles democracies as warmongering nations after RAF strikes Krupp Works again. Führer predicts 1941 will see greatest victory in Germany's history with the complete defeat of Allies, end of war.

My bandages were off. In the mirror I could see that the scratches on my forehead, nose, and cheeks were healing. Mama had told me not to pull off the scabs; she didn't want me to have scars on my face. Jan told me that I looked like a soldier who had fought the Indians. I said I had been the only survivor of Custer's Last Stand. The gashes on the crown of my head, he said, were where the Indians had tried to scalp me. Touching gently with my fingers, I could feel the stitches. They would be there a bit longer, Mama said. I was proud: those stitches would leave scars. Using our hands as pistols—forefinger pointed out like the barrel, thumb in the air like the hammer, thumb snapping forward with each shot—Jan and I spent hours creeping around the house, battling with Indians who returned fire from behind the furniture. Jan and I were always badly outnumbered, like Custer's army, but we were better shots than his soldiers. We never lost a battle.

Sinterklaas day had been a wonder. We had put out our shoes, and Mama had put out one of Margy's little baby shoes. Too bad for her. It was so small, there was hardly any room for gifts! We had sung "Sinterklaas Kapoentje" and "Daar Ginds Komt de Stoomboot." Papa had assured me that Sinterklaas would come. I worried that he didn't know we were in America. I worried that he only left presents for Dutch children who lived in Holland. Papa suggested that we leave him a particularly special snack and an apple for his horse. Coming all the way from Holland, he would be especially hungry. Jan and Mama received ice skates. Mama said there would be lots of skating in Stratford. I had scads of chocolate and a winter snowsuit and mittens. Margy had received a pink snowsuit that made her look round as a ball, as fat and squat as a baby snowman. Tante Ge had knitted it. Margy laughed when Mama put it on her and tried to push off her hood.

Now we were at Aunt Rose Churchill's in Farmington. She had a really big house with a big staircase and a big living room. And the Christmas tree! I had never seen one so tall. Almost to the ceiling. The star at the top looked like a huge diamond. Ornaments everywhere and angel's hair on the branches. Some of the ornaments were beautiful birds, and they looked almost alive. Garlands decorated the staircase and the mantel. The house inside and out looked better than a Christmas card.

I didn't know all the people. The Churchills and Slaters weren't really related to us, Mama said, but they were such good friends that we should call them "aunt" and "cousin." It didn't make sense to me. Cousin Johny Slater was a big as my brother Jan. His baby sister Shirley was smaller than Margy. We were supposed to call their mother Cousin Theo. Tante PC and Oom Alex who were our real family had come for Christmas dinner. There was a lot of noise! Mama had told me that when we reached Stratford, I might go to preschool. I hoped it would be as noisy and fun as this!

Needing to pee, I went upstairs to the bathroom off the hall. At home I didn't lock the door when I went to the toilet, but with all these people around, it would be better if I did. The handle on the lock looked like a golden butterfly. It was hard to turn, but I turned until it clicked into its locked position. The bathroom was just a toilet and a sink, not a real bathroom. I did my peepee and washed my hands. Mama would like that! The soap was the color of honey; I could almost see through it. I washed my hands twice. I liked the smell of the soap, like pine trees. The hand towel was soft and fluffy.

I hung up the towel and tried to turn the golden butterfly latch. It was stuck. I turned harder. It hurt my fingers to press that hard, but the latch wouldn't budge. I tried again. And again. Darn. It wouldn't move. I knocked, and then I knocked louder. No one heard me. I listened a while. I thought I heard someone come up the stairs. I knocked again.

"Someone in there?" said Tante PC.

"Yes," I replied.

"Is that you, Alex?"

I said yes again and that I couldn't turn the lock. She tried to open the door, couldn't, and told me to wait a moment.

I could hear her call, "Marge!" and then Mama's voice, first from far away, then at the door. She also tried to open it. Locked. "Alex?" she said. "Can you turn the lock?"

I told her that I couldn't, it was stuck. She explained that it was the kind of lock that turned. I knew that. She told me to try again. I tried again. Still stuck.

"Are you turning the right way?" she asked.

"Of course," I said. How stupid did she think I was, but I tried the other direction just to please her. Wouldn't budge that way either. Then I could hear Jan. He also told me that it was a turn lock. They didn't understand! I knew how to do it, but it was stuck.

Mama and PC talked. I heard PC say she'd call the fire trucks. PC was getting worried, and I didn't understand why. After a few minutes Mama told me that the fire trucks were coming. Now this was becoming exciting! I watched out the window. First I heard the sirens, then a fire car with a flashing light pulled up and two firemen got out. I couldn't see them at the front door, since it was right underneath me. PC let them in, and I could hear them stomping up the stairs. They talked with Mama and then tried the door. Locked.

"Alex?" one of the firemen said. "Try to turn the lock."

This was stupid. Everybody told me the same thing. I tried again. "I can't," I said. "It's stuck!"

After some more talking, the firemen said they'd call for a ladder. I heard Aunt Rose say that there was one in the backyard. I looked out the window again and watched as the two firemen put the ladder against the house. One came up, and we laughed through the window at each other.

"Are you scared?" he asked.

"No! This is like being rescued!" I yelled.

He asked whether I could open the window lock so that he could get in. It was a turn latch between the bottom half and top half of the window. "Sure," I replied. I put down the toilet seat, clambered up on it, and turned the lock. It was a little stuck, but it turned. The fireman slid the window up. He tousled my hair, telling me I was a smart boy. Then he put his head into the bathroom, leaned his chest on the windowsill, slid in a little, and stretched way out. He could just reach the lock. He tried to turn it.

"Stuck," he said.

"That's what I was telling everyone," I told him. "They thought I didn't know how to do it, but I did. It's stuck!"

He laughed. "You're right," he said. He pulled a bit more into the bathroom to get a better grip on the lock, and this time it turned. Mama and PC rushed in. Mama had tears in her eyes. The fireman and I were laughing. Mama hugged me while the fireman backed his torso out the window and climbed back down the ladder.

A few minutes later the two firemen, Mama, PC, Jan, Johny, and I were in the kitchen. Mama gave us hot chocolate and the firemen hot coffee. I sat on the fireman's knee. Later I gave Mama a big hug.

"You shouldn't have worried, Mama. There wasn't any danger. There weren't any Nazis to kill me." She hugged me back, saying she was glad I was all right. I kissed her to make her feel better. She had been worried about nothing. I could take care of myself!

Hoofdstuk 25

15 maart 1941: Nazi troops crowd Yugoslav and Greek borders, mass in Albania, Hungary, and Romania in preparation for thrusts toward Belgrade and Athens. British forces engage German and Italian armored units near Benghazi.

Snow lay deep on the sidewalks and lawns. Tree branches in the park drooped under its weight. Cars parked along the streets lay buried, abandoned apparently, awaiting the spring thaw, when roads would once again become passable. It had been years since I had seen a snow like this. When the Elfstedentocht—a 120-mile ice skating race and tour through Holland's eleven northern cities—took place a winter or two ago, and the country closed its schools and government for the day, there had been hardly an inch of snow to accompany the hard freeze. Snow and cold were uncommon in Holland. Indeed, the Elfsteden race takes place only once every three or four years, because in the intervening years there isn't enough ice. I had been fourteen years old when I had last seen a winter like this. That was on the farm in Westwood. Father's brown and white cows stood camouflaged in the fields, up to their bellies in the drifts. Father made snow ice cream. He would scoop up a big bowl of soft white snow and we would stir in maple syrup, heavy cream from the cows, and vanilla flavoring. Delicious.

Christmas and New Year's at Rose Churchill's had been great fun, but hectic. My brother Alex had visited with Mary and their daughter Lexa. PC had been there much of the time, along with Rose and Theo of course. Cousin Cal and Tubby Sizer had come up from Bethany for New Year's Eve. Tubby didn't much like the children; he had no patience for them. So it was fun, but losing little Alex in the bathroom had panicked me. And then he had been so sweet afterward. "You shouldn't have been afraid, Mama," he had whispered. "There weren't any Nazis to kill me." He had been right, of course.

We arrived in Stratford in January, at the Royal Netherlands Legion training camp. The Dutch military had received us with excitement. Not many of the Stratford troops had fought in Holland. With Dutch

153

precision, everything was ready. Carl had his commission, his office, and his adjutant. Our quarters were waiting: 13 Front Street, Stratford, Ontario. Right behind the house was a big park, wonderful for the children to play in. At least, it would be once spring arrived! Right now our yard and the park were buried deep in snow.

The house was two stories, with steps up to the front porch, the front door opening into a foyer with a staircase up to the second floor balcony. An old Canadian-style row house, clad in shingles blackened with age, similar to the houses on either side. Indeed, similar to every house up and down Front Street. Dreary, sad, gloomy. Large rooms inside and spacious, but dark and drafty with inadequate heat. Despite layers of clothing, I shivered continually. On the plus side, it was large enough for the five of us. The maid quarters—without a maid—were at the rear of the house, leading to a back door into the yard and down a slope to a small stream. The adjacent park was on the far bank. An unhappy house, but a yard perfect for a family with children. We had shipped our luggage on leaving Cheshire, and it had stood waiting for us on the second-floor balcony upon our arrival.

I had registered Jan in the small school organized by the Dutch community. Alex and Margy were still at home with me. Jan passed his school hours speaking Dutch, but at the house I read to all three children in both Dutch and English. When we had lived in Brussels, before we moved to Eindhoven, Jan was just learning to sound out words. His first sentence had been, "I heb soif." I have thirst. Our maid spoke French with me, and that first sentence had been trilingual—English, Dutch, French. It had worried me at the time that he would speak a confused potpourri of phrases. But that did not happen, and I had blissfully continued reading and speaking to him in our two languages.

I soon found the Dutch community here less to my liking. In Groningen and Eindhoven, we had had many friends, couples whom Carl and I both enjoyed, with whom we played field hockey and tennis and bridge, and with whom we visited and partied. Here there were many single men, some single women, and many couples who drank too much and partied too hard. Early on, we stayed late at a party. As the evening drew to a close, a bowl was passed around. Car keys and house keys were dropped into it. Carl and I hesitated: What was the purpose of this? C'mon, c'mon! we were urged. Throw in your keys! Carl laughed, and we both shook our heads as the others booed the party poopers.

When the bowl was full, it was passed around again for the men to draw, sight unseen, a key from the collection. Laughter exploded as the woman to whom the key belonged would signal, and the man would kiss her or hug her or fondle and tease her, whatever she allowed. Soon the bowl was empty, and the couples so joined left arm in arm, laughing and flirting. Carl and I left together. We went to only a few parties thereafter, and when we went we quitted the scene well before the bowl was passed.

Winter was cold and dark and snowy. I pulled Margy in a little sled, and Jan and Alex slid down the lawn toward the stream. I had hoped to skate, but snow lay deep on the ice on the ponds, and there was no public rink or other cleared ice available. It was dark when I awoke, and darkness came early in the afternoon. I soon wearied of the cold, the snow, and the darkness. Stratford was, I decided, a sad town. So I was looking forward to Carl's new commission. We didn't know when or where we would be sent, but both of us were longing for a change. Stratford and the army here were an interlude. There was no purpose, no action. Stratford was an army storage depot, a huge warehouse where goods and men arrived and were placed in storage until they could be shipped out to where they could be put to some useful purpose.

The bright spot was the coming of the queen. The queen was coming, the queen was coming! The community was in an uproar. The military was sprucing up the army base. Buildings were being painted, fences repaired, a house where she would be staying was being outfitted. The ladies were organizing teas, a dinner, and a ball. When we learned that it was not Queen Wilhelmina but Princess Juliana, the future queen, who was coming, that did not dampen spirits one bit.

The visit was the bright spot of that dreary winter. Carl, as one of the officers, was involved from start to finish, as was I, as an officer's wife. Alex was selected to precede Juliana as she made her official entrance into the hall, where she would address the Dutch community. He was to sprinkle rose petals along her path. He was deemed old enough to be able to perform this task, young enough to be cute, and charming enough, with an impish smile under a head of blond hair, to amuse the crowd. Juliana rewarded him with a tiny ring, which he lost that same day and cried over for hours. He had been excited at the start, devastated at the end. As Carl and I went through the reception line for the formal introductions, Juliana gracefully commented on Alex's charm. He was the same age as her Irene. Should we betroth them? we joked.

Hoofdstuk 26

6 april 1941: Stukas bomb Belgrade as Nazis invade Greece and Yugoslavia. Goebbels issues order to cleanse Europe of all Britons. Moscow and Belgrade sign a treaty of friendship and nonaggression.

Mama was smiling more, hugging us more. Every day after school, she would put Margy in the stroller and take Alex and me for a walk in the park. The snow was melting, and there were puddles of water everywhere that we could jump into. If I did it just right, I could jump, land on my two feet like a toy soldier at attention, and splash water all around me without getting wet. The little stream at the back of our garden that ran around the park was roaring with water. Alex and I threw sticks into it, and we could watch them swirl and speed downstream, faster than Alex could run, even faster than I could run.

Today it was sunny, and Mama let me take off my snow jacket. She hung it on the handle of the stroller. Spring was coming, she told us. Under the melting snow drifts, she explained, the crocuses were poking their little green heads out of the ground. When the snow melted and they could feel the sunlight, they would bloom and spring would be here. Alex and I were excited; we could already envisage the green shoots. "Like hundreds of green soldiers marching to attack the Nazis," Alex said, laughing. Mama laughed too, but said that we shouldn't always think about fighting and war. The crocuses would be beautiful, she said, and would smell sweet. Yes, I said, not like soldiers. They are usually dirty and smell awful, especially if they have been wounded and are all bloody.

Mama laughed. "Enough, enough! No more soldiers. No more war."

Alex had run ahead of us, and he called, "Look, Mama!" He ran back toward us. "A baby squirrel. He needs help."

Sure enough, on the ground near a big tree was a tiny squirrel. At first it looked like a mouse, it was that small. It was lost and didn't know what to do.

157

"Can we take it home? Can we keep it?" Alex and I both begged. It was so cute, so furry, so small.

"We'd need to feed it from the eye dropper," Mama said. "It's too small to eat nuts."

"Yes, yes!" Alex and I said. "We can help feed it."

So Mama leaned over and gently picked up the tiny animal. "Yow!" she yelled. "Ow!" She dropped the squirrel quicker than a cowboy could draw his revolver. Her hand was red with blood, which ran down her wrist and stained the cuff of her winter jacket.

"He bit you!" Alex said. "Traitor. He's a traitor."

That was the end of adopting the squirrel. It was also the end of our stroll. Mama took us home to bandage her hand. Alex and I followed her as she pushed Margy's stroller. We could see drops of blood on the path, and we began tracking them as if we were living in the Little House in the Big Woods and had wounded a deer that we were following to finish off.

On another day in the park, Alex found a toy gun. The stock was made of wood and the barrel was metal. The two parts had become unfastened, and someone had thrown it away. Mama let us keep the two pieces. The spoils of war, we told her. A dead Nazi had left it. Where was the Nazi? she asked. His buddies had carried him off to bury him, I explained. At home, we fastened the barrel to the stock with tape and began shooting at the soldiers hiding behind the chairs. It was an awesome gun, wickedly accurate and totally deadly. Capturing weapons was an important byproduct of winning battles. The spoils of war! To pillage was the infantryman's right and reward.

A few days later, we couldn't go for a walk. Papa was getting ready for a military parade, and he and Mama were upstairs. It was sunny and warm. Alex and I decided to go feed the ducks.

"Me, me," lisped Margy. She was sixteen months old, hardly old enough to go with us.

We found bread in the kitchen, and the three of us slipped out the back door and down across the yard to the stream. The ducks saw us coming and quacked and gabbled with hunger and excitement. The snowbanks were wet with melting snow and slush, grass was showing on the lawns, and mud was everywhere. The stream was roaring with water, full from the melting snow. Alex and I threw bread to the ducks. One of the drakes was quick and mean. He gobbled up most of the crumbs. We tried to throw past him to the other ducks, or throw one to him to our left and quickly throw some to the right for the other ducks. Margy caught up to us and again squealed, "Me, me!" We gave her some bread, and she started down the bank to the water's edge. She took no more than a step or two when she slipped in the mud and slid down the bank on her butt, as if she were sledding. And then she was gone! She slid right in and the water grabbed her and pulled her under.

"Margy!" Alex screamed. "Margy!"

I took off for the house. "Papa! Mama!" Alex was running with me now. I got to the back door. It was locked. Alex pounded on it, yelling for Papa and Mama. I left him and bolted around the house to the front, screaming for Papa and Mama as I opened the door. In a flash, Papa appeared at the top of the stairs. He had just changed into his dress whites for the parade. He had hurt his leg a few days earlier and was leaning on two crutches.

"What happened?" he roared.

"Margy! Margy! She fell into the river!"

I had never seen Papa move so fast. He threw off the crutches and bounded down the stairs, Mama right behind him. "Where?" he yelled as we raced around the house.

We ran to the stream, and I pointed to where Margy had fallen in. Mama ran to where I pointed, but Papa ran the other way. I wondered why Papa wasn't running to where I pointed, and then I realized he was running downstream. He was right. With the stream moving so fast, she wouldn't be where she fell in! I ran after him, but couldn't keep up. Suddenly, way ahead of me, I saw Papa jump into the water right up to his armpits. He was half floating, half walking, sliding with the current. I saw him grab for something, and then I saw Margy's pink snowsuit, with Margy in it, as he lifted her out of the water. In a moment, Papa was out of the stream, holding Margy upside down by the ankles with one hand. With the other hand he was slapping her back as water gushed out of her mouth. We started back toward the house where Mama was waiting.

"Is she okay?" she called.

By now Papa was holding Margy in his arms, cuddling her, while she cried, squealing with fear.

"I panicked," Mama said, explaining why she had run upstream. "I don't know what I was thinking. Oh, Carl, you saved her!" She took Margy and comforted her.

Alexander H. ter Weele

"You can thank Ge," said Papa. "That knitted snowsuit that Ge made saved her. It filled with air and kept her more or less afloat. I could spot the pink even in that muddy roil of water."

When we reached our backyard, Alex was waiting for us, standing and crying. "Margy, Margy," he wailed over and over with tears streaming down his cheeks.

I put my arm around his shoulders as we walked back to the house. "She's okay." He was still crying when we all reached the front door. "She's okay," I repeated. "Mama will give her a warm bath and she will be fine."

"Can I take a bath with her, Mama?" he asked. "Without me, she may be afraid of the water."

Alex smiled when Mama said he could.

Hoofdstuk 27

2 februari 1942: Japanese planes strike Netherlands Timor. US ships blast Japanese strongholds on Marshall and Gilbert Islands. US guns on Corregidor disrupt Japanese troops massing in Manila Bay. Russians claim victories as German tanks retreat near Dnipropetrovsk.

We returned to Stratford from our Christmas and New Year's vacation, which we had spent in Connecticut with Alex and PC. No sooner had we started our vacation than President Roosevelt announced on the radio that Japan had attacked Pearl Harbor. It had been a somber Sinterklaas. While the children searched their shoes for goodies left by the good saint, Carl and I worried what it might mean for us. Would Carl be ordered to join the Royal Netherlands forces in the Dutch East Indies? After all, he knew Java and Sumatra, having lived there for seven years. Roosevelt had immediately declared war on Japan; and then, a few days later, declared war on Germany and Italy as well. And sure enough, hardly had we returned to Stratford than Carl received new orders. He was to leave the next week, not to Jakarta and the East Indies, but to Curacao, to Willemstad, capital of the Dutch West Indies. After a year of Stratford, waiting in limbo, nothing to do, bored to tears, suddenly, he was reassigned. No advance notice. No discussions, no warning, no gossip, just "Go. Next Monday."

It took our breath away. On the one hand we were happy. Stratford had pleased neither of us. Carl hadn't enjoyed his job, which had consisted of lots of make work and some managerial logistics—the Dutch troops in England needed toilet paper, toothpaste, boots, and whatever. And I hadn't much enjoyed the Dutch military community. People coming and going, often here for only a few days or a few weeks, most of them simply waiting, waiting, and waiting for orders. They were young men in the main, with few couples and even fewer with children. And too much drinking, too much carousing, too much partying.

So we were pleased to be leaving, but Carl would be back in the war. I had no idea how dangerous the West Indies might be. There was vague talk of submarine attacks on the islands. And while we had no regrets about leaving Ontario, it certainly would have been nicer to have a bit more notice. Five days … Carl arranged an extra week for me and the children in our house, but off he went. I clung to him at the train station, and he kissed away my tears.

"I'll be waiting," he promised. "Come as soon as you can. I'll arrange a house right away. Just think, no snow." He smiled and touched my cheek. "Sun, sand, and swimming."

I waved as he boarded and then, with tears still in my eyes, I headed back to Front Street and the three children. As soon as I could finish packing, we were leaving. Although we had another week to stay in the house, I was determined to leave the day after tomorrow. Without Carl, there was no way I would stay in this godforsaken town longer than that. I was short, I expect, with the children while I packed, but two days later we boarded the train from Ontario to New Haven, Connecticut. What I couldn't take with us, the military would box up and ship. If it didn't get to us, good riddance. The last days had been exhausting, but we were on our way. I never turned my head. There was no reason to look back on Stratford.

We arrived in Cheshire in February 1942. The boys, of course, loved Cheshire and Jinny Hill Road and PC and Alex. They adored roaming the fields behind the house. They would return breathless to tell me of rabbit tracks in the snow in the old vineyard, or a fox that they had seen slip out of sight over the stone wall. They missed their father. Without him, there would be no hunting! We would be there for two weeks. Carl had already cabled to say he had a house waiting for us. Two weeks was too short a time to worry about putting Jan back in school. That would wait until we were installed in Willemstad.

But how to get to Curacao? I talked about it with Alex and PC. First we had to get to Miami. We could go by bus or train, but it would be a long and cumbersome trip for me with the three children and all of our luggage. From Miami it would be possible to find a boat, or to fly across with Pan Am. There were flights every fortnight from Miami to Willemstad. I had never yet flown in an airplane. My older brother Josh had learned to fly. He had flown regularly from Hyannis to No Man's, initially to visit the island and later to visit the daughter of Father's caretaker. I didn't remember Josh well. He had died when the plane he was flying went down. He had been much older than I—he the first and

I the last of the six of us—and had long since left home when I was being raised in Westwood.

After thinking about it, Alex decided he would drive us to Florida. His car opened in the rear to a large compartment, perfect for our luggage. The three children could sit on the rear seat, Alex would drive, and I would join him up front. We knew a few people who had driven the fifteen hundred miles of the East Coast. The Post Road went the whole way. It would take us a week or so. With Alex driving, the trip would be far easier for me. Gas was expensive because of the war, and there would be places along the way where there would be shortages, but Alex had six five-gallon drums that he would fill and store in the back of the car, and we would keep our gas tank as full as possible.

So off we went. I kissed PC and Mary good-bye, and the children waved as we left Jinny Hill Road, the car packed to the brim. Jan pointed out the Sleeping Giant to Alex, off to our left.

"He's lying on his back. That bump is his head, that one his stomach, and over there are his feet." Alex laughed, and Jan cautioned him to be quiet. "We don't want to wake him. He might roll over and squash us!"

The trip had started. Down Route 10 to Hamden to pick up Route 1 at New Haven. Route 1 was known as the Boston Post Road between Boston and New York. The postal service had used the road from the first days of the founding of the nation. We would be on the Post Road for the next week. It went from New England all the way to Miami. At least the weather was propitious. A warm sun spoke of an early spring. The children were full of excitement, and Alex and I were in good humor. Of my siblings, he was my favorite. Big and blond—not as big nor as blond as Carl, but big and blond nonetheless—and rarely out of sorts. Easy to get along with, with a quick smile. He was the fifth and I was the sixth of the siblings.

As we began, we would pass through West Haven, Milford, and Stratford (yes, another Stratford!) on the Post Road. The Post Road ran right through the heart of all the major towns and cities on the East Coast. We would see them all. That was the good news. The bad news was that in many of the towns, it would be slow going. At Stratford, however, we picked up the brand new Merritt Parkway. It had just opened a year earlier. We were able to bypass Bridgeport, Fairfield, Westport, Norwalk, Stanford, and Greenwich on the way to New York. The parkway was two lanes in either direction with a greensward between. A wonderful invention! We hoped to traverse New York in the early afternoon and spend our first night in New Jersey.

The journey was slow. We spent the first nights in Howard Johnson hotels, clean, new, and bright with their orange roofs. The boys liked them: the roofs were the color of the jerseys of the Dutch soccer team. And in their restaurants, Howard Johnson boasted twenty-eight flavors of ice cream! The boys were also excited by the view of the Empire State Building from the George Washington Bridge as we crossed from New York into New Jersey; and they spied the Empire State Building two or three more times as we started the descent through New Jersey.

And then the trouble began. One of the tires went flat. Alex jacked up the car and put on the spare. At the next town, he had the blown tire fixed. In Delaware, again a flat. Alex again changed tires, but this time we learned that the blown tire was too damaged. It couldn't be repaired. Alex tried to buy a new spare, but it was impossible. There simply weren't any available; supplying the Allies meant that civilians could not buy tires. So far we had had no trouble purchasing gas, although we had used one of our jerry cans at a stretch in Maryland where service stations were without gas. So on we went, without a spare, our fingers crossed.

In Georgia, disaster struck. Another flat. Alex jacked up the car, removed the flat tire, and flagged down a passing driver. He agreed to drop Alex and the flat at the first service station down the road.

So off Alex went, leaving the car with three tires and me with three children. No sooner had he left than we all needed to pee. Down the embankment we went. Under some friendly white pines, we relieved ourselves. As we climbed up the embankment, I heard a passing car stop down the road and then back up. As I cleared the embankment, I saw a GI standing in front of our car. When he spotted me, he whistled appreciatively and greeted me with a broad smile and a, "Hi, babe! Trouble?"

He obviously liked my looks. Another two steps, and his smile faded. He spied the three children in tow. Hopes dashed. No hot date, this. He put on a brave recovery smile and offered to help. We chatted for a few minutes. When he learned that I was headed to join my husband, that my brother would be back shortly, that I was cared for, that I was, in short, unavailable, he smiled, pecked me on the cheek, and waved good-bye to the children and me. A watchdog? No, I didn't need one. Three youngsters was defense enough!

Hoofdstuk 28

9 februari 1942: Japanese launch attack on Singapore, bombard US fortifications at Manila Bay, unleash assault on MacArthur's defense positions on the Bataan peninsula. The Axis advance in Libya halted by British near Tobruk. Russians drive wedge into German lines laying siege to Leningrad. Nazi U-boat sinks oil tanker in Atlantic off US coast in daring midday attack, similar to attack and sinking the day before of tanker off the New Jersey coast.

Oom Alex returned with a tow truck, which pulled our car and took us all to the garage. Oom Alex explained to Alex and me that it would be a few days before the garage would be able to find a tire. All the tires were being sent to England to equip army jeeps and trucks. We pretended that our car was a captured German personnel carrier that we were towing back from the front lines.

Oom Alex and Mama decided we would continue on by train, and that he would stay behind until the car was fixed and drive back to Cheshire alone. With our luggage stacked on the platform, Alex and I pretended we were GIs headed for the front. Mama and Margy were our wives. Soon they would be waving to us and crying as our train pulled out of the station. We would be brave, smiling at the coming danger, and we would comfort them as they worried for our safety. We would pat our rifles and tell them we could protect ourselves.

Our train would be arriving on the track next to the platform. A freight train was on the next track, one track farther from the platform. It was just standing there, not going anywhere. Mama bought sandwiches and drinks in the depot, but there was no place to sit on the platform. Oom Alex picked me up and sat me on the edge of an open baggage car of the freight train. He placed my drink next to me and then placed Margy on my other side. As Margy and I sat on the edge of the baggage car, our legs dangling above the track, he stood next to us, watching for our train to arrive. There was no one at the station except us and the station master. He had on a neat hat with a shiny visor that he placed on my head for a minute. Maybe I would be conductor someday, he said. Or an engineer. Usually the incoming train didn't stop at this station, he explained. The station was too small. But he had sent a telex by dit-dit-dit dot-dot-dot, asking the engineer to stop and pick us up.

I hopped off the baggage wagon when Alex told me he had found a vending machine with big balls of chewing gum in it. They were all colors, red, blue, yellow. The orange ones were almost exactly the color of Dutch soccer jerseys. We heard the train whistle and ran back to Mama.

The train pulled in, and Oom Alex and the station master quickly loaded our luggage onto it. Since this wasn't a scheduled stop, they had to be quick. No sooner did we have everything on board than the station master waved at the engineer, the doors closed, and we started off.

Mama waved good-bye to Oom Alex. Just then Alex screamed, "Margy! Mama!" He was pointing. "Margy! There!" Margy was still sitting on the edge of the baggage car with her drink and sandwich next to her.

Mama rushed toward the front of the train to tell the conductor. Alex was sobbing, "Margy. Margy. My little sister!" I tried to comfort him, but he sobbed louder. "My little sister. I love her. I love her!"

Mama came back to us. I could see she was worried. "It will be okay," she said to us. "The conductor will stop the train at the next station." She kissed us both. "He telexed back to the nice station master to ask him to take care of Margy."

"When will we see Margy, Mama?" Alex asked, still crying. "How will we get her back? What if the freight train left with her on it?" He began to tremble and shake. "I love my little sister. She's so small!"

Mama hugged Alex, but the more she hugged him, the more he cried.

The train slowed and stopped. We were at another small station, even smaller than the last one. There was a concrete platform with no roof and a tiny shed. There were no travelers, no one except a station master. He walked to the front of the train. No one got on the train and no one got off. A few of the passengers were asking one another why we had stopped.

A few minutes went by. The train seemed to have shut down. The only noise was Alex's sobbing and his occasional murmurs of "Margy," and "My little sister," and "I love her so much!" His crying made Mama start to cry too.

The door at the front of our car opened, and the conductor made his way down the aisle toward us. He had a telex in his hand, and he was smiling. "She should be here in a few minutes," he said. "As soon as they received our telex, they put her on the freight train and it left. It's not more than a few minutes behind us."

Mama smiled, a big smile of relief.

"The station master and your brother saw your daughter as soon as we pulled out of the station. Apparently she was never in any real danger."

"She's all right?" Alex whispered to the conductor.

He ruffled Alex's hair. "Yes, big brother." He picked Alex up, held him so that he could speak to him face to face. He was a big Irish-looking man with a ruddy face and a deep laugh. "Yes, your little sister is fine. She's probably sucking a big lollipop right now. We should see her in three or four minutes."

Alex was smiling through his tears. The conductor handed him to Mama, searched in his pocket, pulled out two lollipops. "Green or red?" he asked Alex. Alex asked for the green. The conductor gave it to him, and then gave me the red one.

Sure enough, in no time the freight train pulled up alongside us and stopped. Three burly railway workers hopped down, one of them cradling Margy. They were joking with her, spoiling her. She was laughing, and yes, she had a big lollipop in her mouth. The man carried her onto our car, and as soon as he put Margy down, Alex kissed her on the cheek. Now he was laughing too. Wow. He had really been worried.

Hoofdstuk 29

16 februari 1942: British surrender in Singapore. Japanese forces converge on Thaton in drive to take Rangoon railroad. Dutch set fire to Shell oil fields and facilities in Palembang as Japanese troops land on Sumatra. Tokyo claims thirty-two ships sunk in Strait of Malacca. Japanese troops mass on Bataan in preparation for attack on MacArthur's forces there. Germany drawing on reserves as Soviet counterattack advances toward Poland.

Carl was waiting for us at the dock. We had reached Miami, spent a night in a hotel, and found a boat that was leaving the next day for Willemstad. Fewer than twenty of us were on board. It was not that much different from running over to No Man's Land from Woods Hole. I guessed the vessel had probably previously served as a fishing boat. There had been one scare: a German submarine had surfaced less than a half mile from us. She had looked us over and after a few minutes had sounded. The captain was relieved, but he had not been overly anxious. So far from home, he said, the subs saved their fire for bigger game, mostly the tankers that carried Shell oil from Aruba to the Allies. Our little ship was not worth one of their torpedoes.

Behind the dock, Willemstad was alive with color. The houses were shaped like those along the canals of Amsterdam or Delft: narrow—perhaps three windows wide—and about four stories tall, topped by a gable. Many in brick, the rest in wood. But unlike Holland, the houses were painted a riot of colors—bright green, magenta, pink, powder blue, yellow, and all against a clear sky and eternal sun. I had not yet set foot on shore and already I loved Curacao. What a glorious contrast to dull, drab Ontario!

It was a relief to see Carl. In Stratford he had been bundled in an overcoat, his face winter pale. Here, his khaki uniform had short sleeves and he was tanned already. He waved and smiled and blew us kisses from the small dock. It was only a moment before his bulk was pressed hard against me and his arms wrapped me in a hug. How quickly I had forgotten his size and strength.

A moment flashed before my eyes. We were first married, in Amsterdam in a crowd jostling to see a football game. Ajax Amsterdam versus Juventus of Turin, a "friendly" match. A small group of male Italian fans pushed up to me, flirting. One of them obnoxiously complimented my looks in Italian, suggesting that he would like to get me in bed with him. Carl told him to leave me alone, that I was with him, that I was his wife. The man shrugged. So what? His friends cheered him on. The man gestured and suggested that he could please me more than Carl could. Looking at Carl, daring him, the man reached down and fondled my derriere. There was a flash of Carl's fist, a single punch, and the man was on the cobblestones. Suddenly there was space around us. Carl was gesturing to the fan's friends, smiling, inviting them to take him on. They put up their hands and backed off. Carl laughed at them, told them to help their friend up, and the two of us continued on.

Carl's hug now was comforting. It was a joy to be loved by this man, a joy to know that he would protect me. The children swarmed him, also excited to see him. It had been hardly a month that we had been separated, but it seemed far longer than that.

Carl bundled us into a staff car. He introduced me to Wanga, his driver, who dealt with our luggage and delivered us to Gaito 6. Our house! Oh, my. Two maids awaited us. Would I get along with them? Yohannita, tall, willowy, and dressed to attract. Vain, perhaps? Shieshie, short, plump, and the darker of the two. Quick to laugh. Both were about twenty years old, perhaps in their early twenties. Wanga, spiffy in army khaki and with a lean, athletic look, was probably a year or two older. He carried our luggage into the house while I introduced Jan, Alex, and Margy to the two maids. They laughed and smiled with the kids, obviously at ease with young children. Yohannita took instantly to Margy, captivated by her blond hair, fair skin, and twinkling eyes.

The two maids spoke the local Papiamento with each other and with Wanga, and a broken Dutch with me. Wanga's Dutch was fluent. He'd had some schooling and had worked a number of years for the Dutch military. My first impression was that I would be able to get along with the two maids. I hoped so. Wanga, of course, would be working for Carl, on base, at his office, chauffeuring him. He was paid by the military, Carl's aide-de-camp. The two maids were paid by us and would be my charges. It would be hard for me to like them as much as I had liked Rita in Eindhoven. Rita and I had confided in each other as sisters; she the younger one, asking for advice on how to treat her boyfriend. But at first glance it appeared that it would work with the two maids, different as they were. Yohannita more reserved, concerned about her looks, correct in her manners. Shieshie, her clothes a bit frumpy, a constant laugh in her throat, outgoing and easygoing.

The house would work. From the street, one entered the front yard—framed by a chin-high hedge—through an arched trellis, thick with bougainvillea. In three steps one reached the low porch with two chairs for watching the passersby. Inside it was quiet and pleasantly dark, an oasis from Curacao's perpetual sun. Upstairs, one bedroom for Carl and me, a second one for the boys to share, and a smaller one for Margy. A large yard out back, perfect for the children, especially with the hedge all around and more bougainvillea. At the back of the yard was a small shed where Shieshie and Yohannita slept. The sun, the flowers, the Caribbean breeze ... What a glorious change from Stratford's ice and snow and dreary black afternoons! I did not yet know what Curacao would bring, but the climate and the flora were certainly to my liking.

As it turned out, Curacao became a perpetual vacation, fifteen months of relaxation. Wanga took care of the garden. Yohannita became Margy's nursemaid. Shieshie did most of the cooking. Together the maids cleaned the house, washed the dishes, did the laundry—by hand!—and the ironing. Yohannita's extended family and female friends came by the house regularly. Always at these visits, Yohannita would have Margy on her hip. She would spend most of the visit showing Margy off, extolling her fair hair and complexion. When I let her, she would take Margy to the market, ostensibly to shop for vegetables, but I knew she covertly enjoyed the attention garnered by the blond toddler on her hip in a world of dark-haired humanity.

The children and I spent entire days at the Baby Beach, a lagoon with a white sand beach, palm trees, a dock, and tidal pools on the reef that were alive with crabs and multicolored fish. The water was so clear, you would swear it was possible to reach down and touch the fish swimming along the bottom, even though you knew it was ten feet deep.

Carl and I could dine out or spend evenings with friends as much as we wished. The Dutch military crowd here was preferable to the hard-partying transient group of Stratford. There were quite a few other soldiers with families, and postings were more permanent, so to speak, often for a year or longer. Nonetheless, we didn't find many couples that we truly enjoyed. In part, this was due to an officer corps jostling for positions and promotions. Each newly arrived officer was a threat to those already on the island.

Carl was assigned to manage logistics for the artillery defenses. Not strategic issues of the island's defense, but the administration of supplies, personnel, equipment, and maintenance. It was not an exciting assignment, but necessary, and it kept him busy. It also kept him out of the direct line of backbiting and nastiness amongst the chiefs of staff. I suspected that the level of this nastiness was directly proportional to the distance from the theater of war: at the front, winning battles and keeping one's troops alive kept the officer corps busy. Less time, therefore, to jostle for promotions. Here the danger was intermittent. Submarines firing torpedoes on tankers at sea every few days, or surfacing to fire their deck guns at the oil storage tanks at the refinery on Aruba every month or so. No danger to speak of on Curacao itself. Thus, the chiefs of staff had time, too much time it seems; and backbiting was the game, their favorite game, a game that vied with the real war for its viciousness.

On April 8, 1943, we celebrated our tenth wedding anniversary. Fourteen months had gone by on this island in the stream. I loved it here. We decided against a party, and Carl and I dined out quietly, just the two of us. He spoiled me by going to a small outdoor restaurant, local and simple, but with the freshest of fish. I say *spoiled* because Carl would normally shun a seafood restaurant. While I adored fish of any ilk, he rarely ate it. We reminisced about our wedding, which had taken place at St. James Church, Hanover Square, London. I had been staying at Brown's Hotel with Father while our bans were published. Had that been a wait of a fortnight? Were the life-size wooden carvings of the two dogs—Brittany spaniels?—still guarding the foyer of St. James? We had been so amused by them that we adopted Barbara, our black English cocker spaniel, two weeks later. After the ceremony, a quick glass of champagne with our small coterie of guests—all five of them—and off Carl and I went on the train to Southampton, boarded the ferry to Ostend, and back on the train to the Hotel Metropole in Brussels. And there, like this evening, we dined on shellfish, a delicious moules frites, at Chez Leon, just off the Grande Place.

Here we were, ten years later, not London, not Brussels, but Willemstad. We would not have dreamed it. With three youngsters too, and me six months pregnant with our fourth. We had always talked of having four children, but with the war, we had postponed that thought until now.

Carl and I decided that I would return to the States for the coming birth, which would be in late July. As we talked, we decided I should leave Curacao toward the end of May. PC had offered to find a place for me. Her Lexington Avenue apartment in New York, which she used during the week when she was in the city for her job with Simon & Schuster, was far too small for me and the three children, but she would find something near the city so that she could live with me to help out with the kids. She would be off during the day of course, but even so, having her with me on the evenings and weekends would be a godsend. Rentals tended to be by the month, so Carl and I decided she should find something starting June first. I didn't want to risk travel after my seventh month.

Hoofdstuk 30

26 juli 1943: New York Mayor La Guardia sees hope for slight increase in supply of eggs, meat; warns city will boycott $1 eggs. American and British bombers smash Kiel, Wustrow, Rostock, Hamburg, Warnemuende to destroy Baltic ports, shipyards, aircraft factories. King Victor Emmanuel of Italy strips Benito Mussolini of premiership, ousts Fascist cabinet, appoints Marshal Pietro Badoglio to form new government, continue war. Two hundred Allied planes bomb Japanese base in the Solomon Islands.

It was awful. We hated being here. Alex was pushing and pulling on the upper bunk of our double bunk, hitting it against the wall. Thunk, thunk, thunk. Margy was across the room in the dark, crying in her bed. I asked Alex to stop. He wouldn't. Before going to bed, he had pulled all the buttons off his pajamas and thrown them into the trash. He had been crying while doing that. I went over and cuddled Margy. Eventually, both she and Alex fell asleep.

I returned to my own bed and cried quietly. Why were we here? Why had Papa and Mama put us here? We didn't even know these people! Mama had explained that our cousin Cal Sizer was being very nice to let Papa and Mama stay with her and her husband, Cousin Tubby, so they could be near the hospital where she'd go to give birth. But Cousin Cal's house wasn't big enough for Alex, Margy, and me. So we were staying with these nice people, neighbors to Cousin Cal. Neighbors? Not really. This house was at least a mile from Cousin Cal's house. And nice? They were old and didn't even remember our names. We called them Mr. and Mrs. Gorilla. Mama had said our stay wouldn't be long. As soon as she recuperated from the birth, we'd all leave Bethany, Connecticut, and the Sizers and go back to Bronxville. And she said it would only be for sleeping; we would be at Cousin Cal's house during the day. Was Cousin Cal really a cousin? She was older than Mama! It seemed funny that she was our cousin.

Papa and Mama had told us that we should be excited. We'd soon have a new baby brother or sister. But living with the Gorillas had squashed any excitement we were supposed to have. A few days after Papa had arrived in New York, we'd all driven here; and it was only a short time later that he and Mama left in the middle of the night to go to the hospital in New Haven. When Papa came back from the hospital, he was excited to tell the three of us that we had a baby sister. Her name was Fenneke. He laughed and said that when they were driving to the hospital, while Mama was having the contractions that told her she was about to have the baby, she said she was starving. She suddenly had a craving for onions. They had pulled into a White Tower and bought a hamburger, even though the contractions were coming fast. She ate the hamburger with lots of onions on it in the car because they needed to hurry. They got to the hospital and Mama gave birth only five minutes later. That was close!

Two days later Papa brought Mama and Fenneke from the hospital to Cousin Cal's house. Meanwhile we were stuck sleeping in Gorilla Land. Every time Alex and I started to play war, the Gorillas would tell us to stop. So when they weren't looking, we would shoot them. We used silencers of course, so they wouldn't know they were being killed. We'd already shot them hundreds of times and they didn't even know it.

Then Papa had to leave. He told Mama that he might be transferred from Curacao to Bonaire. He wasn't sure yet. He'd let us know. When Papa kissed us good-bye, he said he had arranged for Tante PC to come to drive us all back to Bronxville.

At Cousin Cal's, Margy was allowed to play with Cousin Cal's doll collection. She had to be careful, because the dolls' heads were breakable. Porcelain, Cousin Cal said. Margy could only touch the dolls with Cousin Cal present, could only play with them sitting on the rug, and wasn't allowed to change their clothes. Cousin Cal had to do that. She was afraid Margy would pull off the tiny buttons or tear the lace. The dolls weren't baby dolls; they were ladies wearing grown-up clothes. Cousin Cal said they had belonged to her mother and her grandmother. Since Cousin Cal was already old, her grandmother had lived a really long time ago!

Hoofdstuk 31

19 augustus 1943: More than 3,000 Allied planes hit German installations across the Netherlands, France, and Germany in record twenty-four-hour period, destroying a secret Nazi research facility on the Baltic coast, airfields, manufacturing plants, troop staging centers. American Third Division captures Messina as Germans flee Sicily. Russians regroup, resume advance on Kharkov front after a three-day retreat in face of crushing Nazi counterattack. Allied planes in the Pacific theater bomb Wewak in New Guinea, and Allies score victory in sea battle near Vella Gulf in the Solomons. Nazi U-boats sink two tankers off coast of Venezuela.

I was relieved to get away from Bethany. Living in someone else's house was uncomfortable. Cousin Cal had tried to be nice, but we didn't know each other well; and her husband Tubby was stuffy and set in his ways. Cal had felt Tubby wouldn't be able to handle three young children, so she had suggested Jan, Alex, and Margy stay with some neighbors who needed a bit of extra cash and would be pleased to board them. That had been a disaster. The children had cried. Alex had ripped the buttons off every pair of his pajamas, and all three of them—including Jan, despite that he was eight years old—had wet their beds. It was awful. Cal urged me to stay longer so that she could help with Fenneke, but the moment Carl left, I had to get out. The ten days before the birth with Carl there had been bearable, but the two days in the hospital and then three more days with Cal and Tubby, with Carl gone and Tubby constantly fussing about Fenneke's crying ... For my own sanity, and especially for Jan, Alex, and Margy, I had to escape. PC picked us up and brought us back here to the rental house in Bronxville.

She, of course, goes to work, leaving every day at 8:00 a.m. and is generally back at 5:30. I've taught the boys to memorize our address here, repeating over and over "15 Kraft Avenue, Bronxville." It's home now to them. They settled in during the seven weeks we were here in

June and July, before the debacle in Connecticut. Still, the house is too big, too dark, too drafty, too much like every other house up and down the street. Porch out front, darkened and dank shingles, dim interior. Forsaken and sad. Bronxville reminds me of our depressing stay in Stratford. PC had committed us to three months' rent, June, July, and August, and we just extended that through September. With luck we will be going back to Curacao before the end of September, but if Carl is transferred to Bonaire, we'll have to wait until he arranges accommodations for us there.

I'm worried about schooling for Jan. He's been in and out of schools. A half year in Cheshire in kindergarten, speaking English; and then the rest of that school year in the play group organized by the military in Stratford, in Dutch. Then a half year in Stratford in first grade in the public school, in English, and the second half of first grade in Willemstad in Dutch. The only full year he had with a single teacher was second grade in the same school in Willemstad. There he adjusted well: the teacher said he had mastered reading and writing in Dutch. I needed to go this week to enroll him here in third grade, which starts right after Labor Day. In English. That will be difficult for him, not the speaking, but the rest. And how long will that be? A week or two? A month? And then back to the islands. It has been difficult for him, not so much the learning—I've helped a lot with that—but the adjustment. New school, new teacher, new classmates, different language.

PC is a great help. She is, of course, her usual domineering self and wants to run my life. That's the way she is. I suppose it's always that way with a big sister, especially one who is thirteen years older! But she means well. She does her best with the children, but she is not a natural with youngsters. She's never been around them, has no children of her own, and being self-centered and short on patience are not good qualities for a mother. For all that, after Bethany, Bronxville is a pleasant respite, and I'm grateful to my sister for her help.

Hoofdstuk 32

9 september 1943: Italy surrenders as Allies land near Naples. Stalinist forces advance to Dnieper River, now control the Donets Basin, a key steel-making region. Neutral Portugal weighs joining Allies. US Navy raids Marcus Islands as Allied planes bomb Madang in New Guinea and strafe Japanese troops on Salamaua, New Guinea.

Alex and I had the soldiers set up on the treads of the big staircase that rose from the front hall. It was a perfect place for the Americans to take a stand. Whether it was Alexander the Great or Julius Caesar or Napoleon, great generals knew how to use terrain to their advantage. George Washington had been a tyro. He had tried to defend the indefensible and had not only lost the island of Manhattan to Cornwallis, he had almost lost his army. How could he have been so retarded not to have realized that the redcoats could surround him with their fleet and pound him into submission? What a *stommerd*! But here, with the Americans arrayed on the steps, the cannon behind—a step higher—the muskets at the front, and the cavalry poised in between, Hitler and his Nazi troops had to charge uphill. As the troops advanced, Alex and I swept them off the treads to their death. Once again the battle was ours!

The blood having been spilled, the heat and thunder of battle over, Alex and I sat quietly on the stairs. Mama was taking a nap with Margy and Fenneke. Tante PC was at work. Alex told me how he had sneaked out of bed last night and sat right where he was now, halfway down the stairs. Mama and Tante PC had not yet gone to bed and were chatting in the living room, just off the foyer. Alex kept himself hidden and listened to the conversation. He was a spy gathering intelligence, he said.

Mama was telling Tante PC that she was pleased for Papa. He had received the transfer he had wanted: commander of the prison camp on Bonaire. Not that it was an exciting posting, but he would be the highest ranking officer on the island and therefore free of the nasty backbiting of the top command on Curacao. Bonaire was a nothing island, he had

179

explained to Mama. There was the prison camp and, next to it, a hamlet, nothing more than a fishing village with a harbor. He had inquired about schooling for the two of us. Yes, Alex would be going to school too, and he had been excited to learn that.

Mama didn't know when we would be joining Papa, though. He wasn't certain of the date of his transfer, and he wanted to arrange a house for us before we came. She didn't like the sound of it. We might be stuck here in Bronxville for longer than she wanted. She was anxious to get back to the sun and warm weather and Papa. The last thing she said was that Shieshie, Yohannita, and Wanga would be going to Bonaire with us. Mama had asked Papa to arrange that if he could. Alex and I exchanged grins at that news. Then Alex had scrambled back to his bed. Mama and Tante PC were turning off the living room lights, and he didn't want to be caught out of bed.

Alex was a good spy, I thought. I was particularly happy to learn that Wanga was going with us to Bonaire. He was the best kite maker in the world.

We dismantled our troop positions on the stairs and put the toy soldiers and cannons into their box. Mama, Margy, and Fenneke were still sleeping, so we decided to scout the basement. It was a big basement, under the whole house. Because it was dark and scary, we took a flashlight with us. Most of the space was empty. Right in the middle squatted a great furnace. We called it the octopus. The door to the firebox had tiny holes; those were the eyes of the octopus. Up above were its arms, ductwork spreading to various rooms like huge ... Arms, Alex said. Not arms, I told him. Tentacles. I know that, he said.

Over in the corner, two partitions, about as high as Alex was, squared off to make a small room. Under the basement ceiling and right above that small room was a door just large enough to crawl through. It was too high for us to reach. It was the coal chute entrance, we concluded. The furnace had once been a coal furnace. It now burned fuel oil. The coal had probably been stored in the corner surrounded by the partition. We decided not to go in there: coal dust lay thick and looked dirty. Alex decided it was where the Nazis burned Jews. That was what Hitler did.

On the other side of the basement was a high window. It was ajar, just a smidgen. Like the entry for the coal chute, the window was just large enough to crawl through. Could we reach it? No, it was way too high. We checked the drawers of an old dresser. Empty. Farther along

was a table with a chair. One of the legs of the table was broken. That
was it.

The open window intrigued us. It appeared to go outside, but it was
dark beyond the window, even though it was a sunny day. We decided to
take a look. With both of us pushing, we shoved the dresser against the
wall, under the window. I got on the dresser; my chin was even with the
window ledge. The glass was dirty, but I could see that the window
opened underneath the front porch. The lattice around the porch cut off
any exit into the garden. Under the porch it was dark. Like a cave, I told
Alex. He wanted to see and climbed on the dresser, but he was too short
to look out the window. I jumped down, got the chair next to the broken
table, and sat that on the dresser. Now Alex could see everything.

Let's go caving, he said. Spelunking, I said. We managed to open the
window. I boosted Alex through, and then climbed on the chair and
followed. It was neat in there. Our own world. We could see through the
lattice and watch cars go by on the street, but no one could see in. The
ground was dry, and we could crawl around easily on all fours.

"Hold on," Alex said. "I have an idea."

He climbed back into the basement, and I waited, listening to car
motors. Down the street, a mom called for one of her children. Our cave
smelled of dead leaves. When Alex returned, I had to lower myself onto
the dresser to help him back through the window. He had brought two
candles from the dining room table and a box of matches. Great
thinking, I told him. He made two small holes in the dirt using a splinter
from the porch and set the candles into them. I lit the candles. Perfect!
Now we had light. We decided to ask Mama if we could camp here, get
our blankets and spend the night. Why not? Even if it rained, we'd be
dry.

We squatted on opposite sides of the candles, pretending they were a
campfire and we were Wild Bill Hickok and Davy Crockett. We had
shot a bear and were going to roast it over the fire. No, we decided it was
a deer. Venison would taste better. We held our hands out to the two
candles, warming them in the heat of our campfire.

A siren sounded in the distance. Fire engine? Police? Ambulance? At
first it was a tiny sound. As it got louder, we listened with interest.
Would it go by our house? We could hear it blaring, and watched
through the lattice of the walls of our cave. It was going to pass right in
front of our house. Even better, with its lights flashing and sirens blaring,

a fire engine stopped in the street right in front of us! It was a huge hook and ladder truck, the most exciting kind.

The firemen piled off the truck. We heard the front door of our house open and Mama call, "Here! Here!"

A couple of firemen charged up the sidewalk and onto the porch while others ran around each side of the house. What was going on? Then we head Mama say, "Smoke." The firemen were yelling, "Where?" and "Not in here," and "Nothing over here." Then three or four of them pounded down the basement steps shouting, "Down here! Smoke!" And, a moment later, "Furnace looks okay."

Another instant and a fireman's helmet and face appeared at the window, peering into our hideaway. The head turned away from us and we heard, "It's okay, guys. It's in here." A pause. "No! No hoses or pickaxes. It's okay."

The head turned back to us and the big red face under the helmet smiled. "What are you guys up to? You scared the bejeebers out of your mother." He laughed. "Blow out those candles and c'mon out of there."

He helped us back through the window and onto the basement floor. It was hard to see. There were a lot of people and a lot of smoke.

The fireman who had lifted us down took us up the steps. "Here are your pyromaniacs, ma'am," he said when Mama came over. "Two candles." He gave those to Mama. "Matches." He gave those to her as well. "Playing under the front porch. No fire this time." He shrugged. "Next time they might not be so lucky."

We watched as the firemen piled onto the back of the truck, hanging onto the handholds. The siren blared as they pulled down the street. Alex and I glanced at each other. We were in trouble. We looked at Mama. Big trouble. We were glad we weren't soldiers. Soldiers were shot for disobeying orders.

Hoofdstuk 33

2 februari 1944: British and American forces expand Littoria beachhead in Italy, take Aprilia, advance on Rome. Red Army drives wedge into Nazi front south of Leningrad. First Japanese soil attacked as US Marines and Army invade Marshall Islands; amphibious troops storm ashore, take Roi-Namur and Kwajalein.

This time we flew from Miami to Willemstad. The boys were in seventh heaven. Margy was worried, largely, I suspected, because I was worried. Fenneke was asleep in my arms. The Pan Am airplane—an airship, as they called it—was moored to the dock. It rested on a big fat belly, a floating whale, with a pontoon under each wing for stability. The boys scrambled across the floating gang plank as if they had done it a thousand times. Margy held tight to my skirt as I held tight to the railing with one hand and cradled Fenneke on my shoulder with the other. Once everyone was strapped in their seats, the engines sputtered and caught, and we couldn't hear ourselves think over the roar of the propellers. The plane rocked like a boat as we pulled away from the dock. The boys were laughing, Margy squeezed my hand, and I held tight to the arm of my seat. Once well out into the bay the captain idled as he checked his instruments, then he told us to hang tight. I didn't need to be told. My knuckles were white from hanging on.

The roar of the motors when we had pulled away from the dock was the purring of a pussycat compared to the howling as we started our takeoff run. I glanced at the boys. They were laughing together with excitement. With the plane—the ship!—careening through the waves, the captain started to rock the craft left and right. All part of the takeoff process, I knew, but the rocking unnerved Margy and me. The effect on the boys was like a big ice cream cone on a hot summer day: smiles ear to ear, laughter, pure enjoyment. They would be slapping each other on the back if they weren't strapped into chairs. When we finally broke free from the water, their ecstasy was complete. Little by little, as the plane gained altitude and the engines settled into a constant roar, the fear ebbed from my body. I even began to understand how my brother Josh had been so taken with flying.

Every time we saw a fishing boat, the boys pulled a lever as if to open the bomb bay doors, pushed the release button on the end of their armrests, and called out "Bombs away!" A few seconds later came their "Ka-boom," and then, "Got him," or "Direct hit," or "Enemy sunk." I pitied the Cubans. As we flew over Cuba's eastern tip, the boys simply annihilated entire villages. The carnage was indescribable.

When it came into view, Curacao showed itself as the tropical paradise it was. The waves breaking on Noordpunt; the black lava stone of Sint Christoffelberg, the highest point on the island looking hardly larger than a small hill; Kaap Sint Marie curling protectively around Bullen Bay. We started our descent toward Willemstad and its large harbor, and I could see the bright colors of the houses, the sun glinting and sparkling on the water, the sky so utterly blue, so utterly clear. Yes, Josh. Yes, my older brother whom I hardly knew, I can understand how and why you loved flying! And somewhere down there, Carl waited for us.

A surge of happiness washed over me, overwhelmed me. The Bronxville interlude was supposed to be just three months. Then we had added September. Carl had let the rent on Gaito 6 in Willemstad lapse, living temporarily in the barracks as he awaited orders to transfer to Kralendijk on Bonaire. October, November, December. We kept extending our lease at 15 Kraft Avenue. Finally Carl received his orders. He was to report to his new command on January 1. It didn't take him long to find us a house. I decided to stay in Bronxville until the end of Jan's first school semester. We didn't stay a day longer than that, even though our lease was through the end of January. Too bad.

The surge of happiness that overwhelmed me made me realize how awful the stay in Bronxville had been. Worse than Stratford; there, Carl and I had been together. In Bronxville I had had PC, but even she and I had worn on each other after the first couple of months. Neither of us had expected the three months in Bronxville to grow to eight months. The constant expectation that I was about to depart and the regular disappointments and monthly lease extensions—it was like a pregnancy continuing a week beyond the expected date of birth, and then another week, and another. Emotionally draining. And such a dark house and awful weather. Darkness and cold and icy rain. I remembered now how pleasant Willemstad had been, how much I had enjoyed the sun and sand and sea. How relaxed it had made me to have Yohannita and Shieshie to help. And Carl. Carl. God, it would be good to be together again, to have him in bed at night, to have him in bed when I awoke. To know I would see him in a few minutes made me realize how lonely I'd been in Bronxville. Other than the few days when Fenneke had been born, we hadn't been together for eight months.

Hoofdstuk 34

23 januari 1944: Italian capital in jeopardy as American, British, and French units of the Fifth Army surprise Axis powers with amphibious landing just south of Rome. Red Army announces major advances on northern front as it captures Leningrad-Mga-Kirishi railroad. Australian forces in New Guinea close in on Japanese bases of Bogadjim and Madang.

When my superior ordered me to Bonaire, it was, he said, to clean house. The place was a mess. The Red Cross's report after their visit to the POW camp in September alleged prisoner mistreatment, low troop morale, theft of supplies, poor nutrition of our own troops as well as the POWs, unclear lines of command, dirt and disease, tension with the local community, and on and on. On my second day on the job, it was already clear that the report had it all wrong. The situation was far worse than the report indicated. The Red Cross had been too polite in describing the extent of the army's lapses.

Yesterday I had walked through the camp to take a look. It was little more than three Quonset huts used as bunkhouses, another one as a mess hall, and a third for leisure activities. Alongside the outside wall of one of the bunkhouses was a line of sinks. A half-dozen oil drums filled with water, each set on a two-meter-high tripod with a showerhead protruding below, served for bathing. Behind one of the huts was a latrine. The buildings fronted a large rectangular space that had been cleared and was used for assemblies and recreation. A goal set up at each end confirmed football to be the sport of preference. The whole of the installation was surrounded by a high wall of barbed wire, which in turn was surrounded by coils of more barbed wire as a further deterrence to would-be escapees. A hundred meters outside the camp was another cluster of huts similar to the cluster inside. This was where the troops bunked, and that served as our command post.

The camp had been built immediately after the start of the war. The first POWs had been a handful of fifth columnists captured in the Dutch Caribbean colonies right after the war began, here on Aruba, Bonaire, and Curacao; on St. Maarten, St. Eustatius, and Saba; and in coastal Suriname. Just as the Nazis had planted fifth columnists in Holland behind our defensive lines, they had recruited Germans living in our colonies to disrupt transport systems, particularly oil transport, and to attack Shell oil installations—both the refinery on Aruba and its oil wells in Venezuela. As the war progressed, each time a German submarine or other craft was captured or a marauding party caught coming ashore, another handful of prisoners would be added to the rolls.

My secretary was welcoming the mayor of Kralendijk in the adjoining room. After my walk through of the camp yesterday, I had met with the members of my small staff individually, to gain their perspective of their personal job responsibilities, their achievements, and the problems they faced. It rapidly became clear that no one had a job description; that there was no chain of command; that decisions were ad hoc; that everyone did everything, and that as a result, no one did anything. Who scheduled guard duty? Who ran the mess hall? Who purchased and stored supplies? Who kept accounts? Who was in charge of the armory? What was the schedule of daily prisoner activities? Who was charged with prisoner relations? Which prisoner spoke for the imprisoned? Where was the log of prisoner complaints, the record of sicknesses? Who was charged with ground maintenance, keeping prisoner quarters clean, checking and repairing fencing? Who was responsible for community relations? For staff training? In almost all instances, the answer was a shrug, or a half-hearted "Jan and Gerrit usually," or "Piet did it last week," or "Hendrix, I think."

Today I wanted to gain the mayor's perspective of the state of our relations with the community. The POW camp was tiny—seventy troops and some sixty prisoners—but when the island's men were out fishing during the day, we outnumbered the onshore population of women, children, and old men. Given that both the military and civilian populations were small, and that we were isolated together on this small speck in the ocean, it was imperative that we get along.

The mayor was ushered in by my secretary. A small man, skinny and quick as a monkey, old as tanned leather, quick dark eyes under the straw hat that had done little to protect him from the ocean sun and breeze. A fisherman, like everyone else in Kralendijk. Probably unschooled and illiterate, and undoubtedly smart as a whip when managing a trawler, its crew, and the currents and winds that raged among the islands of the Lesser Antilles. He was mayor because he was recognized by his peers as the shrewdest among them. Within seconds, we liked each other. He thanked me for meeting with him, noting that he had never met the previous commander during the three years he'd been stationed on Bonaire. I had known that, as I knew that the previous commander had never set foot inside the POW camp and had never met with any of the POWs. I offered the mayor a Camel to replace the twisted bit of paper he was about to light up. A real cigarette! He accepted the offer with genuine pleasure. As we both inhaled, I wondered aloud if it might be possible to find a secretary for me from among the townsfolk to replace the soldier presently serving in that capacity. It would provide a salary to a local, and would immediately create a channel of communication and exchange between the military and civilian populations.

We had hardly gotten through such initial small talk when both of us paused in midsentence. Gun shots. The *pop-pop-pop* of pistol fire at a distance. To those ignorant of small firearms, it would sound like the innocent snapping of castanets. Then I heard the roar of a jeep accelerating and voices raised in cries of confusion. I strode to the door to the anteroom just as my adjutant opened it from the other side.

"Captain!" He pointed across to the prison compound. "Escapees!"

Verdomme, I thought. *My second day on the job and we have a prison break.*

I called in the guard who had seen the flight. Five men, he reported. Somehow they had gotten hold of wire cutters and the keys to one of the jeeps. It had taken only seconds for them to snip the strands of barbed wire and make a run for it. And they had at least one pistol.

While he rattled on with the confused tale, I interrupted. "Boats?" I looked at the mayor. "Where on the island are there boats?"

"Not many spots." He waved toward the docks of Kralendijk. "Here, of course. Two other places. The small jetty near Pink Beach. Gerrit Janssen and his brother Klaas usually moor their trawlers here in the harbor, but sometimes if it's calm they moor them there, nearer their house. And Tim Wouter moors his sailboat offshore where he lives."

"Where's that?" I asked.

"At Lacre Point," the guard replied hastily. He was anxious to be in my good graces. "Right near the salt pans."

I looked at the mayor for confirmation. He nodded assent.

"Three men at each of those two spots," I instructed my adjutant, "armed with rifles. Guard those boats. Quickly." I paused. "And after that's done, alert the guards at the harbor. I don't want any boats sailing from the docks with escapees."

The latter order was irrelevant at this time of day: all of the thirty or so of Kralendijk's trawlers were out working.

Off he went at a run, legs flailing. I asked my secretary to call in Klijnstra and Bergman, my two underofficers. With escape routes blocked, there was no further rush. We could now organize the next step: rounding up the escapees.

Our meeting was short. Our first priority was locating the stolen jeep. There were only two real roads on Bonaire: the beach road that circumnavigated the island, and the other that cut across the middle from Kralendijk to the opposite shoreline. Off those roads were a few dead-end tracks that led into the brush or down to the sea. I would take the beach road to the north, Klijnstra would take it to the south. Bergman would take the road across the island. We would all meet at the juncture of the roads on the far side of the island. Three other jeeps would follow on those three routes, but they would poke around any of the dead-end trails that showed recent use. Three men to a jeep with rifles and walkie-talkies. Keep in touch.

As we left the prison compound, I ordered my driver to drive to my house first. I wanted Margery to know what had happened. Her face went blank when I told her about the escaped prisoners, and she started to shake as I handed her one of my service revolvers—"just in case." She clutched me, murmuring, "The war, the war." After a moment, she let me go.

"Sorry," she whispered. "It overwhelmed me. I was being sucked back to the front. It felt as if we were in Berlin." She smiled awkwardly. "I had almost forgotten that there was a war." She gave me a quick kiss. "Be careful."

I got in the passenger's seat of the open jeep, instructed the soldier in the back to have his rifle at the ready as I laid mine across my knees, and we headed north.

The driver said his name was Nico; he had worked for Shell in the oil fields in Venezuela before the war. A big man, bigger than me. He looked out of place driving the jeep, the steering wheel too small for his hands, the seat too small for his bulk. He belonged in the cab of an enormous lorry. He drove without a care in the world, throwing up a cloud of dust behind us, bouncing and swerving, tearing up the countryside. The private in the back hung on for dear life. His name was Smit. He'd also worked for Shell before the war, but as an accountant in Shell's Willemstad office. Small of stature, squinting through his glasses as if he was half blind, looking every bit the accountant he had been. I hoped he knew how to shoot.

The landscape was desolate—thorny brush, stunted divi-divi trees, black rocks. As we crested rises, we could see the blue of the sea in the distance, always to our left as we circled the island. All three of us scanned the brush for signs of a jeep, Smit looking left while I concentrated on the right. Nico seemed to look everywhere except the road, which had been wide enough for two cars as we left Kralendijk, but had dwindled quickly to a track the width of the jeep. As we drove, I wondered what awaited us. Five men, at least one pistol. Apparently no rifles. They could be dangerous if they jumped us, but at a distance the pistol or pistols would be no match for our rifles. If we could avoid an ambush, we'd be all right.

As we approached the junction of the coast road and the road that cut across the island, we could see a jeep. That would be Bergman: his was the shortest of the three routes we were patrolling. He waved as we neared, obviously excited.

"They're at Lacre Point!" he shouted. "Hendrix was waiting in the road there when Klijnstra arrived."

Hendrix, I guessed, was one of the three troops we had dispatched to guard Wouter's anchorage.

"They found the jeep, the sailboat is still moored offshore. No sign of the escapees."

I nodded toward his walkie-talkie. "Tell him that we're coming. Tell them to do nothing until we get there."

We all clambered back into the two jeeps. Nico headed out as if he were a gazelle with a starving cheetah right behind him. It took me a few moments to slow his pace. We weren't about to be eaten, but we did want to arrive alive. Bergman's jeep followed in our wake.

As we approached Lacre Point, I could see the acres and acres of salt pans running from the edge of the road in descending terraces to the sea. The terraces were irregular in shape, their form, curves, and size dictated by the topography. All were perfectly flat and level. Each pan was covered by a film of water perhaps a half inch in depth. At the downhill edge of each salt pan, a spillway led to the salt pan below. Small windmills on spindly steel legs turned rusted blades in the trade wind, pumping water from the sea to the topmost salt pans. From there the water would leak down from terrace to terrace until it spilled back into the waves below. Every week or two the pumps would be stopped, the last of the water in the salt pans would be left to evaporate, and the salt crust covering the pans would be harvested. Primitive and ingenious.

We pulled over to speak to a man, his wife, and their ten-year-old boy, who were raking the salt in one of the dry pans into wheelbarrows. Their shanty could be seen pinched between the salt pans and the sea. Not much of a house, but the view? Spectacular. Had they seen the escapees? No, they hadn't. Five men. If you see them, let us know. Be careful.

Hardly a mile farther, three jeeps came into view. The two on the road in front of Wouter's house would be those of Hendrix and Klijnstra; the one dumped into the brush a few hundred yards farther on would be the POWs'. Wouter's boat bobbed at its mooring. Two soldiers sat on an overturned skiff on the shore. Good. That blocked any chance of flight in that direction.

"Any sign of them?" I asked as we pulled up and cut the motors. From the jeeps, I could see a kilometer or two in all directions. Hendrix and Klijnstra both shook their heads. "Anybody home?" I nodded toward the house. Again no.

"What do you think?" I asked. "You've been looking it over. Where do we start?"

Along the shore it was rocky; inland there was heavy brush. From the direction Nico and I had just come, the salt pans offered little cover. If someone wanted to hide, the brush would be where they'd go. If someone hoped to escape, they'd probably stick to the shore, hoping against hope to find some sort of boat. I walked to the jeep the escapees had dumped off the road. No footprints that I could see. But the jeep was on the ocean side of the road. I decided we'd begin by working along the shoreline, starting at the house and moving away from the salt pans.

"Two men here," I said, indicating our three jeeps, "and two over there at their jeep." I waved toward the overturned skiff. "And the two down there stay where they are. Anything moves"—I tapped the walkie-talkie—"let us know immediately. The rest of you come with me." I started toward the beach. "Fan out. Twenty meters apart. Stay in line. Cover each other. Don't forget, they have at least one pistol."

One of the men looked at me questioningly. "If they shoot?"

"Return fire. Shoot to kill." I paused. "But let's not let it get that far. Let's bring them in peacefully."

The six of us spread out in a line, me at the end near the surf, the other end 150 yards inland up toward the road. The walking was difficult. The brush thick, anywhere from knee high to chin high, and the terrain under the brush treacherous with lava rocks, both fixed and loose, with bumps and holes hidden below, lying in wait to trip us. Along the shoreline, breakers pounded on huge boulders and outcroppings, shooting white water high into the air. Or the waves ran a few meters up the shingled beach, where the slope of the land was more peaceful. I'd taken this end of the line: if I were an escapee, this was where I'd take a stand. Protected by the rolling breakers on one side, I'd pick a spot to hide behind some boulders, where I'd have a view of my surroundings. Each time I approached a potential hideout of this sort, I slowed my pace, moved forward cautiously. As I had told the men, the only real danger was an ambush.

The going was a slog. After the first hundred meters I was drenched with sweat, continually mopping my brow with my handkerchief. The sun beat down on us, the brush scratched at our legs and torsos. The breeze from the trade wind helped, but mostly it was hot. The men had been calling back and forth at the start, laughing at one another when someone stumbled and fell. After the first half kilometer they were mostly silent, focused on their walking and on scanning the brush near them for any sign of the POWs.

After about forty-five minutes, we reached an area where the land dipped, and we could no longer see Wouter's house or his boat. Ahead the land rose again, and our struggle to push through the brush intensified as we began up the incline. At the end of an hour, we would turn and sweep back. And then a shot. All of us ducked instinctively. Curiously, the shot didn't frighten us. Presumably it had been fired to kill one of us, but the sound of the pistol, it was definitely a pistol, was childish in this wide open space, seemingly less dangerous than the noise of the breeze and the breakers.

The man at the far end of the line yelled, "I see them!" He pointed at a spot perhaps a hundred meters in front of me. "Over there, between those two big rocks."

"Move back!" I yelled at the men. "Move back out of range." After we had all moved back, I ordered them to surround the POWs. "Janssen." I pointed to the man farthest from me. "Circle around to the shore on the other side." And to the four who had been working the middle of the line, "And you guys spread out to trap them in the semicircle. Each time you see them, fire over their heads. Let's keep them pinned down where they are. Don't let them break out."

In a few minutes the six of us had taken positions in a wide arc around the two rocks the POWs were crouched behind. We were out of pistol range to all but the luckiest shot, but within easy killing range for our rifles. We assumed that the five escapees were together, although we'd seen no more than a movement now and then from at most two people at a time. Janssen had begun to move toward the rocks where the escapees were hiding. Proceeding along the shoreline, he was scurrying from one rock to the next, careful to stay out of sight. He closed to within a hundred meters with little trouble, then to seventy-five meters, and then ever more slowly to fifty meters or so. As he started to move toward the next rock, one of the POWs straightened from behind the boulders and fired. Janssen fell from view. Wounded? Dead? I called out.

He answered with a laugh. "He couldn't hit an elephant at ten paces! He wasn't even close." But he stopped his approach, hiding where he was.

We baked in the sun for ten minutes, thirty minutes. Without shade, we were all perspiring, wiping sweat to keep it out of our eyes. Time was on our side. We were not in danger. They were. We could move back to Wouter's house for shade and water if and when we needed to. They couldn't. After an hour, I decided to try to end the standoff. The hopelessness of the situation would have sunk in on the escapees by now. They had been here an hour longer than we had with nothing to drink and no way to escape.

Time to give them a way out.

I stood up, moved completely into the open where they could see me. *"Heren!"* I called, using a voice of authority, an officer speaking to soldiers. In German, "Let's talk."

I moved toward them through the brush, keeping to the open, making sure I could be plainly seen from the rocks where they were

194

hiding, holding my white handkerchief up high. I was now within a hundred meters, then seventy-five. Then a shot. The crack of the pistol was still that of a toy gun, but the buzz of the bullet near my head spoke eloquently. I stopped. Despite the instinct to duck into cover, I pretended nonchalance. After a moment I repeated, more casually this time, "Let's talk."

I could now see two of the POWs standing up, one holding a pistol. All I could see of the pistol, on which my attention was transfixed, was the hole at the end of the barrel. Perhaps in my subconscious I thought I would see the bullet as it came out of the barrel and have time to duck. Still speaking German, I continued calmly, "Look. We have a problem. I am here to bring you back to the prison camp. You are here trying to escape. Right now, we can do neither." I paused. "If we continue as we are doing, someone is going to get killed."

I took off my hat, took off my pistol belt, careful to be obvious as to what I was doing. Hung the hat and the pistol belt on a bush, stood my rifle up against it as well, and then held my two hands high in the air, my white handkerchief in one of them.

"Let's you and me talk. You have the pistol. If you want, you can kill me. If you do, you know that my comrades will bring in reinforcements and that all five of you will be killed as well. None of us wants that to happen." I chuckled. "Especially me, because I would be first!"

I started forward, trying as much as the brush would permit to act as if I were strolling with my sweetheart in the park on a Sunday afternoon. I trusted that being spoken to in German would make the escapees less inclined to shoot. That black hole of the pistol pointing at me was, however, unnerving. So far, the POWs hadn't said a word. Nor had the pistol moved. I continued my imitation of a nonchalant stroll. Sweat ran down into my eyes. I wanted to wipe my brow with my white handkerchief, but thought better of it. A movement toward my face might cause that trigger finger to twitch.

I was close enough now to make an easy instep pass to either of the two men I could see. If we were on a football pitch. If we were playing football. But we weren't playing. I stopped walking. Still speaking in German, I suggested to the two of them that the pistol was making me nervous, that this was no way to welcome their new commandant. My heart was pounding. I hoped my voice sounded like I was making an amusing jest and not like the dirge of the drumbeat in my chest. Over my shoulder I called to my troops, "Stand up so you can be clearly seen. Put down your rifles."

When the five of them were in plain view, I turned back to the POWs. "How about pointing that pistol in the air? It's making me feel unwelcome."

The pistol pointed at me did not budge. Time froze. Behind the two POWs, the breakers roared and crashed on the rocks, stark contrast to the serenity of the distant horizon, where the blue of the ocean morphed seamlessly into the blue of the sky. The eternal trade wind blew across the waves. Two gulls cried forlornly. The three of us stood, hardly blinking. It was the moment when a bird dog was on point, dog and bird transfixed, mesmerized, tied by an invisible bond, neither able to budge.

I gathered myself. Time to break the stalemate. "Let's talk first," I suggested. "Then you can shoot me if you want."

The pistol moved. The arm holding it dropped a few inches, and the barrel was no longer pointing at my forehead. If the finger on the trigger twitched now, the bullet would hit my abdomen. Why, I thought, did that make me feel better?

"Are you German?" the armed POW asked.

"Not exactly." I pointed to my uniform and tried to chuckle. I hoped I sounded carefree and amused. "I'm from Enschede."

There was a flicker of recognition; he seemed to know Enschede. I sensed a turning of the tide.

"Just across the border from Gronau," I added. "Near Munster and Osnabruck."

At the mention of the German towns, the pistol barrel dropped a few more inches. I breathed a sigh of relief. If the finger tightened now, the bullet would hit the brush somewhere near my feet.

The POW spoke again. "My grandfather owns a farm near Rheine." Wistfully, he added, "Before the war I spent all my summers there." He seemed to be speaking to himself. "In Ochtrup. He had cows. I would milk them every morning. In the dark." He was remembering. "And again in the evening before nightfall. Then Oma would serve us a supper of cheese and brown bread and fresh milk." He paused. "Do you know Ochtrup?"

Rheine and Ochtrup were even nearer to Enschede than Munster and Osnabruck, though not as near as Gronau. His grandfather and my family lived within a few miles of each other. Now that the pistol was no longer pointed at my head, I had a moment to look at the man himself. Hardly a man at all. Nineteen years old? Twenty? Called up by the Führer from the Hitler Jeugd at the age of sixteen? His grandparents and my parents were basically neighbors.

"I've been in Rheine," I told him. "I know where Ochtrup is. My father has a farm in Hengelo." It was a small lie. Not even really a lie. We did have a farm in Hengelo, and it was where Vader was living when he died, but it was more of a gentleman's farm. Vader was largely retired then, but still making his living from his bakery in Enschede. I figured I was better off to sell myself as the son of a farmer than as the son of a merchant.

"C'mon," I said. "Let me sit down and let's talk." I took a tentative step forward. "We have a problem to solve. I think we can solve it in a matter of minutes." I took another small step forward, watching the German's reaction. He wavered for a moment. "Go ahead, it's all right. Keep the pistol pointed at me, but let me sit down."

I moved to his side of the rock. Yes, there were five men in all. The two men to whom I had been talking sat down across from me. The other three, who had been crouching out of sight, now stood up and moved back a few feet, wary. The pistol was still at the ready but not pointed directly at me. That was a good sign.

"Look," I said, watching the five men, sizing them up. They were all young, about the same age as Mr. Pistol. "Before we begin solving our problem here"—I gestured at the six of us and the five soldiers standing in the brush fifty meters from us—"you could do me a favor. As you know, I became the commandant of your camp just two days ago. I was sent to clean up the mess here on Bonaire. Headquarters thinks the camp has been run poorly, that you and the other POWs are being treated unfairly."

I could see I had them now. Their heads nodded subconsciously in agreement.

"I plan to meet tomorrow with the whole camp. I want to introduce myself."

They were trying to remain expressionless, as if in a high-stakes poker game, yet each face twitched ever so slightly. I had dealt them a card they had not expected. They were surprised that the commandant would think to meet with the POWs. It would be a first, as well I knew.

"When I meet with everyone tomorrow, I'll be telling them that I want to know the problems we all have. Food, clothing, schedules, organization, job assignments, health, housing, interaction with my troops …" I let my voice trail off. "I want to be certain that everyone knows that I'm serious about wanting to learn what the problems are and serious about wanting to deal with them." I paused. "I'll be asking you and your friends to designate a committee to compile a list of problems, report them to me, and work with me to resolve them."

I could see they were listening. Their eyebrows rose slightly, questioning. They were wondering what I wanted from them.

"What you could do for me is to alert your friends of the purpose of our meeting tomorrow. And when you do—and this is the important part—please make it clear that I am serious about this matter. I want to make changes. I want to improve camp conditions. My orders are to clean up the mess, and I need their help to do this."

Slight nods of assent from the two sitting across from me, mimicked after a short pause by the three others. For a minute we continued to glance back and forth at one another in silence, but now that my speech was over, it was time to deal with the matter at hand. The aside had bought me some time and, I hoped, some good will.

"Okay. Look, you guys are in a pickle. There are three spots on this island where there are boats. Here"—I gestured down the coast toward Wouter's house and his sailboat—"at Pink Beach, and in the harbor at Kralendijk. I have troops guarding all three spots." I let that sink in for a moment. "There's no way you can get off the island." I let it sink in some more. Their faces showed that they believed me. "Right now you are surrounded by five rifles. There are six more up at the house. If I pick up the walkie-talkie, I can have thirty more rifles here in an hour." I shrugged, palms up. "If you resist, you will either be captured or killed."

A particularly large wave punctuated my remarks, spraying the six of us with foam. They were looking at me, wondering what my next move would be.

I changed pace, gesturing at the five of them and at myself. "You and I have been swept into a war. Before your country invaded mine, we were neighbors. No matter who wins the war, after it's over, we will be neighbors again." I focused that remark on Mr. Pistol. "No matter who wins, at the end of the fighting, everyone in the camp will be set free. You will be set free, either by the Germans or by the Dutch. Maybe this year. Maybe next year?"

The three men standing shifted their weight from one foot to the other.

"Being a prisoner is no picnic, but I promise that things are going to be better." Another pause. We listened for a moment to the breakers. "Return to camp, go free in a year?" I pointed to my five soldiers. "Or shoot it out and be killed?"

A long pause, and then Mr. Pistol asked, "What do you do to us if we surrender here?"

I rubbed my chin, as if thinking. "Down the road a bit I saw a big pothole. What say if we go there and the five of you spend a half hour filling and repairing it?" Their eyebrows rose again in question. "Then we could say that you were out of the camp on work release. Work release … An important first step in the commandant's new program to better relations between the POWs and the community."

"That's all?" Mr. Pistol asked in astonishment. "No punishment?"

"Not if you hand over the pistol." I smiled. "And you need to promise to participate in the new work-release program that I will be announcing tomorrow."

I took the pistol with my left hand and shook Mr. Pistol's hand with my right. His shake was tentative. As I began the circle of shaking hands with each of them in turn, each grip became firmer. After completing the round, I shook hands once more with Mr. Pistol. This time his was a firm grip, a solid clasp. We both smiled. We were equally relieved. I slapped Mr. Pistol on the back. He was almost young enough to be my son. The six of us started through the brush back toward the road. I waved to the five troops to shoulder their weapons and join us.

The filling of the pothole went quickly, especially since I ordered my soldiers to help. The drive back to Kralendijk was another matter. Our lives were in constant peril, not because of the POWs, but because Nico insisted on displaying how fast a jeep could go on a dirt road when safety was of no concern. Upon returning to my house I was almost killed again, this time by Margery's hug. I joked with her that I was in more danger of dying from the ferocity of her squeeze than I had been from the pistol pointed at me by the escapees. She wasn't smiling. Tears came to her eyes as she squeezed harder. Being reminded of the war had shaken her, but it took just a moment for her smile to return and for her to plant a kiss on my cheek.

Hoofdstuk 35

7 maart 1944: US Air Force loses sixty-eight planes as eight hundred US heavy bombers, mostly Liberators and Flying Fortresses, protected by Mustangs, Thunderbolts, and Lightnings, wreak havoc on Berlin. Marshal Zhukov's troops continue assault, take Odessa-Lwow railroad; Moscow reports 15,000 German deaths in the two-day offensive. Fifth Army advance at the Anzio beachhead in Italy stalls. On the Asian front, troops under Lieutenant General Stilwell mount attack in northern Burma.

Despite its inauspicious start with the prison break, Bonaire turned into a whirl. Carl had whisked us onto a boat in Willemstad and off to Kralendijk. No Shieshie, no Yohannita, no Wanga. The town was no town at all, hardly more than a fisherman's pier, a cluster of fishing shacks, and a clutch of a dozen or so houses. The remainder of the island reminded me of No Man's Land—almost no hills except at the north end; no trees; a wilderness of thick brush; and everywhere the sea. In contrast to No Man's were the persistent cacti, the lava rock of the coast, and the delicious tropical breeze. Other than the houses of Kralendijk, the gravel and sand roads, and the fishing shacks, the only sign of man was the prisoner of war camp—hardly more than a few tin shacks surrounded by frightful fences of barbed wire—and the salt pans on Lacre Point at the south end of the island. The nearest swimming was at Pink Beach, almost a half hour by the gravel track we called the coast road. Electricity came from the town generator that fed the few houses and the POW camp. I could set my watch by the generator: its roar commenced promptly at six each evening, and the silence was deafening at ten, punctuated by darkness as the lights went out.

Carl had announced that our stay would be short. He had hardly been assigned when he learned that he would be posted to Aruba. Thus the decision that Shieshie, Yohannita, and Wanga would not come with us. That our time there would be short transformed our stay into a holiday visit. Our house was the largest in Kralendijk, which said little. The windows had no glass, only louvered shutters that I opened wide to the sun and sea air each morning and shut tight every night to quiet the breeze, to observe the blackout restrictions, and to keep out the cats. We had almost no furniture, which made the airy rooms with their twelve-foot-high ceilings seem uncomfortably empty. The entry of the house was up long wooden steps to a porch that overlooked the town "square"—no more than a small hard-packed dirt space shared by four or five small houses and our rather larger one, and a small warehouse.

The town pier was abuzz with activity at dawn, when the town's dozen fishing boats cast off. The rest of the day the hamlet appeared deserted but for an occasional old man or two fishing from the dock, or a mother with a clutch of children headed for an errand at the town's only "store," another euphemism for the front room of one of the houses on the square that was lined with shelves stocked with canned and dried goods. Refrigerators were a luxury unknown on Bonaire. The only fresh food on the island was fish, available on the town pier every evening when the trawlers returned from their fishing. The military sent us a boat once a week with food for Carl's troops and the prisoners of war, including any items that I ordered through Carl's supply officer. There was no meat, except for the ubiquitous cans of Spam.

Not much to remark about in the hamlet, although I did write to family and friends about the cats. Feral cats roamed everywhere in the town. Their main focus was the offal of the fishery processing plant next to the pier, where each day's catch was cleaned and iced. The heaps of guts, fins, scales, and bones attracted both flies and cats. The latter were suffered. They were preferable to rats, which were the alternative. So cats roamed everywhere in the hamlet. Each household took measures to protect itself against the marauders. Dogs, shuttered windows, cat-proof walls surrounding gardens.

The evening Carl and I returned from the good-bye party for the commander Carl was replacing, we entered the house to find one of these wild cats right in the middle of the dining room table, feasting on the remnants of our dinner. We had not yet learned the necessity of closing the shutters upon leaving the house. Carl pulled his service revolver out of its holster and waved it at the cat to frighten it. The cat was unfazed by the danger posed by an unholstered weapon and did not abandon his meal. Carl approached, spoke loudly, and the cat grudgingly leaped to the floor. It backed away a few feet, apparently assuming it would finish its meal once Carl, the intruder as the cat viewed it, left him alone. Carl waved his pistol some more; the cat, not knowing my husband as I did, stubbornly held its ground. Carl aimed the pistol and put his finger on the trigger. While the cat had not been worried about a pistol being waved in the air, it apparently was aware of the danger of a pistol pointed at it. Just as Carl squeezed the trigger, the cat leaped for the sill of the open window and disappeared into the night. Where the cat had sat on the floor there was now a hole. Carl was dumbfounded by his miss, appreciated the kiss from me to assuage his pride, and was embarrassed for weeks thereafter every time I teased him as we sat at the dinner table and looked at the hole in the floor.

Hoofdstuk 36

22 maart 1944: Nazi troops sweep into Hungary to smother resistance to German occupation there. Analysts expect Bulgaria and Romania to share Hungary's fate in the next days. Red Army makes gains against Germans, secures another strategic crossing of Dniester River. Marines under virulent air cover sweep ashore, overwhelm Japanese forces on Emirau Island, establish US air base 600 miles from Truk Island.

My birthday! My birthday! No sooner did I wake than those words sang in my head. March 22, 1944. I could do the arithmetic, though I didn't need to. Nine years old. Papa had said that he had a special present for me, a surprise. An exciting surprise. I brushed my teeth, threw on my clothes. Alex was already in the kitchen. He was always awake before me. He yelled, *"Gefeliciteerd!"* and spanked me nine times while I was standing. I laughed. He couldn't hurt me. He tried to spank harder; I just laughed more. Mama said happy birthday and gave me a hug and nine kisses. Papa was already at work.

Mama made me scrambled eggs and toast, my favorite breakfast, and I drank orange juice. Because it was my birthday she didn't make me drink my Klim. Klim was horrid stuff. Because of the war, we couldn't buy real milk. Klim was *milk* spelled backward. And it was truly backward stuff. A white powder that came in a yellow can as big as a cookie jar. Mixed with water, it was nasty. Mama always made us drink a glass for breakfast and another for lunch. Good for our bones and teeth, she said. Icky, we said.

Right after breakfast, Mama let me open one birthday present. A Dutch football team jersey! As we waited for Papa to come—Mama said she expected him in an hour or two—I put on the jersey, and Alex and I went down the stairs to play football in the town square.

Under the overhang of our porch was a big door that swung open, like a garage door. It was kept closed by a hasp with a padlock. Behind

205

the door was a kind of cellar where Mama stored all her canned foods, soaps, toilet paper, brooms, mops, rags, and other junk. She called it her super pantry. Carlos, our new helper, kept the space organized, put everything in its place in there for her, and fetched for her whatever she needed. He wouldn't let us in there, wouldn't let anyone in there. Mama's rule was that if anything went missing, it came out of Carlos's pay. Carlos made sure that nothing was ever missing. There were only two keys to the padlock. Mama had one, Carlos had the other.

The big door made a great football goal. Alex and I never called it *soccer*. We always said football, or *voetbal* in Dutch. Everyone in the world said football. Even in England it was football. Only the Americans called it soccer. The Americans were retarded. Even worse, American kids didn't even know the rules of the game.

Alex played keeper. He set up in front of the cellar door, and I took penalty kicks. Sometimes we changed places, but that wasn't much fun. Alex wasn't strong enough to take penalty kicks, and he could never score on me. The cellar door made a great goal. If I shot near the edge, though, Alex would argue that I had missed. Since we needed a referee to decide if it was a goal or not, we decided that I would be the referee. It made sense. As a shooter, I had a better angle, I could see the goal better. The keeper can't see the goal as well as the shooter can. Anyway, I was older than Alex. After a while, he agreed that I would be the ref.

With Alex in goal, I would take five shots, like a shoot-out. If I made three, I won. If I didn't, he won. We always played for the World Cup. No friendlies for us. I was always the Dutch team, and today was even better: I had on my new orange jersey. Usually I told Alex he was the German team. We hated the German team. Sometimes I would let him be France or Italy.

As soon as Papa returned from the POW camp, he and Mama and I climbed into the car. Mama had packed a big picnic basket full of food ready for our lunch. At first I thought we might be going to hunt goats, but Papa hadn't brought a gun. Alex wanted to come with us, but Mama said that he had to stay with Margy and Fenneke and Sofia, the maid. She was okay, but nowhere near as nice as Shieshie or Yohannita.

In about the time that it takes me to dribble the length of a football pitch, Papa parked the car at the pier and announced that we were going fishing. Alex and I had fished off the pier before, so I didn't see how this was much of a surprise, but then I realized Papa had rented a boat. We were going to fish off a real fishing boat! I should have realized it right away. During the middle of the day there were never any boats moored at the dock. They were all out fishing. Papa laughed at the smile on my face. Wow! No hand line from the pier to catch flounders. Real tackle, rod and reel, to troll for tuna. The sun played brighter on the water than it ever had, the pelican sitting on the piling of the pier seemed to smile at me. My lucky day! I could feel it—I was going to catch a big one. And I meant it, a really big one!

Captain Diego gave me a hand as I stepped across the gunwale. Sinta was his first mate. Both of them had faces like the sailors on board Captain Horatio Hornblower's *Lydia*: wrinkles, creases, skin tanned like leather. They were real seamen, real fisherman. Papa was also excited. Mama should have been frightened like Lady Barbara Wellesley, but she wasn't. On Cape Cod and across to No Man's Land, she had done a lot of sailing. She had even sailed on the Mediterranean and off the British coast with Grandfather Crane. Mama was amazing. She had traveled a lot, done a lot of stuff, but I'd bet she had never caught a tuna as large as the one I was going to catch today!

Captain Diego cast off, and it wasn't long before we were bouncing and swaying through real waves. Every time we bounced, the bow threw spray into the air. Once in a while I got wet, but most of the time the spray just caressed me, and my lips tasted salty. We were really on the ocean! The dock and the houses of Kralendijk receded in the distance, although if I looked hard, I could still make out where they were.

Sinta rigged a rod for me and showed me how to hold it using a belt with a leather cup attached to it. I had to place the butt of the rod in the cup and hold the rod with two hands. To reel in, I had to pump the rod and then reel as I eased the rod's tip back toward the bait. He had attached a treble hook to the line—big hooks, much larger than I had ever used, bigger than my small finger. To that he threaded a long strip of squid.

He cast the line and showed me how to let it run out behind the boat. I could see the strip of squid dancing on the waves, then diving into the water, and then dancing on the surface again. The bait was a long distance away, about as far as I could kick a ball with a really good kick. After a few minutes, my arms tired from the strain of tugging on the rod. Sinta showed me how to fasten the rod into a holder on the gunwale at the stern. Wow, that was neat! No hands!

After a while, Mama opened the picnic basket. She had made egg salad sandwiches. She said she was sorry she hadn't been able to make my favorite, a ham and cheese sandwich. There were lots of chickens on the island, so getting eggs was no problem. But because of the war, the only meat was Spam and, occasionally, iguana and goat when Papa had the time to hunt. She also had a bunch of cute baby bananas, bananas no longer than half a pencil and fat as two fingers. Before Curacao and Bonaire, I had never seen bananas so small. Best of all, there was no Klim. Mama had made lemonade. Getting lemons was also no problem, although she had to be careful not to use too much sugar. Sugar was rationed. We could only buy it when we received a rationing card.

A hit! Sinta grabbed the rod and set the hook with a sharp tug. He handed me the rod, but I couldn't hold it by myself. The fish pulled too hard. So Sinta sat me on his lap and helped. At first I couldn't see the fish, I could only feel him tug, but then he started to jump. Sinta shouted. He was laughing and swearing in Papiamento. A tuna! He was far bigger than Fenneke, maybe even as big as Margy. He looked black some of the times, indigo when the sun flashed on him, and glittery silver on his sides and belly. As he pulled and jumped, Sinta kept telling me, "Let him run!" and "Slowly, slowly." He didn't want to break the line. Papa was laughing and yelling, while Mama was worried the fish would pull me overboard. After a while, Sinta told me to start pumping and reeling, though not too hard. Little by little, the line got shorter. Then Sinta asked Papa to help me with the rod while he scrambled for the gaff. We maneuvered the fish nearer the stern, and with a quick thrust, Sinta gaffed the tuna and heaved it into the boat. As it flipped and flopped, Sinta clubbed him. He still moved, but now it was rigor mortis. I had read about that.

Papa scooped me into his arms and hugged me as Sinta measured the tuna. Thirty-five inches!

"Wow!" Papa said, putting me down. "When I was nine years old, I was fishing in a canal and catching fish this long."

He held up his two hands, showing a fish nine or ten inches long. Mama also hugged me. This was my best birthday ever.

It was the only hit we had, but I didn't need another. This one was great all by itself. Mama was already planning how best to prepare tuna steaks for dinner.

As we neared Kralendijk, Papa wondered how awake his troops were.

There was a no-boat zone off the island just in front of the POW camp. To avoid prisoner escapes and possible rescue attempts, machine gun emplacements ringed the barbed wire of the camp. More gun emplacements fronted the camp where it ran along the rocky coast. Boats were forbidden within two kilometers of the shore at that point.

As we neared Kralendijk, Papa told Captain Diego to set a course parallel to the coast, along the shore. Captain Diego protested. The course Papa was instructing him to take would pass right in front of the POW camp, smack through the middle of the no-boat zone.

"Can't do it, sir," the captain said. "Not allowed. They have orders to shoot us."

Papa laughed. "Exactly. Those orders are mine."

Diego protested again. Mama sided with him, but Papa just chuckled, "My boys know I'm on the boat. I want to see what they'll do."

So Diego changed course and we headed for the POW camp, parallel to the shoreline. Nothing at first. In front of us a buoy marked the start of the no-boat zone. As we closed on the buoy, Mama and I jumped as if stung by a snake. A machine gun had frightened us with its rattle. Splashes appeared on the water in front of us. It was exactly like in the Horatio Hornblower books: the captain would fire his cannon across the bow of the ship as a warning. This was exciting! Mama kept saying Papa's name, and Papa laughed and told Diego to turn the boat around and run back to the pier in Kralendijk.

Captain Diego asked Papa how he would punish the troops who had fired at him. The brig? Papa told him that as soon as he found out who the responsible parties were, he would give each of them a week's leave. Diego seemed surprised.

"Orders are orders," Papa said, "even though it might have been difficult for them since they knew they were firing at me." He laughed again. "Maybe it wasn't so difficult. They were probably laughing themselves silly!"

Hoofdstuk 37

28 maart 1944: Luftwaffe rains explosives, incendiary bombs on London for more than an hour while the RAF pounds Berlin, Leipzig, and Weimar. Russians make gains near Voznesensk, Beltsy, and the Dniester River. British imperial forces drive back Japanese on invasion route into India.

School, school, school. Mama said I didn't like it because I had had too many teachers. She ticked them off for me. Did I remember the playgroup in Cheshire with Mrs. Singer, the fat lady with the big glasses? In her house up the road on Jinny Hill Road? No, I didn't remember. Then in Stratford, the *kleuterschool* run by the army? I did remember that, with Mevrouw van Bos and the really neat indoor playground. She'd had a jungle gym and a sandbox in her classroom. And then the public preschool in Stratford, with Mrs. … What was her name? Mama wondered. The young, cute one, blond, big blue eyes? Then she remembered—Miss Overton. Yes, now I remembered too. I had taken the bus with Jan in the morning. I had gone only two days a week, and Mama would walk me home at lunchtime. Jan came back home later on the bus. I had really liked Miss Overton.

Then what? Mama said. The year before, in Willemstad, I had gone to the *kleuterschool* for a few weeks with Jeffrouw Steen. Did I remember? In her house? I did remember. She was old and tall and ugly and nasty. Mama had taken me out of her school and started me in Jan's school five mornings a week. Yohannita had walked me there every morning and walked me back for lunch. That teacher, Mevrouw de Haan, had been okay. And after Willemstad, in Bronxville, I started real kindergarten. Miss James. I nodded. I had really liked her. And Jimmy had been my best friend. He and I had played soldiers at recess, and we had shot all the girls. They were spies.

And now, Mama said, you will finish kindergarten here in Kralendijk. She had met Mevrouw Hendrik that morning, and she seemed very nice. Mama explained that the school was all one big room sort of divided in half. Mevrouw Hendrik taught the younger children in half of the room; the teacher for the older ones was Mevrouw de Jong. Jan would be with the older students. There were about eighteen pupils in all. And yes, some of them would be way bigger than Jan, who would be with the third graders. One of the girls would be an eighth grader. Wow! That was old! I liked it that Jan would be in the same classroom.

Mama laughed. "You have already been in six schools. This will be number seven! You must be really smart. Some people go to only two or three schools during their whole life. And for you, it's been like Ping Pong, one school in Dutch, then one in English. This one will be in Dutch." She hugged me. "You and Jan are really special."

Mama was wrong. She had said that I would like Mevrow Hendrik. I didn't. She was strict and mean, and she would use her ruler to hit my friends on the knuckles. She hit so hard, they would cry. That was mean. Nobody liked her. We called her Mrs. Big Butt because she had the biggest rear end you've ever seen. It was like a giant football that wasn't inflated enough. It squished and squashed back and forth every time she walked.

The only good thing about school was recess. The playground was almost as big as our classroom, with a high chain-link fence all the way around. The bigger boys played football. We hung old rags on the chain-link fence to mark the goal posts. Jan could score on the far goal from his own goal. Most of the little kids weren't allowed to play; the big boys would tell them no. But Jan was one of the best players, except for two older boys in sixth grade, and he told the boys to let me play. That was the best part of school. Jan scored a lot. When I got a goal, the big boys would cheer and say, *"Mooi!"* or *"Goed zo!"* I was kind of their mascot. And sometimes we would play marbles. My shooter marble was almost all green, with a bit of clear and a bit of white. I kept it on the nightstand next to my bed at home and in my pocket at school. Some of the boys were really good at marbles.

And then one day, I finally got revenge on Mrs. Big Butt. Henkie was pulling his little sister's hair, and she was crying. Piet, Toop, and Karel were trading marbles and had begun to argue. Herman was passing notes to Miep. She was his girlfriend. Yuk. She didn't even know how to kick a football. Then Mevrouw Hendrik swooped in with her ruler. Everybody had to place their hands flat on their desks. She made her way around the classroom, snapping her ruler across knuckles. And she wasn't even fair.

She hit the boys harder than she hit the girls. She skipped Anneke and Piet. Anneke and Piet were her pets. Most of the girls were crying. The boys tried not to. Then Big Butt snapped her ruler across my knuckles. Boy, did it make me mad! And I hadn't even been bad!

As she turned away from my desk, her voluminous butt was bouncing right in front of my desk, right in front of my face, right in front of my nose. I grabbed my ruler and slapped that butt just as hard as I could. It made a sound that was half *splat* and half *splosh*. Boy, did that feel good!

The whole class went silent. Big Butt turned around. Her face was beet red with anger. She was about to explode, and I imagined there would be red globs of her stuck all over the walls and ceiling of the classroom. Nobody breathed. Everyone waited for the explosion. She was mad, but I was madder. I placed my ruler back on my desk, waved my finger at her, and told her that if she ever hit me with her ruler again, I would tell my father and she would be in that POW camp so fast, her head would spin.

Boy, talk about scared! Her face went from red to white quicker than an Abe Lenstra penalty kick takes to reach the corner of the net. Without a word, she went back to her desk. The kids didn't whisper a peep, not even when the bell rang. But outside the school, everyone was pounding me on my back, and the little kids were telling the big kids what I had done. Everyone was describing the sound of the ruler when it hit Big Butt. I was proud to be the kid whose father could put the teacher in jail!

At dinner that night, Papa asked how my day at school had been. It was the moment I had been waiting for. I hadn't told Mama because I wanted to be the one who told Papa. So I spilled it out, how mean Big Butt was, how she had hit everyone with her ruler except Anneke and Piet, how she hit the boys harder than the girls, how kids were crying, how she hit me even though I hadn't done anything except maybe talk, how big and squishy her butt was and how it bounced and jounced when she walked, how I had hit her back and how red and mad her face had been. And then, proudest of all, how I had waved my finger at her and told her my papa would throw her in the POW camp if she ever hit me again.

How I got upside down, I don't know. Papa was holding me by the ankles with one hand, way up high. My head was hanging toward the floor. It made me think of the poster in my room of Abe Lenstra upside down in the air, doing a bicycle kick with the football flying by the

213

keeper. Before I could finish that thought, Papa was laying into me with the other hand. It was a big hand. He could hold a football in one hand and throw it as if it were a baseball. Why, oh, why was he giving me a spanking? Wasn't it true that he was my papa and could throw anyone in jail to protect me?

For a moment, I was stunned at the spanking. Then all my thoughts and my blood and the pain in my butt tumbled down into my head, and I was crying and gasping for air. And then I was lying on my bed as my bedroom door slammed shut. Through my tears and confusion, I could see my poster of Abe Lenstra, upside down doing the bicycle kick, the ball headed for the net. Usually I imagined it was me kicking the ball. This time I was the keeper, confused, baffled, beaten. Where had I gone wrong?

I was in the doghouse with Papa and Mama for a few days, but it was worth it. At school I was everyone's hero. Almost all the kids asked me to sit next to them the next time desks were shuffled. Big Butt moved us around every few weeks. Every time there was a game of marbles, they begged me to play with them. The big boys talked even more with me when we played football. Everyone started calling me Triple B or just Triple. Triple B meant Big Butt Basher. They'd yell, "Hey, Triple, pass me the ball," or "Great score, Triple!" Nobody told Big Butt why I was now called Triple, but she must have known something was up, because every time someone used the name, they'd smile in her direction. School was way more fun now. And Big Butt had stopped using her ruler. I still couldn't figure out why Papa hadn't been proud of me, but I had learned one thing: if you hit your teacher, don't tell Papa about it! That had been a nasty spanking.

My next big day came early on a Sunday morning. Every morning in Bonaire was a beautiful morning. There was always the sun, the clear sky, a bit of a breeze alive with the aroma of salt and sea and happiness. I wasn't always the first one awake, but rarely was anyone out and around before me. I loved the morning. Jan never wanted to get out of bed. He was grumpy and sleepy in the morning. Margy and Fenneke always seemed to be asleep. Papa and Mama arose on days when Papa had to work, but if they had the chance, they stayed in bed. I couldn't understand how they could forgo the thrill of a new day, the excitement of being there as the world awoke.

At the start, not a soul. As the first light softened the darkness, the shadows of men left the houses and headed for the boats at the town landing. Then a cat might stretch and search the corners of the square, or a neighbor would open a shutter, or a seagull would drop from the sky on a scrap of food. A second gull would follow, and a squabble over the scrap would ensue. Later Tante Tien would open the door to her little shop and set baskets of fruit and vegetables outside. Bit by bit the scene would be peopled: a man too old for the trawlers bringing eggs for Tante Tien to sell, two women talking outside their front doors, two or three children coming out to play. How would anyone want to stay in bed? If there wasn't anything to watch, there was a good book to read, books about war or football or sailing or whatever.

That morning I was at the window overlooking the square. It was another perfect day, not a soul in sight. Nothing but quiet. Well, not exactly quiet. Three or four gulls were flying high and squawking at each other. Carlos was the first person I saw. He pedaled into the square, parked his bicycle under our porch, unlocked the padlock on the garage door, and disappeared into Mama's super pantry. I went out on the porch and down the steps to talk to him. The big door was closed. I noticed the hasp with the dangling padlock. I realized I could slip the bar of the unlocked padlock through the hasp and lock Carlos in. He'd be a prisoner of war!

In a trice I had the door secured, with the padlock unlocked so that I could open it and free Carlos. This was a great prank. I ran up the stairs onto the porch and waited to see what would happen. It took only a few minutes before the door rattled. Carlos was trying to push it open, but with the padlock through the hasp, he was as tight as a POW behind a barbed-wire fence. At first the door rattled gently, then it began to shake. Next Carlos was roaring with anger.

That was when I should have run down to free him so that we could have a laugh together. But he began yelling swear words, and I panicked. If I let him out, he wouldn't laugh with me. He'd not only be mad, but he'd tell Papa. And I would be upside down again like Abe Lenstra with Papa whacking my behind. I scooted back to bed, closed my eyes.

I was asleep. I was asleep when Jan awoke. Asleep when I heard Mama wake Margy and carry Fenneke down to breakfast. Asleep when Jan arrived to wake me and tell me it was time for me to eat my breakfast. Nobody said anything about Carlos. It was only later in the day that any of us learned that Carlos had been locked in the pantry. A neighbor had heard him pounding on the door and freed him. Carlos had been both pleased to be liberated and roaring angry, but neither he nor anyone else had any suspicion of who had locked him up. Needless to say, I remained as silent as a spy with his life on the line. I didn't tell Jan. I didn't tell Margy. I didn't tell Mama. I especially didn't tell Papa. That lesson had been learned. Telling Papa was a bad idea, a really bad idea.

Hoofdstuk 38

24 april 1944: On this day, day seven of the greatest air offensive the world has ever known, more than 1,000 British, Canadian, and US planes pounded Nazi airfields in France and Belgium, and decimated Dusseldorf, Mannheim, and other Reich cities. Allies assert death of Luftwaffe in sight. Admiral Nimitz and General MacArthur join as army troops pour ashore from the Pacific navy fleet to corner 60,000 Japanese troops on Dutch New Guinea.

This was the easiest of our moves. We'd come to Bonaire knowing it would be a short stay, so we'd taken nothing more than our clothes. Our personal possessions were still in storage on Curacao. Bonaire had been an interlude, a tropical vacation. Carl was now assigned to command the artillery installation on Aruba. We loaded ourselves on the interisland ferry from Kralendijk to Willemstad with our suitcases. Fenneke was on my hip, Margy held on to my skirt, Jan and Alex galloped ahead. They were scouts reconnoitering the German gun emplacements. Carl directed the loading of our baggage while keeping a watchful eye on the boys.

Bonaire had been fun, as any vacation is. Carl's job had not been terribly demanding once he cleaned up the mess he had found upon arrival. The staff of the POW camp was small, but it had been in disarray when he arrived. The International Red Cross had warned the Dutch military that the camp did not meet international standards, that something had to be done. So Carl had been sent to clean up the administrative mess; it had taken him less than a fortnight. Clear lines of authority, clarity on responsibilities ("every job with a man, every man with a job"), daily/weekly/monthly schedules and timetables.

Clarity established, the only job for him was enforcement. He called it discipline. And heaven knows, and the camp's staff knew within an hour of his arrival, that Carl knew discipline. The first offense, even the smallest one, and every corner of the camp could hear his megaphone of a voice as he chewed out the offender. The second offense led to

217

immediate punishment. Within two minutes, the offender was in the mess hall peeling potatoes.

On the other hand, he was quick with praise when jobs were done well and on time. In a fortnight, the camp had been transformed from grouchy, lazy disorganization into smart, snappy efficiency. Within a month, the initial fear he had inspired in the men had transformed into admiration for him and a quiet satisfaction among themselves at the quality organization they had become. Even the POWs were happy—if prisoners can be happy. They grumbled less about their food and treatment, and found the work-release program Carl initiated, which let them out from behind the barbed wire enclosure to work on upgrading the town pier, painting the dilapidated fish processing plant, and filling potholes in the dirt roads near the town, a pleasant change in prison life.

My worry had been the school. Jan had adjusted well, but Alex had gotten away with murder. After the incident when he slapped Mevrouw Hendrik, I met with her and made Alex apologize. Despite my insistence that she control him by any appropriate means, she let him run wild. Alex had truly frightened her by reminding her that Carl was the supreme authority on the island. Alex was creative. His quick mind and impish smile were infectious, and it was what made him so lovable. But he needed to be controlled. Once he had sensed he had the upper hand with Mevrouw Hendrik, all hell had broken loose. The class had become unmanageable. It was close to the point where the lovable imp in Alex had turned into a spoiled brat, a teacher's terror. Perhaps the school in Aruba would be better.

The move from Bonaire to Aruba took us through headquarters in Willemstad. Carl was caught up in a whirlwind of work during our three days there. His staff, his troops, his budget—and more importantly, the scope of his responsibility—would be larger by two orders of magnitude. In the hotel at Willemstad, I suddenly realized how small Bonaire had been. In Kralendijk, there had been an occasional cat in the street during the day and total slumber by 10:00 p.m., when the generator cut off. Despite the war, Willemstad was a vibrant ... what? Large town? Small city? The contrast with Kralendijk was one of night and day. And the hotel, just a reasonable hotel as hotels go, was luxurious in comparison to the house we'd been living in. Shieshie and Yohannita were excited to see the children and excited to be going with us to Aruba. Carl had already arranged to have Wanga transferred, and Jan and Alex were making plans with him for the new kites he would fashion for them.

Two days later, all of us were on the ferry from Willemstad to Oranjestad. Carl had visited Aruba briefly two years earlier as part of his orientation when the military had first introduced him to the islands. Wanga had family there. For Yohannita and Shieshie, though, this was a trip to another world. For the most part, they had lived their lives in their shantytown on the fringe of Willemstad. The half dozen trips they had made in their lifetimes were from their shantytown to downtown Willemstad. The boat trip was an exciting journey for all of us.

Yohannita had captured Fenneke, and Shieshie had Margy by the hand. Carl had taken the boys to the wheelhouse to show them around and to chat with the captain. I had taken ownership of one of the two deck chairs. It was delicious to feel the trade wind on my cheeks. I closed my eyes, luxuriating in the warmth of the sun. My mind wandered back to Cape Cod, to Yarmouth, to Cataumet, to Falmouth, to Barnstable, to the outer beaches on Sandy Neck and Truro, to the pitch of the waves in Buzzards Bay and the rip of the currents on Vineyard Sound on the trips from Woods Hole to No Man's. PC and Alex had confirmed that the island was now totally under the control of the navy. How sad. Such a peaceful, idyllic spot now an outpost of this war.

The thought of the war brought me out of my reverie. The war did little to touch what were called the ABC Islands, but when it did, it was inevitably attacks on Aruba. Bonaire, of course, was empty. Curacao was by far the most populated. But Aruba was strategically the most important of the islands. Carl had told me that one of every sixteen barrels of oil consumed by the Allies came from Aruba. Shell Oil—or Dutch Shell, as it was called here—had established leases to drill in Venezuela eons ago. Concerned about making large investments in both plant and equipment in an unstable, developing country, it had constructed its refineries on Dutch soil, under Dutch government control, on Aruba. Oil pumped in Venezuela came to Aruba in tankers, was stored and refined and stored again, and then shipped by tankers to the war zone.

The tankers, the oil refineries, and the storage facilities were high priority targets for the Reich's submarines. There weren't many of them here in the Caribbean. The distance to Germany was great; and the long voyage across the Atlantic, a space controlled largely by the Allies now, was difficult and dangerous. And that distance created resupply problems for them. These were solved in part by the subs stopping on the smaller islands for food and water, which they bought or commandeered as necessary. Diesel fuel was obtained by training guns on wayward tankers and threatening to sink them unless they sold their fuel. Rearming, however, demanded the long trek back to Hamburg for torpedoes and ammunition. So the upside was that there were not many German subs in the Caribbean. The downside was that those that were here focused their efforts on Aruba.

Carl would have PT boats armed with torpedoes and depth charges to patrol the waters around Aruba and to pursue subs that were spotted. But his main weapon was the artillery battery with its variety of cannons. I was not privy to its strength, but it was an impressive installation; certainly more than a few score and likely a few hundred of gun emplacements. Carl had tried to reassure me by saying that attacks on the island were sporadic. He saw that as the glass being half empty: we wouldn't be attacked much. I saw the glass half full: sporadic meant that we would be shelled from time to time. As a mother, I couldn't help but think that one shell was all it would take to destroy a house and kill its occupants.

When approaching Willemstad by boat, one is taken by the curve of the beaches and the gaiety of the pastel-painted houses. In contrast, the Oranjestad skyline—or more precisely, the lower end of Aruba—was dominated by the black steel associated with manufacturing. Chimneys hundreds of feet high belched smoke into the tropical sky. Gantries, derricks, trucks, piping, great steel docks, and tens—no, hundreds—of oil storage tanks squatted like giant black toads, each the size of a small hill. Curacao and Bonaire: pristine tropical isles, antithetical to the concept of war. Aruba: dirty, black, smoky, smelly, constructed of steel, built to fuel the engines of war.

The sight propelled me back to our flight through Germany, and shivers ran down my spine. These past two years, whether we were in Stratford or Bronxville or Curacao or Bonaire, the war had seemed a distant mirage. Here we were geographically no closer to Germany, but suddenly the war slapped me in the face. The war was here. Carl might as well have been sent back to defend Grebbeberg. We were an ocean away, but this was the front. Cannons were aimed at us. We would be fired at. It was cold comfort that the firing would be sporadic, as Carl had said. The firing on the Western Front during WWI had been sporadic, and it had killed millions.

I took a deep breath. I had decided to come. Bronxville had been truly horrible. There was danger here, but it was not a great danger. Carl was here. It was where the children and I belonged. We would deal with the danger as and when it threatened.

Just then Carl and the boys clambered down from the wheelhouse, laughing and talking together. All three of them started telling me about the captain. I couldn't focus on the story as a wave of emotion choked me at the joy being shared by these three males who filled my life to the brim, who made me happy beyond all bounds. *Aruba*, I thought, *here we come. Do not snatch from me this togetherness.* The boys were still laughing, each pulling me by the hand as the ferry gently bumped the pilings, the motor roared for a moment in reverse, and then stilled.

The drive from Oranjestad to Sint Nicolaas took less than a half hour. I hadn't realized how small the island was. Oranjestad to Sint Nicolaas was hardly ten miles along the coast road. The ocean was gorgeous, the island more curious than attractive. The beaches were tempting, the island reefs protecting them from the surf, but inland there was little foliage other than the divi-divi trees scattered across the landscape. Hardly more than scraggly bushes with gnarled trunks as high as a man's head, the foliage and branches grew sideways on the downwind side of the trunk. The trade winds were sometimes gentle, sometimes stiff, sometimes storm blown, but always from the same direction. So the little foliage there was on the island all grew sideways, like weather vanes. We passed Hooiberg. The hill had a Papiamento name, but the Dutch called it Hooiberg—the haystack. Obviously volcanic with loose lava rock tumbling down its sides like black glaciers, it was not a mountain at all, as *berg* would imply. No more than a hill, and not even a very large one at that.

As we neared Sint Nicolaas, the landscape became oil storage tanks, cheek to jowl, shoulder to shoulder, black and ugly. As we passed downwind of them, we were slapped in the face by the stink of the oil refinery. It was an odor black as pitch, suffocating, permeating, dominating. As the children and I gagged, Carl tried to assure us that as long as we stayed upwind of the refineries and upwind of the acre upon acre of storage tanks, there would be no smell. Right then, downwind of whatever, it was cold comfort to know that if we were not here, there would be no smell, that we would be able to breathe.

Our house stood apart, by itself on a hard-packed dusty space; an older house, built well before the war. Beyond was a development of low cookie-cutter houses, built by the military for the married troops. Enclosing our house was a chin-high fence of four-strand barbed wire, with cactus planted into it as an additional thorny barricade. The cookie-cutter houses had tiny yards enclosed by eight-foot high brick walls topped by shards of glass set into their concrete tops. The local population was poor, not dangerous but given to petty thievery. To one side of our house, perhaps fifty yards from it, was another prewar home, this one surrounded by a great green hedge that enclosed trees and other greenery. Abandoned? Or inhabited by a recluse?

To the left a street led toward the main gate of the army base, a "city street," flanked by sidewalks and houses on each side. In short, except for our home-to-be and the other older house, this was all army housing, army built, a wartime addition that linked the army base to the shanties on the edge of the old town.

Wanga pulled our car through the barbed-wire gate and into the yard. Other than the green of the cactus hedge, the yard was a desert. Without irrigation, nothing grew on Aruba, other than the divi-divi trees. The house stood on knee-high cubes of concrete, high enough so the children could crawl under, and high enough that I could bend over and see the yard on the other side of the house. At least the children couldn't hide or get lost under there. At the top of each cube was a moat as wide as the length of my thumb and about that deep, filled with an oily, tarlike substance. A defense against ants, Wanga explained.

Inside, the house was plain Jane. Great square rooms, high ceilings, shutters on all the windows that we would close every evening in accord with the blackout regulations, to make it as difficult as possible for U-boats to identify targets for their guns. Three bedrooms: one for Carl and me, one for the boys, and one for Margy and Fenneke. A dining room and a serviceable kitchen, with a four-burner gas stove, stone sink, refrigerator, and an expansive table in the middle of the room for food preparation and eating. A large pantry for storage, but no cupboards, no counters, no countertop appliances. But with Shieshie and Yohannita to help me, none of that was necessary. Many hands make light work. A few feet behind the house, within the yard, sat a minuscule cottage for the maids, with two tiny bedrooms, a bathroom, and a sitting room.

We piled out of the car, the boys scouted the terrain, and Shieshie and Yohannita took charge of the two girls as Wanga carried our luggage onto the wide veranda fronting the house. Carl curled an arm around my waist as we stood side by side watching the children. The house was utilitarian, unadorned, but it would serve. With the children already laughing and running, we would make it our home. With luck we would be here for a while, and we could settle in and be together. I tilted my face up, and Carl leaned down to kiss me. We smiled. It didn't take much to make me happy, just this big man and four children squealing with delight. More happiness here than anyone could want.

Hoofdstuk 39

5 juni 1944: US Fifth and Eighth Armies capture Rome as Nazis withdraw to northwest of capital. US Liberators and Flying Fortresses out of British bases bomb Boulogne and the French coast, encounter little Luftwaffe resistance. Thirty Japanese Zeros downed over Truk and Biak.

Wanga had finished painting the beds green. He had been building them for some days. Tomorrow, he said, when the paint dried, he would put them in our room. We would be able to sleep in them tomorrow night! Twin beds exactly the same size. One for Jan, one for me. Before he had made the beds, he made kites. A box kite for himself, and two warrior kites, one for Jan and one for me. The box kite was tethered in the yard, tied to the stake he had driven in the ground. It went high. I mean, really high. You could hardly see it. Once Wanga got it up, he just left it. It never came down. It had already been up for more than a week. Jan said that with the trade wind, Wanga could leave it up forever.

The fighting kites were the best, though. Wanga showed us how to make them dip and dive, how to make them climb. He said that the dimensions of the kite itself, the lengths of string that made up the halter, and the shortness of the tail were the keys to a fighting kite. When the kites were finished, he broke some bottles and ground the shards of glass into a sandy grit, and then he dipped a length of kite string nearest the kites into glue and then into the grit of glass. When the glue dried, three meters of the kite string was a sharp, dangerous razor. He repeated the process for the tail of the kites. Thus armed, the kites could slash other kites or their string, cutting them up or cutting them down. Slashing another kite, thus destroying it, was the best fighting technique. Cutting its string won the fight, but the kite would flutter down and live to fight another day.

When Wanga fought with our neighbors, the dads, he always won. If I fought kids my age, I could sometimes win. Most of the kids had been flying fighting kites for years. I learned that the trick was to position my kite above the enemy kite, dive down until the string of my kite touched the other kite, and then quickly release my string so that the kite string would run out and the sharp string would slice like a saw. Of course, the enemy kite was trying similar attack techniques. The quickest, most agile kite and the flyer with the best strategy won, at least most of the time. Sometimes a kite flyer would lose control of his kite, but the ensuing out-of-control maneuver could prove to be a winner, if the uncontrollable dive smashed and cut the enemy kite.

Wanga would sniff at that. "Just luck," he'd say, and we'd go home to repair the kite or start from scratch and build a new one. The best part of kite flying in Aruba was that we could fly anytime we wanted to. The wind was always right.

As Jan and I got to know the neighborhood, we became more and more curious about the nearby old house that was surrounded by trees, bushes, and an almost impenetrable hedge. No kids seemed to live there. No cars ever went in or out. If somebody did live there, we decided they must be old and mean. The place was scary. We often prowled around the hedge, peering through to try to make out if anything was going on; and a bit frightened that suddenly someone would appear in the yard and yell at us for spying on them.

After a few weeks, we concluded no one lived in the house. Then it dawned on us that this was a safe house for German spies. Spies in our backyard! Our prowling became even more furtive, more cautious. Spying on an old, mean neighbor demanded care, but spying on spies … This was war! We now combed the area outside the hedge. Since we never saw anyone going in or out, we concluded there must be a tunnel into the house from a point outside the yard. Look as we might, we couldn't find the entrance to a secret tunnel.

One day we were in our yard playing stick ball when a white delivery van stopped at the gate to the old house. Jan told me to put down the bat. We played catch, appearing nonchalant, but watching every move of the truck. The house was the length of a football pitch from our front gate, but our view of the hedge around the house was unimpaired. A man got out of the truck from the passenger side and unlocked and opened the gate. The driver pulled into the yard, and the man who had opened the gate now closed it and snapped the padlock shut.

"C'mon," Jan whispered to me. I wanted to go straight to the hedge to spy on the truck, but Jan led me up our porch steps and into the house. "Diversionary tactic," he said. We went out the back door of our house, crawled under our barbed wire fence out of view of the old house, and doubled back at a run to arrive at the rear of the old house. We crouched outside the hedge, panting hard from the run, and peered through the hedge. By moving a few yards, we could see the van. The man who had opened and closed the gate was directing the van as it backed up. When the van neared the shed, which we had earlier decided was a large dog kennel, about half the size of a one-car garage, he signaled for the driver to stop. He swung open the large door, and the van backed right up to the kennel. The large door obscured our view; we couldn't see the back of the truck or into the shed. The driver shut off the motor, and the two men disappeared into the shed.

"What are they doing?" I whispered.

Jan held up a finger to his lips to shush me. We couldn't see what they were doing, but we would be able to see them if they came out or left. We lay down on our stomachs, watching. Spying was often like this: wait and watch. Jan and I had read every one of the books in the Hardy Boys series, many of them twice. Frank and Joe Hardy both knew that impatience had led to the death of many a spy. Jan and I wanted to move to another location, but did not dare to get closer. We were well hidden where we were, so we waited. Jan sort of dozed off. I listened. No sound from inside the shed. I could hear some dogs barking in the distance. The rooster in the henhouse in our yard crowed a few times. If I looked up, way, way up, I could see Wanga's box kite floating high in the sky.

A long time later I heard a sound in the shed. I poked Jan and held my finger across my lips. We had been lying there forever it seemed, but we were both wide awake now. The two men exited the shed, and the driver pulled the van a few feet forward while the other closed the door. He then walked to the gate, opened that, let the van drive through, closed and padlocked the gate, and off they went.

We lay there a few more minutes and then prowled along the outside of the hedge, closer to the dog kennel. "Let's sneak in," I whispered.

Jan shook his head. No. What if the two German spies returned? "No. Let's go home. We'll wait a bit, see if they come back, then we'll come back."

We both knew that haste was also the demise of many a spy. Detective work required caution and courage; Frank and Joe Hardy knew that. It was crucial to know when caution should rule, and when courage should drive one to action. Anyway, we were hot and thirsty.

"Home for some lemonade," Jan ordered.

"Okay, but then back to puzzle out this mystery," I replied. We often pretended that I was Joe and that Jan was Frank.

An hour later we were back at the hedge, lying flat on our stomachs. We peered through the hedge and watched. Nothing. I was impatient. Jan told me we should wait ten minutes, and I reminded myself that it was never a good idea to act hastily. After watching a while longer, Jan nudged me. We crawled to a spot where we could wiggle under the hedge.

"I'll cover you," Jan whispered, "while you reconnoiter."

One to stay back, one to advance. If one was captured, the other could escape to fight another day. I ran across the open space to the dog kennel. My heart was pounding, but all remained quiet. I opened the large door. The space inside was empty, completely empty. Not a paper, not a bottle, not a piece of furniture, nothing on the walls. I couldn't believe it. What had the two men been doing in here for two hours?

I backed out of the shed and motioned to Jan to join me. Silent as a shadow, he arrived. I pointed to the inside of the shed. Jan was as astonished as I was. After a moment we concluded that there must have been something in the shed that the two men had loaded into their truck.

"Let's look for clues," I whispered.

On our hands and knees, we crawled across the wooden floor searching for spillage: grain, seeds, powdered cement, a fragment of paper, whatever.

"Look!" I pointed to a ring in the floor. At first it seemed to be just a ring. Upon closer scrutiny, it was the handle to a trap door.

Jan seized the ring and lifted the trapdoor, which opened on hinges. Below, a dark space, a hole. "We need a flashlight," he said.

I offered to go get mine. We had flashlights next to our beds—which was handy during the nighttime blackout periods—but Jan said we'd both go. We were too scared to stay in the shed alone. We closed the trapdoor, shut the shed, wiggled under the hedge. A few minutes later we were back at the hedge, each of us with a flashlight. We again lay on our stomachs and watched the yard for a few minutes. Nobody there. While we had been frightened to go into the yard the first time, it had been a vague, unspecified fright. Now it was a specific fright of two men and a trapdoor.

We shone our flashlights into the space below the trapdoor. We could see a room the same size as the shed above it. Cardboard boxes were stacked against the walls. I wanted to descend the ladder, but Jan stopped me with a hand on my shoulder.

"Look." He flashed his light on one box. "Camels." And then he moved the beam of light. "Lucky Strike."

"Cigarettes," I muttered. That explained what the men had been doing. They hadn't emptied the shed into their truck; they had been unloading cigarettes from their truck into the shed, into this secret space, to hide them here.

"Let's get out of here," Jan whispered.

We'd been frightened to this point. Now we were petrified. We really were Frank and Joe Hardy. Stolen goods! We weren't dealing with imaginary German spies, we were dealing with real-life thieves! We closed the trapdoor and the shed and bolted for home.

In our room we discussed what our next steps should be. Should we lie in wait, surprise the men when they returned, and capture them? No, we concluded. They might have guns, and we didn't have any. What would the Hardy boys do? In most of their stories, when it became really dangerous, they went to their father or the chief of police. That decided it: we'd tell Papa, and he would send his soldiers with their guns to make the arrest. Meanwhile, we took an oath of secrecy—we'd tell no one. We didn't want the story to leak and have the men flee before they could be arrested. Oaths of secrecy were important to good detective work. We wouldn't tell Mama or Margy or Fenneke. Nor Wanga. And especially not Shieshie or Yohannita. Those two blabbed everything to everyone. Blabbermouth women were the bane of every detective. So we swore an oath of secrecy. We wouldn't say a word to anyone except the chief of police. Which in this case would be Papa.

When Wanga pulled the car into the yard with Papa in it, just before supper, we ran out and gave him his big evening hug. "Mum," I whispered to Jan, and nodded toward Wanga. We'd play it cool until we could get Papa alone in his office. Then we'd let him lean back in his chair with his hands clasped behind his head and his feet on the desk. That was the best way to spill the beans.

As soon as we were in the house, I took Papa's hand. I tried to make my voice deep and somber. "Jan and I need to speak to you."

Jan took his other hand. "It is a matter of utmost urgency," he said softly.

"Jan and I have sworn an oath to tell no one but you," I added.

Papa looked impressed at our adult behavior. We knew at once that we could trust him in this matter. We had a problem, however. Papa did not have an office in the house, so we had to settle on the dining room. It was a shame we didn't have a swivel chair for him. A regular old dining room chair would have to do. He sat on one side of the table, and we took chairs across from him. We had another problem, though. The two blabbermouth women—Shieshie and Yohannita—were coming and going, setting the table for supper.

I jerked my head in their direction and looked questioningly at Jan. How could we speak in front of them? "English," Jan said. The Blabbermouths didn't speak English. Mostly Jan and I spoke English with Mama but Dutch with Papa. He raised his eyebrows as we started in English. I cocked my head toward Yohannita and Shieshie. "Blabbermouths," I explained. Papa nodded knowingly.

I let Jan do the talking. The last time I had been excited to tell Papa a story—the story of how I had put my teacher in her place—it had ended with me hanging upside down being spanked. I'd learned my lesson: don't tell Papa anything that he might see as naughty behavior. Wasn't it possible he would be angry that we had trespassed on the property of the old house?

"Cigarettes?" Papa was suddenly as excited as we were. At first he had been bemused, thinking Jan and I were playing a game. Now he understood that this was for real. I mean, really serious. Almost a matter of life and death.

"Yes." Jan nodded vigorously. "Cartons and cartons of them."

I remembered what Joe often said. "Yeah," I said, trying to imitate Joe's nonchalance. "We caught 'em red-handed. Caught 'em with the goods."

Papa rubbed his chin with his hand. "Black marketeers. Running cigarettes, like the old rum runners."

Now he was deadly serious. "Don't get even close again to the old house," he warned. "Those men could be dangerous." He lifted his finger in warning. "They're breaking the law. They could shoot you if they thought they were going to be caught."

He sounded like Mr. Hardy. I nodded knowingly. "Witnesses are the bane of the criminal." I paused to let that sink in. Then I added,

"Witnesses must be erased."

I could see that Papa was impressed by my grasp of the situation.

"What should we do?" Jan asked.

"Nothing," Papa said. "You two do nothing. I'll put some of my men on it. We'll put the old house under surveillance and arrest those guys when they return." Jan and I nodded. That was a good plan. "They'll be back soon," Papa went on. "They'll be back as soon as they have a buyer for the cigarettes."

He kicked back his chair and stood up. "Good work, lads." He had read some parts of the Hardy Boys to us. He shook Jan's hand first, then mine. "Meanwhile, mum's the word." He winked and nodded toward the kitchen. "Not a word. Especially to the Blabbermouths."

Ten days later Papa's soldiers arrested the two men. They were taken to the jail in Oranjestad. Papa said that Jan and I had done first class detective work and that he was proud of us.

"Case closed," I said to Jan. He and I smiled. That was how good detective books ended.

Hoofdstuk 40

6 juni 1944: Great invasion launched! US, British, and Canadian forces cross the English Channel and land at Caen, Calais, and Cherbourg under heavy enemy fire. Initial reports sketchy, suggest substantial Allied losses.

It seemed that we had been in Sint Nicolaas only a few days when Mama told Alex and me that we would be going back to school. "The change will be easy for you this time," she said, trying to calm our fears. Alex was sitting on her lap, she had her hand on my shoulder. "This school will be in Dutch, just like on Bonaire. I'll walk with you tomorrow to show you how to get there."

The school was farther away than on Bonaire. There it had been hardly a five-minute walk. Here it seemed a long way. The walk was easy for me; I was a lot bigger than Alex. He was whining to Mama, but my mama was no dummy. She knew he was scared to go to a new school. I was a little scared too, but I pretended I wasn't. I mean, I was a third grader, almost a fourth grader!

"Don't worry," I said to Alex. "If you have any problem, just come and find me." We walked farther. "Anyway, the morning won't be long. We go home at noontime for lunch." Mama nodded to confirm to Alex that I was right about going home for lunch. "We'll walk back together."

That helped. Alex figured he could make it through the morning.

The way to school was in the opposite direction from Papa's army base, toward the center of Sint Nicolaas. Our shoes were dusty when we got there; the road was just dirt. The neighborhood around the school was jammed with shacks, little shacks with corrugated tin roofs. In Oranjestad most of the houses had orange tile roofs, but in Sint Nicolaas, hardly any houses had them. Behind the school, the shacks were separated by dirt paths and alleyways—you could hardly call them streets—and garbage was piled wherever people threw it. Alex wrinkled his nose at the odor and complained to Mama. I was older so I was able to pretend that it didn't bother me. I could see that Mama was also doing her best to ignore the smells.

The school was one long, low building that made up three sides of a square. The doors and windows of the classrooms opened onto a covered walkway that connected all parts of the school. The courtyard framed by the three arms of the building was teeming with kids, most of them playing football. Others played tag, and some were on their hands and knees playing marbles or spinning tops. The courtyard could have been a football pitch, it was so smooth and level; but there was no grass, just smooth dirt. The place was a whirl of kids yelling, laughing, and talking.

"The building's like a cloister, Mama," Alex said. "Kind of a noisy, dirty cloister."

Just as he said that, a priest stepped out from the door onto the walkway and rang a big hand bell. In no time, the courtyard was empty as the kids scurried to class.

Alex and I followed Mama as she crossed the now empty courtyard to speak to the priest. All the doors off the walkway opened into classrooms except for this central door behind the priest, which led to his office. I could tell that he was the school principal. Alex and I had never been to a school where the principal was a priest. Mama had already told us that this was a Catholic school. I shouldn't have been surprised, I guess, but it was weird to see a principal dressed in a long black robe and a white clerical collar.

Mama introduced us to the priest. "*Jan gaat dus in de derde klas,*" said the priest, and the four of us walked to a classroom labeled with the number three. There had been some noise inside the room, but the instant the principal appeared, the room went silent. *Wow,* I thought. *They are really scared of the principal.* He spoke with the teacher, Father Herman, who was also a priest. Father Herman welcomed me, and then took my hand with a "*Kom*" and showed me to an empty chair and desk. All the kids were staring at me.

As soon as the principal left with Mama and Alex, the room filled with the buzz of whispers. Everyone was still staring at me, particularly at my feet. I realized I was the only one with shoes. Then, as I looked around more carefully, I also realized I was the only white boy in the room. As the teacher, the priest, shushed us all and began his lesson, I next realized that this was an all-boys school. There were no girls in the class; and thinking back, I recalled that there had been no girls in the courtyard when we arrived. This was weird. No girls, priests as teachers, no white boys, no shoes. As I looked around, I wondered which of these classmates might become my friend.

At the end of the morning, the principal rang his bell, and instantaneously the pupils erupted out of the classrooms in a wave of noisy jubilation. The courtyard filled with laughter and cries of greeting as groups of children collected to walk home together. It might as well have been a party for Queen Wilhelmina's birthday. It was a relief, though, to be freed from the classroom, from the chair to which we had been affixed, hardly moving a muscle, since the ringing of the bell to start the morning. Now we were free until two o'clock, when we would return to the same classroom, the same chair. My classmates had told me that the afternoon was better. We would have a ten-minute recess to play on the courtyard. And the afternoon was only three hours long, not the four hours of the morning.

As the crowd of pupils dispersed, Alex and I were able to find each other. Alex was squinting in the direct sun, which was bright after the relative darkness of the classroom. I could see tears in his eyes, so I took his hand and gave him a quick hug. A really quick one. I didn't want anyone to laugh at us. When my little brother was sad, it hurt me right in the top of my chest, just below my throat. Seeing tears in his eyes made that spot feel as if a football under my chest bones was being inflated, and its pressure was stifling me.

"What's up?" I asked.

"I need to go." He sniffled. "I think I did some in my pants."

In the middle of the courtyard stood a small shack. It was an outhouse. I hadn't gone in there yet, but you didn't need to go in to know it was an outhouse. It smelled. It smelled if you were near it, and it smelled if you were a mile away. In the tropical heat, an outhouse was bad smell central.

"You want to go in there?" I asked, nodding toward the shack. Alex shook his head, and more tears squeezed from his eyes. "Okay. Let's go home," I said, taking his hand and heading toward the house. We were about halfway home when he had more or less stopped crying. "What happened?" I asked.

"I had to go. I raised my hand and the teacher was nasty. He didn't want to let me go during class. When I started to cry, he let me go." Tears formed in his eyes again. "When I went to the outhouse, I almost threw up. I couldn't go in. It would have made me sick." We walked a bit more. When the tears stopped, he added, "So I went back to the class. I had to go so bad that it hurt. It still hurts. I need to go so bad!" He began to cry again. "I think I did some in my pants."

As soon as we were at the porch steps, he rushed to the bathroom. I told Mama what was wrong. She grabbed a pail, ran some lukewarm water into it, and armed with clean underwear and shorts and a towel, she went into the bathroom to clean Alex up. I put my head on my arms on the kitchen table. I wanted to cry. I felt terrible for my baby brother.

Hoofdstuk 41

9 juni 1944: Allies gain ground, expand Normandy beachheads as Eisenhower mourns loss of lives. Germans driven back north of Rome. Japanese cruiser hit west of New Guinea.

Despite the fighting in Europe, Eisenhower's invasion of France, and MacArthur's struggles in the Pacific, the longer we lived in Sint Nicolaas, the further the war retreated from my everyday thoughts. It was like the quiet ebbing of a tide, the lapping of distant waves on the sand, the protective span of beach growing larger and larger and the edge of the sea receding.

The last major attack on the oil refineries on Aruba had been two years earlier, in February 1942, when a submarine, the *Werner Hartenstein*, shelled the island and set ablaze the field of oil storage tanks. That was just after I had arrived on Curacao with Jan, Alex, and Margy. The islands were a turmoil of fear then. These last months, calm had been restored. Yet every evening as the sun set, the war thrust itself into our lives as we all blacked out our homes, and snapped blinders on the headlights and taillights of our cars if we expected to drive that night.

In contrast to Stratford, Carl and I made good friends here. I particularly liked Jannie Klijnstra. A nurse, she had enlisted long before the war, as had the doctor Carl liked. We called him the Dikke Doc. Both had requested assignment to the Dutch West Indies a year or two before the invasion, as a chance to see the world. The Dikke Doc was small in stature but rotund, round as a barrel, with a bright red face and a double chin. His droll sense of humor, infectious laugh, and love of partying made it impossible not to like him. He was well into his forties—older than we—and single.

Jannie looked Dutch in that she had blond hair, blue eyes, and a fair complexion, but she was not at all a tall, stolid, big-boned Dutch Amazon. Rather, she was small and lithe, quick on her feet with the smile of a pixie. She was my age and had been married ten years or so with no children. Her husband was an elementary school teacher back in Zwolle. She confided that their marriage had been insipid, and she had seen enlistment and an assignment to Aruba as an opportunity to revitalize her life. During the week she and I played tennis in the women's league, and on weekends she and Carl and I and, yes, the old and fat Dikke Doc, as well as others, played mixed doubles. Jannie had paired up with one of the young officers, Johan Meer. As he reported directly to Carl, he was reserved when we were all together.

School was not going well for Jan. It worried me. It seemed acceptable for Alex, although the first day had been difficult for him what with going in his pants. Much as at school in Bonaire, some of the older boys had taken a shine to his diminutive stature, quick smile, and his agility and speed playing football. They wanted him on their team. Their protection kept him safe in what seemed to be a raucous school environment. And both boys had learned to visit our bathroom before leaving the house, in order to avoid the cesspool odors of the outhouse at the school.

For Jan it was another matter. A group of bullies were after him. His pride seemed to stoke their anger. I spoke to Father Herman and the bullying stopped in the priest's presence, but under the cover of recess and especially after school, the bullies were merciless. Jan's classroom work did not seem to suffer, and Father Herman especially lauded his written work. Since hardly more than a year ago, in Bronxville, Jan had also received praise for his creative writing—in English then—it was clear he had an ability with languages.

As for the war, it had lurched once again into our lives. Ten days earlier there had been a submarine attack on an oil tanker off the coast of Venezuela. The following Sunday, Carl, the children, and I were picnicking in a little frequented cove that we had discovered at the end of the beach road. To get to the cove, we needed to climb down a fifty-foot escarpment to the beach. The beach, hardly larger than two tennis courts, was snuggled safely from the wind on the island side by horseshoe-shaped cliffs, and was attacked relentlessly on the sea side by pounding surf. The sea was far too dangerous here for swimming, but the beach was deliciously private and perfect for a picnic. A hideaway from the world and from the turmoil of the war and from Carl's military duties. Or so we thought.

The boys had been off, playing at soldiers, of course, but now they were running toward us, pointing out to sea and yelling, "Submarine! Submarine!" Their voices were torn by the sea breeze and muffled by the roar of the surf, but we still heard them. They were right. On the horizon, tiny but distinct, the conning tower and hull of a U-boat was rhythmically rising and disappearing on the waves. Carl scrambled for the two-way radio he carried with him whether on duty or off. Try as he might, though, he could not raise a reply. Batteries low? Cliffs too high? Too distant from the base?

We grabbed the blanket, the picnic basket, and Margy and Fenneke, and scrambled up the escarpment to the car. Too late. As we reached the top of the cliffs, the submarine had submerged. We returned nonetheless to the base, where Carl placed the installation on full alert and ordered his three patrol boats out to sea to search with sonar for the sub.

And then, last night, it had been sirens and cannons. Sint Nicolaas had exploded. One moment we were asleep, and the next our house shuddered from the concussion of the simultaneous firing of a hundred cannons. It was one huge blast, or perhaps more precisely, a hundred huge blasts all within a second or two of each other, creating a terrifying roar. Silence followed, a deep silence, a silence that was frightful in its intensity. What had happened?

The quiet was broken a few minutes later by the motors of the PT patrol boats firing up, heading out to sea. It was only as I turned the radio to the warning channel operated by Carl's military instillation that I realized Carl was not in the house. Little by little the news trickled in. A German U-boat had surfaced a mile or so offshore. It had fired at the storage tanks in what we called the oil field, fortunately doing no damage. Carl had prepared his installation for just such an attack.

As I understood it, he eschewed the more common method of sending a firing crew to each cannon, awaiting the next blast from the U-boat, swiveling the guns in that direction, sighting, and firing. Rather, he had each cannon aimed in a different direction and at a different distance. When the cannons were fired, the shells exploded in a series of concentric circles around the island. The effect was that an attacking U-boat captain would see an enormous explosion, a deafening barrage of guns, and at least a few shells exploding near his submarine. His reaction would be to assume that the entire artillery installation had been lying in wait, knew that he had been coming, and that the guns were closing in on his coordinates.

Indeed, the submarine had immediately sounded, had not fired even a second round. After a half hour, the radio signaled the all-clear, informed us that we had been fired on by a U-boat, that no damage had been done, and that the U-boat was on the run. By then the children were already long back to sleep, and I had only to calm Shieshie and Yohannita and return to bed myself. I spent a few long hours tossing and turning; Carl returned before my sleep did. He told me exactly what I had been telling myself these past hours: that we were safe, that the U-boat was gone, that I need not worry, that the war was in Europe, not here. Our adrenaline was still surging, though, and we made love. We were alive, we had each other, the children were safe. I was so happy, so relieved, that I cried in Carl's arms as we climaxed, cried afterwards as he kissed and caressed me, and cried as we both drifted into sleep.

Hoofdstuk 42

27 juni 1944: Cherbourg falls, and Allies capture 30,000 prisoners. Victory is key to establishment of substantive Normandy beachhead. Red Army takes Zhlobin and Vitebsk in sprint toward Minsk and Polish border. Admiral Nimitz confirms carrier planes attack Guam.

The principal rang his bell. Excitement swirled as papers were stuffed into book bags and friends called to one another as we all emptied from the classroom onto the courtyard. I didn't see Jan, so I walked to his classroom. He was still inside. It had seemed to be a particularly long day. It was hot, and school had been boring. We were all waiting for summer vacation to start. Only a few more days! It would be fun to be able to go to the beach every day, to swim in the clear water, to catch fish in our butterfly nets in the tiny pools on the reef at low tide. Fish of all colors—orange, magenta, indigo, yellow.

School was really boring. Father Frans would read and we would write out what he read. He called it a *dictaat*. Or he would write arithmetic problems on the blackboard, like "4+2=" and "6-1=." We would copy them onto our little slates, write in the answer, and wait for Father Frans to check our work to see if we had it right. We were never allowed out of our seats, and I had learned not to ask to go to the bathroom. As I checked the wall clock for the umpteenth time that day, I decided it was true that boredom was the bane of every schoolboy.

"What's the matter?" I asked Jan. I could see that he was worried. He shrugged, glanced over at Father Herman. I sat next to Jan as he arranged papers and carefully put them in his book bag.

Father Herman got up from his desk. He nodded to us. *"Goede middag, jongens,"* he said with a smile as he went out the door.

"What's up?" I asked.

Jan explained that the bullies had cornered him at recess, had taunted and laughed at him, and then they had told him that they were going to get him after school. He and I peered out the door. Sure enough, Wim and his gang lurked on the far side of the school yard. Nobody else was around. Wim and the others were waiting to ambush him.

Jan and I waited a while, hoping the gang would leave. They didn't.

"Okay," Jan said. "Let's go."

All of the classrooms had one door, the one leading out to the courtyard, with a window next to it, and three windows on the back wall with a view of the corrugated shacks and the network of alleyways behind the school. I started toward the door, but Jan put a hand on my arm. "No." He pointed to the back windows. "That way."

The windows, like the doorway, were just open spaces. No shutters, no panes. So we went over the ledge and down to the ground. We had been walking down one of the alleyways for a couple of minutes when we heard Wim yell to one of the other gang members. They had discovered we were no longer in the classroom. We began to run down the alley, each of us carrying our book bag in one hand. They were like little suitcases. Mine banged against my knees, and it was heavy. Jan urged me on. So far the bullies didn't know which alleyway we had taken.

I started to cry. I was too tired to run more, so I just walked. We sneaked through the pathways between the houses, circumventing piles of trash and stinking heaps of garbage. We were about halfway home when Wim and his friends spotted us. Jan sprinted ahead. I tried to run, but I couldn't keep up. Too quickly, Wim and his gang were on my heels.

Panic gripped me. They were going to catch me, beat me to a pulp. Air in my throat and lungs burned as I tried to run faster. The book bag hit my knees, and I stumbled. Down I went, my mouth in the dirt of the path. Wim and the others ran right past me, almost stepping on me as I lay crying. *"Laat hem maar,"* Wim ordered as they whipped by me. They were after Jan.

I lay in the dirt crying. I was filthy from sliding forward on my stomach after the fall. Slowly I got up, caught my breath, picked up my book bag, and followed in the direction Jan and Wim and the others had gone. I hoped Jan had escaped them. I tried to brush the dirt off my clothes, my legs, my arms. My tears had wet my hands, and I was now streaked with mud from brushing the dirt with my hands.

Around the next set of houses I could hear the fighting. I sneaked closer. Just around the bend in the alleyway, next to a huge pile of trash, Wim and the others had Jan on the ground. They were kicking him, all five of them. Jan would try to get up. They would punch him, and he would fall down, and they would begin kicking him again. They were yelling and laughing, but Jan wasn't making any sound at all. I could see blood on his face and hands. The blood was coming from his nose, but he wouldn't make a sound.

The gang hadn't seen me. I slipped away and headed for home. At the house I cried for Mama. Her face went white when she saw my dirty clothes and dirt-streaked cheeks and nose.

"Oh, Alexje!" she cried.

"Jan, Jan," was all I could blubber, pointing back toward school. Wanga, Shieshie, and Yohannita had gathered around me. When they learned what had happened, Mama, Wanga, and I started back to where I had last seen Jan. I took them to the huge pile of garbage. The gang was gone. Wim was gone. Jan was sitting, partly in the pile of garbage. Blood was everywhere. Just like when they were kicking him, he was making no sound. He seemed dazed. Mama leaned down to him. He looked up at her and quietly, with great composure, he said, "I hate him." There was no malice in his voice. It was just a statement, as if one and one made two. "I hate Wim."

Wanga helped him up. Mama picked up his book bag. Wanga put his arm under his shoulders and helped him walk home. I cried all the way to the house. *My brother, my brother,* was all I could think. My stomach ached to see him hurting. I couldn't stop the tears.

Hoofdstuk 43

24 augustus 1944: Paris liberated. General Bradley sends French Second Armored Division into capital. Russians roar into Romania; the nation capitulates. Davao in Philippines torched as US Liberators bomb city.

"Attention!" I commanded my troops. Alex and Margy stood rigid before me. "Right ... face!"

Alex did a smart right face. I had trained him well. Margy turned ninety degrees to her right, imitating Alex, but her foot movement was all wrong. *These fresh recruits,* I thought, and then shrugged. I had discussed these matters with some of the other generals. We all recognized the need for parade training, but we also all agreed that in the midst of a war, with a limited time to ready the troops, we could let parade training slide. The more important issues—to instill absolute discipline and to ensure combat readiness—were our paramount concerns.

"About face!" I paused. "Left face!"

Again, Alex was near perfect: lift one foot, place its toe in the right spot behind the heel of the other foot, swivel on the ball of that other foot, bring the heels of the two feet together with a click, ensure that the heels touch precisely and that the feet describe a perfect *V.*

"Forward ... march!"

Margy was another matter. Oh, well. She was better at holding her wooden gun to her shoulder, leaning her weight forward onto her lead foot, aiming the gun, and getting its stock properly snug against her cheek. If I had to choose what to teach these recruits as they were rushed into war, shooting was more important than marching.

I marched the troops along one side of the yard, halted them as they approached the corner, faced them about, and marched them back again. "At ease!" I instructed. They spread their feet apart, rested the butts of their rifles on the ground. The last two times I had them at ease, Margy had asked if she could fall out. Because she had asked, I had forced the troops back to the march. This time she didn't ask if she could fall out. She had learned her lesson. Finally, I had begun to instill some discipline.

I waited, and waited, and then announced, "Fall out!"

"Yay!" Margy yelled. "Let's go get some lemonade."

We all headed inside. Mama always had lemonade ready for us. Some stuff we couldn't get, like milk. Mama made us drink Klim, saying it was good for our teeth and bones. Maybe, but horrid for our taste buds. And meat. There was no meat. Chicken Mama could buy, though she said they were tough and cost too much. Spam we could get. Mama would slice it into thin rectangles and fry it with eggs. And Papa would shoot wild goats here as he had on Bonaire. He would shoot three or four for the mess hall and keep a kid for ourselves. And once in a while he would shoot an iguana. Mama would cut the meat into small white cubes. That was really good, much more tender than chicken.

Lemons she could buy, and she made lemonade and put it in long, thin terra-cotta Bols bottles. She would lay the bottles down on the refrigerator shelf. We would hold our glass under the end of the bottle, pull out the cork, let the lemonade gurgle into our glass, and push the cork back in. Usually I filled the glasses. Margy wasn't very quick at putting the cork back in and usually made a mess.

We sat and drank our lemonade and mapped out battle plans. We had to halt the advance of the German battalion that was massing behind the fence on our southern flank. Our scouts had penetrated behind enemy lines in the early morning darkness and reported a force of more than a thousand troops supported by four light cannons, a machine gun nest, and two panzers. Alex and I discussed how we should deploy our forces. We were leaning toward a surprise attack at night by the two of us. We would take grenades, slip past the German guards, and destroy the two tanks, the four guns, and the machine gun nest. The grenades would need to be strategically placed. We would need two men with the ability to work with great stealth and with nerves of steel. It would be no small matter to penetrate enemy lines. The two of us were the perfect choice for such a difficult and dangerous mission. We were confident that we could pull it off.

Margy asked if she could come. We told her that she would need to stay home, that she was too young, too inexperienced, that she would just get in the way.

After lunch we decided to go to the candy store. Our favorite was the licorice sticks, three for a penny. Off we went, all three of us. Fenneke stayed with Yohannita. She could crawl like crazy and had just learned to stand up and walk. Well, to waddle, really. Alex and I were already planning to induct her into our command. As soon as she could walk properly, we would begin her training.

I had checked our piggy banks. Not a red cent. I had thought I had a stuiver, one of those five-cent coins, square but with rounded corners, and then I remembered that we had spent it last week. So our first stop would be the dead-end alley behind the row of shops. That's where the drunks hung out. When we got there, we looked for bottles and found a brown and a green beer bottle. Margy said she wanted a ring.

I held one bottle in each hand, horizontally, their necks touching. I overlapped the necks of the bottles a centimeter or so, so that the lips of the two bottles touched. By sliding the bottles away from each other, but keeping the lips pressed together, I could snap one of the lips off. When it was done just right, the lip would break off from the bottle in the form of a perfect ring. On the third sliding movement, the lip of the green bottle broke off. Margy put the ring on her middle finger. She held her hand up, admiring the ring. She knew she needed to be careful. One side of the ring, where it had broken off from the neck of the bottle, was sharp.

We kept up our hunt for bottles. There were lots of them in the piles of trash, but we needed rum bottles. They were flat, like a hip flask. The beer bottles were worthless, but each rum bottle was worth two cents. When we found one, we would take it to the candy store and use it to buy two cents worth of licorice. On a good day, we could find two or three bottles. Although we sorted through the trash up and down the alley, that day we were skunked. Not one single rum bottle to be found. I picked up two brown beer bottles, and the three of us left the alley and headed toward the candy store. Three doors away from the store, we stopped, and I handed the two bottles to Margy.

She wanted the two of us to go into the store with her, but we begged off. When we had rum bottles, we all went in together. If we didn't have rum bottles, the owner would send us on our way. If the owner's wife was in the store alone, she would sometimes take our beer bottles and give us a piece of candy just to be nice. But if Margy went in by herself, the owner's wife always gave her a piece of candy. Margy was cute. She was fair-skinned and blond, with a radiant smile that would darken with disappointment and melt into tears at the merest suggestion of refusal. Margy was our ace in the hole, so off she went. It took only a few minutes before she returned, sucking a long stick of licorice and carrying two more, laughter in her eyes.

The owner's wife had been alone in the store, had chatted with her, had oohed and aahed over the red, white, and blue ribbons—the colors of the Dutch flag—woven into Margy's pigtails, and had been generous with three licorice sticks in exchange for the worthless beer bottles, fully aware that Alex and I were waiting outside. The conspiracy of four was a conspiracy of happiness. We walked home sucking on the three licorice sticks and basking in the generosity of our coconspirator. Little did she or we know that the smile she gave to a cute four-year-old would be remembered by three youngsters for seventy years.

Hoofdstuk 44

17 september 1944: Patton's tanks drive toward the German frontier east of Metz and Nancy. German civilians stream across Rhine as Allied troops widen the breach in the Siegfried line. Red Army captures Sofia, prepares assault into Yugoslavia.

High noon. Distant machine gun fire. *Verdomme,* I thought. I had ordered no target practice, no live-fire training, no war games, nothing involving a machine gun. *What the hell!* I pushed back from my desk and stepped through my open office door. It was a day like every other day on Aruba—hot sun, the trade wind playing with my hair, not a cloud in the sky. The doors and windows of my office were always open, the floor fan always blowing. Our uniforms were designed for these days, khaki shorts and short-sleeved khaki shirts, and even those were truly too hot for Aruba.

On the knoll above me I could see a half-dozen gun emplacements. Above that was the main lookout tower, which had a view of the whole of our defenses: the dozens of other concrete and steel bunkers with their cannons, pillboxes at regular intervals inside the barbed-wire perimeter, smaller lookout platforms at the higher rises along that perimeter. A guard was on duty twenty-four hours a day in the main lookout tower. From where I stood I could see him viewing the field of Shell oil storage tanks with his binoculars. There were hundreds of those storage tanks squatting like gigantic overturned steel buckets, buckets painted a depressing black, buckets ten-stories high and so large that only two would fit on a football pitch. Beyond the hundreds of oil tanks, rising above them, I could see the top of the steel structures that comprised Shell's refinery. The whole of it was ugly, a sickness, a disgusting contrast to the ethereal blue of the sky, the darker blues of the ocean, the gentleness of the trade wind.

Verdomme! Another burst of gunfire! Who the hell was playing with guns? I could see the guard in the tower looking in the direction of the sound, and then he reached behind him with one hand. I stepped back into my office as the telephone rang.

"Commandant, Snuif here. On duty in the tower watch."

"What's up?"

"You've heard the gunfire?" I grunted assent. "I can't see where it's coming from. Far end of the storage field perhaps." I knew he was still peering through the binoculars. "Maybe as far as the refinery."

"Keep me posted. I'll send some guys over to see what's up."

By now a dozen soldiers had appeared. I asked if anyone knew what was going on, but no one had any idea. I pointed to a sergeant.

"Kuiper, take two guys. Grab a jeep and go see what you can find out." Turning to my adjutant, I added, "Opstall, phone Shell, the refinery or the storage field, see if anyone there knows what's happening."

Other than the two initial bursts of gunfire we had heard nothing more, so I spoke again to Snuif in the tower. "Anything?"

"Nothing, Commandant."

In the background I could hear Opstall on the phone. He had reached someone, whether from the storage field or the refinery, I didn't know. The monotone of the other man's voice suggested a lack of concern. Opstall dialed another number. As he did, we heard a blast. A bomb? An artillery shell? My phone rang. Snuif.

"An explosion, Commandant! Behind the storage field. It looks like it might be at the refinery. A huge cloud of smoke!"

I stepped out my door. He was right. Smoke billowed, black and ominous, high above the storage tanks. All the phones started ringing, and then I heard Kuiper's voice over the walkie-talkie. I left the phones to the secretaries, picked up the squawking walkie-talkie.

"Commandant ter Weele."

"An attack, Commandant! A bomb just went off here at the refinery."

I squeezed the talk button. "Where?"

A pause. He was searching for identification. "Block D. Building D-7. I think it's the pumping station." And then, "German soldiers, Commandant!"

His walkie-talkie went silent, and we heard machine gun fire again, this time a half dozen bursts.

Opstall called from the bank of phones. "An attack on the pumping station at the refinery! It's really confused. Two, three, or maybe four squads of Germans. Machine guns, rifles, bombs."

The walkie-talkie squealed. "Commandant?" It was Kuiper again, his voice less stressed. "Sorry, we had to gun the jeep. They were shooting at us. Not friendly fire." A chuckle. "We saw two squads of soldiers, about five in each group. There are probably more. One of the groups looked to be a bomb squad."

"Opstall, red alert!" I ordered. "Hit the siren, everyone to their stations!"

The siren and the voice speakers echoed immediately across the base. "Red alert! Red alert! To your station. To your station. Red alert! Red alert!" the speakers droned and echoed. Wherever they might be, soldiers began running toward their assignments. We did this weekly, and this time it was not a drill. Most of the assignments were to man the cannon, the machine gun emplacements, and the perimeter defenses. Mess-hall personnel went on duty in the kitchens in the event food or drink were needed. Communications personnel manned radios, telephones, walkie-talkies, and signal flag stations, where the red-alert flags were already being run up. Infirmary personnel headed toward operating tents. One platoon—three squads of a dozen men each—was assigned to appear in full armament at the flagpole in front of my office. We called them the Rats: the Red Alert Team. They would be ready for any assignment, from dealing with hurricane damage to countering a landing invasion.

As I walked the twenty meters from my office to the flagpole, the Rats came sprinting from all directions. As each of the three squads began lining up in their formations, I replied to the flurry of questions. "Yes, the real thing." And, "No, not an exercise." And, "At the refinery. At least two squads of Germans, about five to a group. Perhaps more." And, "Bombs, rifles, machine guns."

Once van den Berg, the platoon leader, and the three squad leaders were at attention, I relayed Kuiper's information. Then to the platoon leader, "Van den Berg, take Witte." I waved at Squad Leader Witte and the twelve troops in squad one. "You guys cut off escape routes. Probably a couple of landing craft. Find them. Cover the shoreline." I pointed at Herman and de Velden, the leaders of squads two and three. "Follow me. When we find Kuiper down near Block D, we'll decide how to divide up and attack. Everyone got it?"

Nods all around. We'd done this sort of thing dozens of times. Some of our guys would slip football scrimmage jerseys over their uniforms and mount an "attack," and the Rats would need to counter them. It was always fun, a game of wits. There was no laughter or trash talk as we raced for our jeeps this time.

The column of jeeps roared out the gate of the base toward the oil refinery and Block D. Halfway there, van den Berg, Witte, and squad one peeled off to the right, heading for the shore. I raised Kuiper on the walkie-talkie, told him who was going where. He said he would be waiting for us a few hundred meters from Block D. It appeared there were three groups of Germans. As he and I spoke, another explosion sounded, and moments later we saw another cloud of smoke. Its billows were oily, more solid than gaseous, a dirty intruder in the ethereal, tranquil baby-blue sky. The Germans were polluting Aruba, this idyllic island paradise, just as their armies had polluted Nederland. God, how I hated war!

We pulled up at Kuiper's jeep. Smoke from the two conflagrations hung over our heads. Kuiper pointed. "D-7 is over there, about three hundred meters." Our training included learning the names and locations of vulnerable targets on the island. The oil storage field and the refinery were chief among them. Having Kuiper remind us of what we each should know didn't hurt, however. "I'm pretty sure there are three squads, kind of small, about five troops each. When they were shooting at us, they were at the pumping station, near the pumping control shed in D-11."

"Okay, guys." I raised my voice so that everyone in the two squads could hear. I pointed straight ahead. "D-7 and D-11 are both over there. Straight behind that is the shore. Once we start firing, they'll probably make a run in that direction.

"De Velden." I turned to squad three's leader. He was career soldier, not a recruit called up at the time of the invasion. "Take your guys, go over there." I pointed to our left. "Be our left flank. Herman." I addressed the leader of squad two. He was smart but young, and he had never seen any live fire. "You and I will take your guys and cover the right flank. Kuiper, you and your two stay here, guard the jeeps. If we do it right, we'll have them surrounded. Try to drive them back to the shore." Pointing, I singled out two of Herman's squad. "You two stay with Kuiper. If they try to squeeze out of our trap, we'll need one or two more rifles here. With some luck, van den Berg and Witte will have located the landing craft and will block their line of escape."

I scanned the troops. They were intense, focused. Expecting live fire does that, I thought. With their assignments clear, I added, "Anyone who surrenders we take as a POW. Anyone who shoots at you, shoot to kill."

On this tiny island, thousands of kilometers from Holland, the order "shoot to kill" should never have been uttered. The Germans dragged the sordes and offal and grime of their war machine across Europe and Africa, tracking blood and hate in their wake, all the way from the Brandenburg Gate to this paradise. I pushed the thought out of my mind.

"Questions?" There weren't any. "Okay, let's move out."

De Velden and squad three rounded one of the huge oil storage tanks to our left and disappeared behind a row of tin shacks that served as supply depots. Herman and squad two followed me at a run around the oil tank to our right. I paused at its other side, where we would need to cross into the open. Beyond the open space, the black smoke billowed from the far end of a row of buildings that comprised part of Block D. That would be the pumping station in flames. Farther, a bit to the left and beyond, a second column of smoke reached skyward. We couldn't quite see its source: probably a portion of the piping of the refinery.

All clear, I thought. We'd make a run across the open to the first Block D building. I'd been holding my left hand up as the stop signal for the eleven troops following me. I changed the signal from *stop* to *let's go*. Half of the squad ran with me. The other half covered us. Midway across the open space, we dove for the ground as a shock wave and the roar of an explosion slammed us. I pinned myself to the dirt. As soon as the shock wave passed, I looked up and realized the explosion was behind buildings to our left, that we had not been under fire.

"Up!" I yelled.

Within moments we gained the wall of the Block D building. I turned and waved for the rest of the squad to join us while we covered them. The fresh column of smoke was near what had been the second column, off to our left. *Good*, I thought. And then, *Good?* Well, it was good in that the explosion was between where we were and where de Velden and squad three were. The enemy was between us.

I told Herman and half of the men to stay there and cover the area we had just crossed. The rest of us would go around to the far side. I gestured to the facade of the warehouse that shielded us and added, "Once there, we'll both move toward the point of the explosion. We'll pin them between us and de Velden."

Herman was ashen. I put my hand on his shoulder. "Don't worry.

Each time we move, my group will go first and you can cover us. Then you can go and we'll cover you. Take a deep breath. Good."

He looked a bit better, and I held up the walkie-talkie. "I'll let you know when we're at the far side of the building and ready to move."

I motioned to my guys and we were off, staying in the shadow of the warehouse, alert yet moving at pace.

At the farthest corner we paused, eying the space between us and the next group of Block D buildings. Nothing that we could see. The three plumes of smoke were ahead of us. De Velden and squad three should be beyond them. The shore was now off to our right. Somewhere in that direction were van den Berg, Witte, and squad one. To our left, our jeeps, Kuiper, and his troops. And between us all, somewhere, were the Germans.

They would be at the ready. They'd already fired at Kuiper with the machine gun. On the other hand, they didn't know from where we were coming. I spoke to Herman on the walkie-talkie as I peeked around the corner of our building to the corner of the warehouse where we'd left him.

"Cover us. Ready?"

At the far corner of the building, some hundred yards from us, he raised his hand in acknowledgment. To the guys behind me, I signaled for us to go.

At a run, we crossed the open space to the next building in Block D. Heart pounding, but nothing happened. We paused, slowed our breathing, signaled to Herman. He and his part of the squad made the run while we covered them. They were now at the far side of our building. The breeze rained ash and soot down on us from the columns of smoke, and we could feel their heat. Beyond the warehouse which we were using as shelter, there were no more buildings. This was the edge of Block D. We could see what remained of the hut that had housed the pumping station, now no more than a bonfire of flame and embers. Beyond the flames and smoke of what was left of the pumps rose the piping and gantries of the refinery. The two other columns of smoke came from under the tangle of pipes. Where were the Germans?

A truck with maintenance equipment was parked at the near edge of the refinery. That would be our next objective. Before I could organize the squad for the dash to the truck, another huge explosion shot smoke and flames skyward from under the refinery pipes. I signaled to my guys, and we were running for the truck. Best to move at a moment of confusion. Halfway to our objective, the machine gun opened up. We rolled, but I realized immediately that the firing was from farther along, not directed at us. We scrambled to the truck. They were firing at de Velden, I supposed. He must be closing on the Germans from the far side. I signaled, and Herman and his guys made their run and joined us. As they caught their breath, I instructed them to circle ahead and to our left. I motioned toward the part of the refinery in that direction. I would take my team straight through, to the spot the firing had come from. The Germans were trapped under the pipes of the refinery. With de Velden on the far side, Herman would surround them to my left. The only opening for the Germans was to my right, toward the shore. They'd make their run in that direction and meet van den Berg, Witte, and squad one.

I ordered Herman and his guys to go; crouched, they made a run to the left. We waited a minute for them to take up positions. My team moved out, but only a few feet at a time, each of us keeping a few pipes or a boiler or metal stairs between us and where we thought the Germans were. The smoke of the pumping station fire was well behind us. We were coming up on the origins of the next two plumes of smoke. Beyond those was the spot of the last explosion.

Even at this distance, we could feel the heat emanating from there. We might as well be approaching the gates of hell, I thought. Swirling clouds of smoke and ash above us, smoldering embers, flames, heat, hate, death … A few more meters, stop, a few more meters. And then hell spoke with shrieks and clangor, spitting death.

At the bellow of the machine gun, we all hit the ground. A scream behind me. One of my guys had been hit. As I had thrown myself to the ground, I had slammed my left shoulder and leg into a piece of steel. Damn those limbs. They hurt. Looking up, I could see the spurts of flame from the barrel of the machine gun. I aimed at the spurts, fired. Once, and then again, and again. The spurts did not stop. I quieted my panic.

Not toward the bird, I told myself. *Not into the flock of rising ducks. Pick out the bird you want to hit and aim at it.* How many times had I been startled by a covey of quail and simply fired at the flock, believing in my haste that since there were so many birds, it was impossible to miss? And then startled by the realization, once again, that it was essential to actually select a single target and concentrate on it and it alone. I aimed with precision this time, on the middle of the gunner's chest, halted my breathing for a moment, and squeezed the trigger. Instantaneous silence. Then not silence. Not more firing from the machine gun; that had ceased. Now it was the roar of the fire and the cry of, "Stop! We surrender! Surrender!"

A white handkerchief waved. At first it was one soldier standing with his arms in the air, holding the white flag. Then it was two, then a half dozen with their hands up, and then even more. I waved my men to follow, and we approached with guns pointed. As we neared, I could see de Velden. His squad had closed in from the far side, their rifles equally at the ready. A moment later, Herman and his soldiers came in from our left.

We herded the krauts together, away from their weapons, fifteen of them. The machine gunner was down. Herman and one of his squad made him a sling. He was lucky. I had missed his chest, hit his right arm between the shoulder and the elbow. As I stood there, I realized there was blood on my left arm and left leg where I had slammed into the steel. De Velden raised van den Berg on the walkie-talkie, told him we had captured the attackers, that he wouldn't be meeting any krauts on the shore, that we were returning to base.

I scanned my men. Everyone was soiled, soot covered, perspiring. In the distance I could hear fire engines screaming, roaring toward the fires. The man behind me who had screamed when the machine gun had started its firing had been hit in the leg. Calf wound, not too serious. Lots of blood, but the bleeding was already being stanched.

As we made our way back to Kuiper, Shell workers appeared in small groups to make an impromptu victory parade. By the time we reached the jeeps, the procession had morphed into an exuberant crowd that cheered and applauded my men. We were dirty and sweaty, but happy. And relieved. Van den Berg radioed from the beach that they had found the landing crafts—three inflatable dinghies—and would be bringing them back to the base. There was no sign of the submarine that had launched the attackers.

Back at base, the troops herded the attackers to the brig. Wanga was waiting for me at my office.

"Mevrouw is worried," he alerted me. "We could hear the explosions and the shooting and see the smoke of the fires from the house. She sent me here to find out what was going on." He suggested that he could drive me home to calm her fears.

I nodded. My clothes were a mess. Soot, ashes, sweat, smoke, dirt, two patches of dried blood. Not dressed for a meeting with the Queen. I chuckled to myself. Seeing me looking like this might frighten her more!

Despite my appearance, she rushed out of the house as we arrived, hugged me on the porch, noted with sympathy that I was limping. Wanted to know what had happened.

I explained the attack and the firefight as we headed to our bedroom, boasting that "my boys" had performed by the book. Once surrounded, with the machine gunner down, the Germans had immediately surrendered. As I stripped out of the filthy uniform and threw it on the floor, she noted the blood on my calf and shoulder.

"When the machine gunner opened fire on us, I slammed into a piece of steel when I hit the ground," I explained. "It hurt like hell but didn't bleed much." Looking more closely, she touched the calf wound. I winced. "Careful!"

"Carl," she murmured, "that's a gunshot wound." She caressed my shoulder. "This too."

We inspected the two wounds. It might have been two bullets, but we concluded probably a single shot had hit me, grazed the top back of my shoulder and then the calf. The bullet must have hit me just before or just as I hit the ground.

"Four inches." She shook her head. "My God, Carl. Four inches to the side and it would have smacked you in the temple." She kissed me on the forehead. "It could have hit you right here." She kissed my forehead again. "Right here." She smiled teasingly. "Lady Luck must love you as much as I do." Her smile faded. "Three thousand miles and five years from Grebbeberg, and, but for four inches, it could all have ended here. Who would have thought it?" She touched the spot on my shoulder. "Oh, Carl, we've been so lucky."

Hoofdstuk 45

25 oktober 1944: British and Nazi forces battle in streets of 's-Hertogenbosch as Brits now occupy half the city. Germans retain a toehold by demolishing bridges over the city's Zuid-Willemsvaart canal. Meanwhile, Canadians lunge north of Antwerp in drives toward Roosendaal and Bergen op Zoom. In the Pacific theater, US planes attack two Japanese fleets near Leyte.

Today was the day! The general and the captain were going to induct us into the army as privates first class. I put on my red and white dress and chose a green one for Fenneke, one that she particularly liked. We had begged and begged Jan and Alex to let us enlist, but Jan kept telling us we were not yet ready for war.

The two of them were waiting in the yard. As soon as we approached, Jan bellowed, "Ah-tennnn-shun." I saluted and stood stiff as a ramrod, just as Jan had taught me to do. Fenneke tried to follow my example. Alex came over and moved her feet so her ankles were touching, and then moved her head and right arm into the correct salute position. He looked over at Jan. With disgust he muttered, "New recruits," and added under his breath, "the bane of military commanders."

Alex joined Fenneke and me in the formation, and Jan marched the three of us around the yard. "Company halt! Left face! Display arms!"

Alex and I knew how to display arms. Fenneke did not. She could hardly walk! Our commander roared, "Show her!" Alex placed her arms and the stick that served as a gun in the proper position.

We fell out, and Jan explained that to be inducted into his army, we had to pass his test of courage. He didn't want any sissies in his battalion. I could tell he had put a lot of thought into the test of courage. He marched Fenneke and me over to the chicken coop.

"You will be incarcerated in the chicken coop for ten minutes," he said. "If you cry or in any way protest"—he paused for effect—"you will have failed and you will be summarily executed."

The chicken coop was a chicken pen made of chicken wire. It was just tall enough for Fenneke to stand in. I would need to crawl. Inside the coop was a laying box. It looked like the low bookcase in my room, with an upper and lower shelf, but each shelf was divided into cubicles just large enough for a hen to make her nest. Jan opened the chicken wire door, and in I went. My red and white dress would get dirty, but I knew better than to protest. Jan would kick us out of his army. Fenneke reluctantly crawled in after me.

At first the chickens moved away from us. There were eight hens and a rooster, a bantam rooster. The hens were all colors of the rainbow, but muted colors. The dark orange one with russet and brown streaks, Lady, was my favorite. We called the rooster Cocky. He was mean. He would peck at anything he didn't like. Fenneke and I were scared of him. His colors were flamboyant—magenta, orange, crimson, and russet mixed with thin streaks of black and brown, and even tinges of aqua and green.

We had never been inside the pen before. The nesting boxes could be reached from outside the pen by opening little doors into each box. Fenneke and I often helped Mama gather eggs. We would open the little door and pick the egg, sometimes two eggs, out of the nest. If Lady or one of the other hens was in her box sitting on her nest, we would slip our hand right under her, feel for the eggs, and steal them away. Under the hen, we could feel her warmth and the softness of her feathers. Wouldn't it be nice to be a little downy chick, warm and soft, hiding under her mama's breast feathers!

The hens were always docile, never pecking at us, and Lady was the sweetest of them all. Mama said that she was the most prolific layer too. After gathering the eggs, Mama would often slip them into a saucepan of cold water, bring them to the boil, and let them boil for four and a half minutes. At the breakfast table she would set them in an egg cup, pointy side up, and lop off their hats. We each had our own special eggcup. Mine had a pink *M* on it, for Margery. We had special tiny egg spoons too, and Mama said they were carved from ivory. She wouldn't let us eat eggs with a silver spoon. The eggs tarnished the silver, turning it black. With salt and pepper sprinkled into the open egg, we would spoon out the white and try to get a bit of the deep yellow yolk in each bite. Since we didn't have much meat to eat, Mama said the eggs were good for us. I always ate the inside of the hat first. Since it was all white with no yolk, it was not as good as the part of the egg under the hat.

Right now Fen and I were not thinking of eating eggs. Cocky was watching us, and we were watching Cocky. Fen started to whimper, and I told her to be quiet. We needed to display our bravery. I tried to giggle to calm her fears. Cocky started to strut back and forth, and each time, the back-and-forth strut was a little closer to us. As he got closer, the look in his eye got meaner. The hens seemed to pay us no heed, but when one of them started to approach us, Cocky flew at her and pecked her, driving her back toward the other hens near the nesting box. That scared Fen, and I told her it would be okay. Jan and Alex were watching to see if we passed the test.

Cocky got closer. He tilted his head left, stared at Fen, cocked his head right, stared at her some more. I was sure he was readying to rush Fen and peck her. Fen probably thought the same thing and began to whimper. Cocky moved in for the kill. If he pecked Fen, she would burst into tears and we would be rejected from the army. I had to do something!

Cocky took another step, raising his wings and readying for the rush-and-peck move. Without thinking, I leaned forward, clapped my hands, and yelled, "No!" As I thrust my body toward him, Cocky retreated in fright. He strutted back amongst the hens, eying us warily, but he kept his distance, unsure of himself. That made me feel good. I had made him scared of me! Fen tensed up, ready to cry, but I told her it was okay. He was scared of us. We had won. We had passed the bravery test. We smiled at each other. We would be inducted into Jan and Alex's army. We'd be soldiers!

Hoofdstuk 46

23 december 1944: German panzers and infantry sweep through Luxembourg into Belgian Ardennes, surround Bastogne, pound General McAuliffe's troops. Nazis cross the Ourthe River, concentrate armor in St. Vith-Stavelot-Malmedy triangle, prepare for lunge past Liège toward port cities. Red Army opens winter offensive in Latvia as 270,000 troops advance on Libau. American Superfortresses smash Nagoya airplane plants on Honshu Island for third time in a week.

The scream of an incoming woke me. The bed shook as I awaited the roar of the explosion. Just as the shell hit Janssen and Klein, I realized that Margery was shaking me.

"Carl, Carl." She put her hand on my cheek in a caress. *"Gaat het?"*

I was wet with sweat. She nestled against me as I murmured that it was just a bad dream. I could feel her turn and her body relax as she dropped back to sleep. A bad dream, I thought. A hell of a dream. The word *nightmare* didn't even come close. After the Dutch surrender, I had put the hours at the Grebbe behind me. Margery had asked numerous times over the years to tell her how it had been. I always just shook my head. I didn't want to remember.

How long had it been? Creeping on toward five years now. At first I didn't want to think about it. Didn't want to remember Janssen's and Klein's bodies ripped apart, pieces flying in a thousand directions. Didn't want to remember brushing their hair, pieces of skin, their blood, bits of bone off my uniform. Didn't want to remember the fighting, the noise, the chaos, the deaths of the men under my command. I had done my part. Had done what I could do. Had tried, but it had not been enough. We had lost. We had failed. I did not want to think about it, did not want to remember.

These last months, though, as the war receded, the soldier in me receded as well. During the fighting, during our flight from Holland, during my assignments on Curacao, Bonaire, and initially here on Aruba, I had needed to stand straight, to command. Regrets, fears, memories of the horror at Grebbe needed to be suppressed, pushed into the recesses of my mind. And then, bit by bit, as threats here on the island ebbed like the lap of foam ebbing down the beach toward low tide, the strength of my will to suppress thoughts of the Nazi onslaught seemed to ebb as well. Memories of the Grebbeberg sneaked increasingly from the dark corners of my mind. After the sub attack six months ago and then the attack on the refinery, it must have been the roar of my own guns that unleashed the dreams. The nightmares began in earnest; and almost nightly, the horrors awoke me.

I tossed in bed, shut my eyes, tried to sleep. My ears, though, rang with our first salvos at the Germans, salvos that had relieved the tension of our weeks of waiting. At first it had almost been fun. The men had whooped as their shots exploded amongst the German cannons. We were in the fray!

The excitement lasted only a few minutes, quelled by the German response. Their cannons outnumbered us, overwhelmed us. For every shot we fired, there seemed to be four or five explosions from incoming. Nonetheless, we had an advantage. We were dug in. Our emplacements provided protection from everything but a direct hit. We were camouflaged. The German guns, to the contrary, were on the move, in the open, protected at most by a farm wagon or a haystack. And we were prepared: we had sighted in almost every one of the spots from which the Germans were firing. Every minute or two there was a whoop from one of our teams as they yelled "Got one!" and "That serves the bastards," and "That'll teach the motherfuckers." It took them only a shot or two at each new target to score a direct hit, and our luck held for more than an hour. Only two men hurt by flying debris, no guns or troops lost. My own luck held as well as I moved from gun to gun, talking to the men.

The first round had gone to us. The German artillery in and around Wageningen pulled back, out of our range. Get a sandwich, I told my troops. Eat. Drink. Restock ammunition. Cool down the guns. Clean and oil them. Take a nap if you can. We did it! You did it! It'll be a while. They'll regroup and come at us again. Take it easy while you can. Let's do it again in round two.

Communications with headquarters had gone down during the shelling. Piet Klein kept himself busy, continually biking back and forth between the Villa Santa Barbara and my command post. We were told what we already knew, that the German artillery at Wageningen had pulled back, that we should remain vigilant, that we expected they would renew the bombardment as soon as they regrouped.

At midday Piet reported that the Germans had attacked Kruiponder to our north in full force. The initial attack had been repulsed by our artillery there, but a subsequent attack from the rear, apparently by turncoat Dutch who were Nazi sympathizers, overran our position there. Officers were trying to keep their troops from fleeing, without success. The Germans were pouring through the breach in our lines.

After his next trip to headquarters, Piet reported that Germans waving the white flag of surrender had approached our lines somewhere up north on the IJssel-Linie, only to open fire when Dutch soldiers stood innocently to parlay with them. Over on the banks of the Rhine toward our south, one of our forward machine gun nests had been overrun and two of our troops killed. That squared with action that one of my gun emplacements thought they had seen earlier.

Later in the day, Piet reported more fighting up north. Not much was known, but it seemed clear that the Grebbe-Linie there was under heavy attack at best, and, at worst, had totally collapsed. We should be prepared for Germans attacking our Grebbeberg positions from that side. While that worried me, the north side of the mountain was not in my field of fire. My compatriot regiments would need to defend us there. After each trip, Piet reaffirmed the reports that German parachutists who had been flown into the areas around Rotterdam, Den Haag, and the Moerdijk bridges in that first wave of airplanes had been pinned down and were no longer advancing.

I continued my rounds among my men, ensuring that they were eating and drinking, that they were bringing in fresh munitions. Most of the ammo was now being brought up from Rhenen by the horses; the first round of shelling had blown out sections of our supply roads. While I was recommending sleep, the men were too keyed up to follow my advice. Piet did the next round of our emplacements with me. I wanted him to tell the men firsthand what he had learned at headquarters. Our firing at dawn to the south of the flooded area along the Waal had beaten back a German column there. That, of course, we knew. What we didn't know was that those troops had abandoned their equipment and fled on foot; and that one of our forward patrols had recovered their antitank guns, one hundred antitank projectiles, firearms, a truck full of ammunition, clothes, foodstuffs, and—to top it off—some twenty-five bicycles. The men loved the spectacle of the Nazis fleeing in panic from the pinpoint accuracy of their shooting.

As the afternoon wore on, we could see German movement beyond Wageningen. Piet reported that Major Voigt's forward command post had fallen and that the major had fallen back. Where? I asked. He didn't know. The next time I saw Piet, he was out of breath. He had obviously biked hard.

We needed to be ready, he said. Germans had been spotted advancing near Heimatten. German artillery, bigger guns this time, was being brought forward to Wageningen, to where they had been when they first opened fire on us. We were to fire as soon as fired upon, or as soon as appropriate targets presented themselves. Given that communication was difficult, I was free to use my own judgment. Headquarters was preparing a counterattack to begin after nightfall, to push the Germans back from the forward positions they were taking. Artillery should be ready to fire over our infantry positions upon orders to soften up those forward German positions.

Confusing? Use my judgment or fire upon orders? Which was it? Piet was standing next to me, holding one handle of his bike while reading from his notes. Go back, I said. I need to be clear about our counterattack. I can't start firing at our own troops.

As we stood talking, all hell broke loose. The German assault began in earnest. Shells screamed, dirt and debris flew in all directions. Smoke shrouded our view and burned our eyes. I heard Piet mutter to me that he needed another bicycle. He did. His bicycle had disappeared. Nothing remained of it but the handlebar he was holding. We both shrugged. It hardly occurred to us that either one of us could have disappeared as easily as the bike had. Off he went to find another bike and to make the next round trip to headquarters, while I made my way to the gunners to order them to return fire.

The next hours were war as one sees it in movies—the roar of incoming shells, of our cannons firing, of explosions. I had to ignore the chaos, ignore the loss of gun emplacements and the deaths of my men by direct hits. I had to push all of that, everything over which I had no control, out of my mind, into the background. Piet continued to bike back and forth. On one run, he told me that headquarters was asking that we take out the tower of the church in Wageningen. A German spotter was directing the Nazi ground attack from there. We took out the tower with our second shot. It was one of the targets we had sighted in long before all this began.

On each run, Piet gave worse information about the German advance to our north. The IJssel River was now totally under German control; the Germans were streaming across it with impunity. Later it was Ede that was taken, and later yet, Bennekom. In our sector we were giving the Germans more than they could handle. We had lost two guns and their men completely. The worst was the hit on Janssen and Klein as I stood within meters of them, with parts of them spattered over my uniform. Unfortunately, one of our beloved 6 Velds had been put out of commission. But we were bloodying the Germans in and to the south of Wageningen. Anything they sent in along our side of the Rhine or between the Rhine and the Maas, we handled with ease. The flooded area between the two rivers squeezed any advance there to a half kilometer or so in width, and we had every inch of that land sighted in with precision.

Finally, some good news from Piet. The French were advancing from the south toward the Moerdijk bridges and Rotterdam. Help was coming from our Allies! I sent him back to headquarters with the news that the German guns near and south of Wageningen had pulled back. I cheered my gunners as I made my round. We're doing it, guys. Keep it up! You've given them hell!

As night fell, our counterattack was to take place. At first we heard that our infantry was advancing from the foot of the Grebbe toward Wageningen. Then it seemed that they had been beaten back. Next came a call to fire upon an SS regiment advancing along the Wageningen-Grebbe road. At first we couldn't spot them in the dark. Where the road turned past Bruin's pastures, where our men used to watch his golden-haired daughter milk the cows, the panzers came into view. With a half dozen shots, my gunners devastated the column. Piet biked that news to headquarters and returned with reports that one of our forward machine gun nests had taken out a flanking action to our south near the Betuwe. There was also a report that the French were advancing south of Eindhoven. Would that mean that Margery and the children would be protected? Or that they would be caught in fighting?

Later, Piet returned breathless. The Germans were attacking the Grebbe and Rhenen from the north. Our position was becoming dangerous. The north side of the mountain was invisible to our guns. Our two compatriot artillery regiments were the ones which would need to help our ground forces defend against the German attack there.

Dawn came with a reprieve of enemy fire, but hordes of Dutch soldiers began to appear, crying and calling, stumbling with fatigue, carrying their wounded, most without weapons. Our troops were in full retreat. At noon the Germans began it all over again, with a vengeance. The shelling engulfed the mountain in smoke and fire, visibility disappeared except when a breeze momentarily cleared the air. My guns were running low on ammunition, and the intensity of the German firing made replenishment all but impossible. The last run for ammo had resulted in two dead horses. If this kept up, we'd be out of shells in no time.

Margery stirred next to me. It was all just a bad dream, I reminded myself. *Go to sleep. It's over. It was long ago. Eons ago. Here in Aruba, you're safe. Close your eyes.*

I turned in bed, but the images kept coming. The rumor spread that Sergeant Meyer had withdrawn his men from the north side of Grebbe toward Nieuwersluis during the night, contrary to his orders to stand his ground. Then the shock amongst our men at the subsequent rumor that General Harberts had him shot as a deserter and had insulted our brothers, the Grebbe's Eighth Infantry Regiment, as "the regiment of the fainthearted." And the news that the Germans to our south had established a forward line that comprised Bextel, Oirschot, Eindhoven, and Valkenswaard. That there was chaos there as our troops retreated through an advance by the French, and a contradictory report that the French were not advancing in that direction but were in full retreat from the Moerdijk bridges.

We could now hear mortar fire, machine guns, and rifle fire on the north side of the Grebbe. Piet arrived breathless. The Eighth Infantry Regiment was exchanging covering gunfire with the Germans as the last of our troops on the Grebbe retreated into Rhenen. The other two artillery regiments, our compatriots on the Grebbe, had long since been ordered back and were already in the town. The Germans were now in the northern edge of Rhenen. They had taken over De Stoomhamer factory and were firing from there at our troops, who were defending our next line of defense on the far side of the railroad tracks.

It was now our turn to move. We were ordered to retreat. We would be unable to cross the railroad tracks on the bridge into Rhenen, which the other two regiments had used in their retreat. Enemy fire from the De Stoomhamer factory covered the bridge and made it impassable. We would need to cross to the south of the bridge, which meant descending the embankment, crossing the tracks, and climbing the embankment on the far side. All of that would be in the open. Our troops holding the far side of the tracks would provide covering fire. We would need to abandon our cannons, since it would not be possible to retreat with them. And, oh, yes, if we had any remaining shells, could we take out the Rijnbrug, the railroad bridge across the Rhine into Rhenen? That would slow the German infantry advance along the tracks from the south and improve our chances of a successful retreat.

My men swore at the retreat order. They were furious. We had been holding our own. The shelling of our positions had ceased. Why did we need to abandon the fight? I explained that we were the last ones on the Grebbe. The German shelling had stopped because German infantry now occupied the eastern and northern slopes of the mountain. Reluctantly, they crawled from their emplacements with their rifles, ready to start back.

Before we leave, I said, we need to destroy the Rijnbrug. Who has any ammo left?

A brief pause, and then Gerrit and Joost said they had three shells. No one else had any ordinance.

We all gathered around their emplacement. The men joked that three shells was two too many. After all, it was one of the targets we had sighted in dozens of times. But we all held our breath as their first shot boomed. A spout of water went up under the middle span, throwing water on the bridge. No damage. A few feet too short. Gerrit and Joost made their adjustment, and the second shot boomed. Again the water spout, this time accompanied by a secondary blast. The shot had not only hit the bridge, it had detonated one of the charges laid by our troops to blow up the bridge, which they had never had the chance to set off. The middle span collapsed into the river, amidst spontaneous shouts of approval. The two gunners exchanged opinions and decided to shoot at the farthest of the two remaining spans. Aimed, fired. Again a water spout, but no further damage to the bridge. One for three. A mild catcall or two from the men, but the bridge was out. They gathered their rifles and headed for the railroad tracks and Rhenen.

As the men started the retreat, I made one more round of our positions. The firing on the Grebbe had ceased. No more incoming artillery, no roar from our own guns. No screaming, no explosions. An eerie, disturbing silence, like a dream without sound. Up close, I could see the debris, craters, smashed trees, smoldering trunks, smoke rising from embers. I could smell the acrid odor of gunpowder. Beyond, the land lay serene, deceptively serene. I stared at the crater that had been Janssen and Klein's emplacement. A few pieces of metal, the remains of their gun, a smashed helmet. Dirt blackened in spots with their blood, bits of bone and rotting tissue and scraps of uniform.

Farther along, the bodies of Broek and Kamp sprawled behind their artillery piece. No sign of injury to Broek, but I had lifted his head some hours ago, hoping to help him. He had been hit by a tiny piece of shrapnel on his left temple. He had died instantly. Kamp's body was missing a leg and part of his chest. He had been alive when I had run to him. He had screamed for my help, seemed to realize there was no help that could save him, and had died within seconds with an expression of disbelief on his face. Some of his blood had stained the cuffs of my uniform. Afink had been in the emplacement with them when the shell hit. He hadn't been touched.

I ran my hand down the barrel of a 6 Veld—we had come to admire these dinosaurs—and then reached the place where the horses had been tethered. Johan had loosed those that hadn't been killed. Most of those had wandered away. Two stood quietly as if awaiting orders. Pieces of dead horse were strewn about. A haunch here, legs, a head. Those that had been injured lay with a bullet hole in the forehead. My beloved Klaas lay on his side, entrails spilled on the dirt, his usually sleek black coat sullied. I spoke to him as I was wont to do. He moved. I had thought him dead, but he seemed to have heard me. For a moment I was angry at Johan. I had ordered him to set the unharmed horses loose and shoot those that were injured. He had disobeyed my orders. Then it came to me—he had been unable to shoot Klaas. He had been as proud of this horse as I was, admired him as I did.

I placed my pistol behind his ear, held it there for a few seconds, murmured a farewell. He convulsed at the report. I looked away, straightened, started down the mountain. South of me the Rhine flowed lazily toward the sea, indifferent to the chaos of the past two days. Downstream I could see the middle span of the Rijnbrug where it sprawled in the water. I picked up my pace when I heard shooting below me, in the direction my men had disappeared. I would need to be there to direct the crossing of the railroad tracks.

I had tossed and turned enough. It was too early to get up but I left the bed anyway, careful not to awaken Margery. There was no way I could fall back asleep, so I might as well get up.

Shieshie was in the kitchen. She greeted me, asking if everything was going well as she poured me a cup of coffee.

Well, yes, I thought. *I guess everything is going well. After all, I'm here, alive.*

The crossing of the railroad tracks to get back behind the new defense line on the edge of Rhenen had gone well, all things considered. We had run and slid down the ten meters of banking to the tracks in groups of three or four, sprinted across the four sets of rails and the few meters of space on either side of the rails, and then scrambled and clawed our way up the banking on the other side to where our comrades were dug in, shooting over us to provide cover. The Germans in De Stoomhaven factory had kept us under constant machine gun fire, but the distance was great enough that the danger was minimal. Two of the men suffered flesh wounds, both from gravel kicked up by the machine gun. The greatest loss was Piet's bicycle, a new one to replace the one shot out of his hand, which against his fiery protestations I had ordered him to leave on the other side of the tracks.

From there it had been mass confusion trying to arrange transport for my men back to the position we had been assigned on the Nieuwe Hollandse Waterlinie. Trucks, buses, carts, bicycles. An army in retreat is by definition an army in disarray. About the time we were digging in, we learned of the capitulation. The Germans had threatened to bomb Rotterdam into oblivion unless we surrendered. So we surrendered. And then the Germans bombed Rotterdam. My men were angry. Angry that we had been given the order to retreat. Angry that we had capitulated. And furious that the Germans had bombed civilians after the capitulation.

As I sipped my coffee, that fury returned, and then it ebbed as I pushed the memories of the Grebbe back into the deep recesses where they had lain these past four plus years. I was disappointed with myself, disappointed that I had let the memories creep out to haunt me. I wouldn't let it happen again.

271

I turned my attention to the taste of my coffee, to its aroma. I sipped thoughtfully. Yes, I would now focus on Margery, on Jan and Alex, on Margy and little Fen. My demons were behind me. For good.

Hoofdstuk 47

9 mei 1945: War in Europe legally ends as Germans sign final, unconditional surrender document amongst ruins in Berlin. Truman warns nation that while the west is free, the east is still in bondage. He instructs Nimitz to prepare plans for invasion of Japanese homeland, calls on emperor to surrender.

The war had ended! The war had ended! Everyone hugged and danced. The streets were full of crowds. Groups of musicians everywhere, each group starting its own parade that jostled and flowed like syrup over a pancake, the musicians in front and dancers and walkers following in their wake. Some groups were moving into town, some moving across town. It was wild and wonderful, everyone smiling and hugging and laughing, some crying with joy. A tapestry of color, a cacophony of sound, a smorgasbord of smells. The men were happy, the women were happier, and the infection spread to the children, who were the happiest of all. Radios blared the news from the open windows of houses. Drivers blew their car horns. I couldn't hear the birds through the tumult, but I knew they too were warbling and swooping. The flowers in the window boxes of the houses were in full bloom, their colors more vibrant than ever, and they swayed in tune to the music. Offshore, the waves glinted with sun and ran playfully to join the gaiety of the island.

The war had ended!

Carl ordered his staff to organize a victory celebration. A reviewing stand was erected just off the beach inside the army base. Seven of Carl's cannons were set on the beach itself. Barbeque pits were dug in the sand, and goat and chicken were roasted over the hot coals. Lemonade and beer flowed. Carl had instructed that Margy and Fen could not come until the cannonade was over. The noise would frighten them. Yohannita and Shieshie would bring them later.

Jan and Alex begged to be there, though. They sat on either side of me, along with Carl's top brass and all the dignitaries from Oranjestad and Sint Nicolaas. There was music and dancing, and speeches from the dignitaries. Carl was the last to speak. He welcomed everyone and spoke proudly of the Queen, the Dutch military forces, the support of the Allies—with special thanks to the United States—of his own troops and staff, and of the victory of freedom over tyranny. His great voice, deep and firm, the resonance of the Dutch language, his blond hair blowing in the breeze, his startling blue eyes, the ocean in the background ... It all emphasized his size and strength. I could picture him a Spartan or a Caesar on the rocky shore of the Aegean two millennia ago; Antaeus with his feet planted solidly on an escarpment with the waves breaking below. The echo of his voice persisted for some moments after his speech ended, and then he lifted his face skyward and literally roared to the gods of old: *"Lang leve de Koningin!"*

The crowd erupted with cry after cry of "Long live the Queen!" As the voices rose to a crescendo, the blast of the cannonade began. The pressure of the explosions hurt the skin on my face. Alex began to cry, and I wrapped him in my arms to muffle the sound. Jan was on his feet, part of the crowd. Each cry of *"Lang leve de Koningin"* was punctuated by the boom of the cannon twenty-one times. *"Lang leve de Koningin"* and the blast of a gun. *"Lang leve de Koningin"* and another blast. Twenty-one times. After the last blast, a deafening silence. The waves lapped on the beach, foam slipped back to the ocean. The breeze felt soft on my skin, soothing the pain of the cannonade. And then the silence broke as the crowd burst into applause, voices cheering.

It was over, I thought. The war was over. Hitler had been defeated. He had been defeated! The fear that he might win, so well suppressed in the caverns of my mind, hidden so well to shield the children, suddenly convulsed me. I should be ecstatic, but my stomach twisted with angst. The pain was excruciating. The roar of the guns had shattered my defense, my ability to inter my fears. I felt sick, thought I might vomit or faint, and I closed my eyes. With Alex whimpering on my lap, the festivities slipped away.

I was suddenly on the train leaving Eindhoven, clutching my children, soldiers running through the railroad car toward me from both directions, screaming at me in German. Out the window Carl was peddling furiously on a bicycle, Loeky was running alongside yelling for him to go faster, and the soldiers on the train began shooting at him. He fell. He was down, hurt, lying in a pool of blood on the cobblestones. The Brandenburg Gate loomed behind him. A soldier stood over him and laughed heartily.

Loudly enough for everyone on the block to hear, the soldier yelled, "Escape to Sweden? Not anymore." He raised his pistol. "You are an enemy of the Reich! I will shoot you!"

Shots were fired. Carl cried out in agony. It was no longer the Brandenburg Gate in the background. It was the Swiss Embassy. A man wearing a fedora and carrying a cane was doing the shooting. I shouted and fled. The fedora ran after me. Under his overcoat he wore a Gestapo uniform. I struggled in a crowd of women, smothered under racks of dresses and skirts, gasping for air. The Swiss Embassy! I needed to get to the Swiss Embassy!

Before me the Führer at a table, checking passports. Behind him three Nazis holding the three children. The children were captured, screaming for me. The Führer mocked my panic, smirked as he pointed a pistol at Jan. The crowd screamed, "Heil Hitler! Heil Hitler! Kill the Jew! Kill them all!"

I crumpled, terrified, exhausted, but then I was running again, Margy in my arms. She was listless, dying. Food! Milk! Shells burst around me. Carl was up ahead astride Klaas, firing a cannon at a panzer. I called to him that Margy needed milk, but he couldn't hear me. The bellow of a ship's horn drowned my cries.

If I could get to the boat, Margy would be saved, but there was a mass of humanity between me and the gangplank. The boat pulling away from the quay, its horn bellowing as the gulf of water between ship and land widened. The ship was gone.

I clutched Margy tighter. She was dead. A parade of soldiers marched by. Nazis. Hundreds of them. Thousands. Hundreds of thousands. Trucks, panzers, cannons, personnel carriers. I would be pinned between the Nazis and the crowd. A band was playing. It was a victory celebration. The Germans had won! Airplanes roared above. The planes bombed the crowd while the Nazis laughed. Arms and legs and torsos and heads spun in a blood-red sky.

"Mama." Alex was crying. It was he on my lap, not Margy's corpse that I was clutching. "The guns scared me."

I hugged him, quieted him. "Me too," I murmured, more to me than to him. My body was trembling. "Me too."

I gathered myself and returned to watching the sea of well-wishers milling about my warrior husband. I murmured, reminding myself, convincing myself, *it is done, the war is over, the Reich is defeated, Hitler is dead.*

I pushed the nightmare from my mind and let the excitement of the crowd lift me. I still clutched Alex. I pulled Jan against my knees, took a deep breath, and made a conscious effort to notice the beauty of the clear sky, the trade wind ruffling my hair, and the bright sea stretching to the horizon and beyond. That helped quiet the tremors that shook deep within me. Oh, Carl, I thought as I watched his troops clamor to be near him. We made it!

Hoofdstuk 48

15 augustus 1945: War ends in the Pacific as Japan surrenders and the emperor cedes to Allied rule. Times Square jammed as hundreds of thousands roar joy at news of victory.

The last months had been a cyclone. I now sat quietly on the lawn. New England in the autumn, my favorite place, my favorite season. Fenneke was inside the house taking her afternoon nap. Jan, Alex, and Margy would be home soon. The school bus would drop them at the foot of the road next to the huge roadside sign acclaiming the Waverly Inn. They would walk here, to this typical New England barn-red house, the first driveway up Jinny Hill Road. My brother Alex had once again lent it to us. Alex and his wife Mary were living in Barnstable on the Cape, in the Leading Wind, their great yellow house with the black shutters and black trim, overlooking Barnstable Harbor. Carl was interviewing for jobs. It appeared he would be offered one with Farrell-Birmingham, where he had interviewed last week.

The boys and Margy had started school in Cheshire six weeks late, but they seemed to be making friends. Jan was in the fifth grade, Alex in second, Margy in first. Their teachers had been alerted that they were coming from Dutch schools. The switch in languages—poor kids; their lives had been a progression of schools flip-flopping from Dutch to English to Dutch and back again—would require a few weeks or more of adjustment, not so much for speaking but for writing. All our married life our practice had been that I spoke English with the children when I was alone with them, and Dutch whenever Carl was with us. Now that we would be settling in the US— Carl was determined to become a citizen and also needed to perfect his command of English—we had agreed to switch to English as our "family language." We instituted the change upon boarding the *Kotika* in Willemstad. I was most concerned about Jan: it would take some time for him to write essays at a fifth-grade level. On the other hand, the school in Sint Nicolaas had been a nightmare for him, although the last months in Oranjestad—we had changed schools for the second year we were on Aruba—had been uneventful. All in all, school here could only be an improvement.

The sun was warm on my face as I tilted my head upward. Autumn, autumn. I adore you, but you make me weep. A season for tears. How could such beauty fill me with such sadness? How could morning frost on the fields and the crimson of the sumac bring tears to my eyes? It was the same sun that had warmed me on Aruba, yet it was not. There it had dominated; this autumn sun was a soft caress. There the trade winds never ceased; here the breeze was a feather on my skin.

The party I had organized just prior to our departure had been wild and wonderful. Long in advance I had conceived it as an October surprise for Carl, as a commemoration of twelve and a half years of marriage. It had rapidly evolved into a going-away party, an end-of-the-war party. Bundles of orders had come flying in. The base was being closed. Everyone was receiving orders, most were of their discharge dates, some for staying on to close down the base or assignment to Curacao, a few for transfer to Sumatra or Java. So we all gathered at the end of August: Jannie Klijnstra and Johan Meer; the Dikke Doc, his doctors and nursing staff; Carl's brass and their aides; my tennis circle and our bridge group; and tens of enlisted troops. Laughter and cheer spilled throughout our house and out the door to a crescendo of singing and swaying of troops on the porch and in the yard. Too much punch, too much beer. Too much, perhaps, if this had been a party solely for twelve and a half years of marriage, but hardly enough for the end of the war.

As the hours of partying wound down, the ecstasy melted into melancholy. The war was over: a time to sing and enjoy! And yet, the war was over: a time for disbanding, a time for good-byes and departures. Jannie Klijnstra, for example. Good-bye to her Johan, to the sun and the sand and the sea, to the camaraderie of the troops. Back to the mist and drizzle of Overijssel, to the flat of the polders, to the husband she had not seen in six years. She had assured me she could make the change, that she would treat these six years as a parenthesis in her life, a pleasant interlude that she would push into the back of her mind. She would not look back, but would readjust to the humdrum of small-town Holland and a stale marriage. I wondered. The war years on the islands and life in postwar Europe were as far apart as the *A* of Aruba and the *Z* of Zwolle. Jannie might be able to adjust, but the adjustment would be painful. I could only hope that it would not crush her. She and I had vowed to keep in touch.

Our departure was far less painful than hers. Yes, there was the sadness of adieus. But for me it would be so I could return to the States. What was I now? Thirty-three. The last two-thirds of my life, I had lived as an expatriate. I was excited at the thought of returning to New England. Excited to see my siblings. Comforted to be able to enroll my children in an American school and to provide them with a stable and safe environment.

And Carl was even more excited than I. To live in the land of wide open spaces and opportunity—he could not wait. The transition back to the small-town mores of Holland, to a land where the houses on the street had rearview mirrors attached to the right and left sides of the living room windows, adjusted so that the ladies could sit in their parlors and see the street to the left in one mirror and to the right in the other, and be able to gossip about who went in and out each door and at what time. That transition upon his return from seven years in the Dutch East Indies had been difficult. To return to Holland now, after the adrenaline of the war? No. He wanted and needed an open horizon, a new beginning.

The arrival in New York harbor three weeks ago had been an unforgettable event. Tugboats tooting their horns, fireboats spraying waterworks into the sky. Carl's cheeks wet with tears of joy, hugging me and the children as we sailed past the Statue of Liberty. Our excitement dockside as we spied PC and Alex, with the orange and white Crane family flag stretched aloft on two staffs, standing at the foot of the pier. And our laughter at their cheek when a Salvation Army band turned from Twelfth Avenue onto the pier, with fifes and drums and horns blaring, and PC and Alex stepped in front of the band, banner held high, marching in front of the musicians as if the parade belonged to them. And our laughter at the buzz around us at the ship's rail as our fellow travelers wondered aloud about the Crane flag. Was it the Jewish Emancipation Flag? The Elks? The Odd Fellows Freedom Flag? The Manhattan Indian Tribal Flag? The children danced to the music of the band, waved to their aunt and uncle, caught up in the jubilation engulfing us all.

After debarking, the kisses and hugs, all of us swarmed to the nearest diner. Milk! Real milk! And hamburgers! After almost four years of that horrid Klim, and of chicken and goat and Spam, here was real milk and a juicy hamburger, a feast of which we had only been able to dream.

To dream, to dream. Carl and I had looked at houses. If he landed the Farrell-Birmingham job, he would need to be near the company's offices in Wallingford and in New York City. We had spotted a house in Weston that split the difference. Stony Acres. We would see. First, he had to get the job. It sounded perfect for him. Farrell-Birmingham wanted to expand into postwar Europe, to sell its equipment as Europe rebuilt its manufacturing plants. Carl's knowledge of European business, his fluency in Dutch, German, and French made him, in my eyes, a perfect fit for the position. He was excited at the contribution he would be able to make both to Farrell-Birmingham as well as to the rebuilding of Europe, particularly his Holland.

I dozed. Fen had not wakened. The bus with Jan, Alex, and Margy would arrive soon. I had a roast in the oven. Carl had promised to be home early, so we would all have dinner together. The warmth of the autumn sun was the warmth of Carl next to me in bed. I could feel him move, encompass me. Autumn, New England. Carl, the children.

A murmur in my ears, the languid murmur of happiness, a whisper of normalcy, a whisper of two words, hardly discernible, fading into the depths of my mind. Two words. We escaped ... we escaped ... we escaped ...